CW01669564

Life in England 1935 - 1955

A Diary for Men

George Patterson

First edition published 2020

Gift Book For Dad
Rugeley
Staffordshire

ISBN 978-1-840-41022-8

The information in this book has been compiled from numerous sources over many years. The author and publisher cannot be held responsible for any errors or inaccuracies.

One or two fictional snippets may have been added for devilment.

Dedicated to all those affected by
the Great Furlough of 2020

. . .

New Year 1935... Can you hear me, mother?

It's a dry and mild winter ... Men wear flat caps, fedoras, homburgs and bowlers ... Women wear brim slouch hats, cloche hats, knit caps and berets ... People take invigorating walks in the English countryside ... The Ramblers Association is formed ... The Greater London Regional Planning Committee proposes a permanent 'green belt' of land around the capital ... Families gather around EKCO Bakelite wireless sets to listen to popular tunes of the day performed by The Savoy Orpheans, The Romaine Four, Paul Whiteman, Jack Hylton, The Selma Four, Jack Howard and Jack Payne ... "Can You Hear Me, Mother?" - 34-year-old comedian Sandy Powell makes the nation smile ... 41-year-old Stuart Hibberd announces the news ... Unemployment is high; currently standing at 2.39 million ... There's public unrest as the new Unemployment Assistance Board takes over responsibility for paying out a 'means tested' dole ... 38-year-old Oswald Mosley makes a rousing political speech to a group of 'black-shirts' in London. A few dissenters in the audience are roundly set upon, and beaten up by Mosley's 'Biff-Boys' ... 68-year-old prime-minister Ramsay MacDonald and his National Government announce details of a plan to deal with the chronic housing shortage ... 29-year-old, convicted baby killer, Frederick Rushworth is hanged by the neck until dead at Leeds. (64-year-old hangman Tom Pierrepoint carries out the execution) ... 20-year-old student Unity Mitford takes lunch with 45-year-old German Fuehrer Adolf Hitler, in Berlin ... "In olden days a glimpse of stocking was looked on as something shocking, but now God knows..." *Anything Goes* by The Radio Three is a popular tune ... The British Broadcasting Corporation's wireless programme schedule for a Sunday is made up of hymns, classical music and lectures given by Rev Cannon H.R.L Sheppard C.H.D.D. Up tempo dance music is avoided on the holy day ... Ramsay McDonald's National Government restricts the number of American 'swing' bands entering the UK in retaliation for a similar restriction imposed on British musicians from entering the USA ... 27-year-old football star Dixie Dean is on the score-sheet as Thomas H. McIntosh's Everton beat Grimsby Town 3-1 in Division One, and move up to fifth in the table ... 33-year-old Alex James scores a hat-trick as George Allison's, league leaders, Arsenal beat Sheffield Wednesday 5-1 at Highbury ... A fantastic new Biggles adventure story called 'Winged Menace!' begins in *The Modern Boy* magazine ... A new Simon Templar novel, *The Saint in New York* by 27-year-old Leslie Charteris, is now available in book shops ... People flock to the cinema ... "On the good ship Lollipop, it's a sweet trip to a candy shop" - 6-year-old Shirley Temple, from Santa Monica, stars in the 'talkie' film *Bright Eyes* ... "Come on lads and lassies, the factory's opened again" - 36-year-old Gracie Fields, from Rochdale, plays northern mill worker, Gracie Platt, in *Sing As We Go* ... 53-year-old sporting hero Jack Hobbs retires from first class cricket ... 15-year-old Tommy Lawton and his friends play football, with an old tin can, on the streets of Farnworth in Lancashire ... More and more houses, all across the country, are being wired for electricity. It's estimated that over half of the nation's housing stock is now connected to the National Grid ... "If you go down in the woods today, you're sure of a big surprise. If you go down in the woods today, you better go in disguise. For every bear that ever there was, will gather there for certain because, today's the day, the Teddy Bears have their picnic" - *Teddy Bears' Picnic* by Henry Hall and the BBC Dance Orchestra is a top selling gramophone record ... 11-year-old schoolboy Billy Wright, from

Ironbridge in Shropshire, plays out with his friends ... Major Frank Buckley's Wolverhampton Wanderers football team lose 2-1 against Preston North End at Deepdale ... 22-year-old outside-left Cliff Bastin scores twice as England's national team beat Ireland 2-1 at Goodison Park ... 'Well-to-do' young men dash along England's narrow roads on Wolf motorcycles ... Advertisements state, 'Wakefield Patent Castrol Motor Oil - A real advance in lubrication.'

Spring 1935... Mass unemployment

The weather is inclement ... Thirty-thousand people take to the streets of South Wales, protesting against the hated 'means test' operated by the new Unemployment Assistance Board ... Thousands more demonstrate in Sheffield and Newcastle ... By contrast, in the booming South-East of England a major house building programme is underway ... A mock Tudor semi-detached residence in Ruislip costs £495 ... A modern mid-terraced abode is Cricklewood costs £395 ... Mortgage repayment rates are extremely low ... Men peruse daily newspapers, and keep up to date with the latest sporting events. The *Daily Sketch*, the *Daily Mirror*, the *Daily Express* and the *Daily Mail* are all popular ... *Reynoldstown* wins the Grand National at Aintree ... Cambridge win the University Boat Race for a twelfth consecutive year ... Sheffield Wednesday beat Burnley 3-0 in a Football Association Cup semi-final at Villa Park ... West Bromwich Albion beat Bolton Wanderers 2-0 after a replay at the Victoria Ground ... 46-year-old jockey Freddie Cox rides *Bahram* to victory in the Two-Thousand Guineas at Doncaster ... 34-year-old Joe Davis is the World's Professional Snooker Champion for a ninth consecutive year - he beats Willie Smith from Darlington by 25 frames to 20 in the final at Thurston's Hall in Leicester Square ... 57-year-old farmer Walter Worthington murders his wife, shooting her dead with a shotgun, at St. Ives near Huntingdon ... David Gordon Nobbs is born at Orpington in Kent ... Brian Howard Clough is born at Middlesbrough ... "You can tell a man who boozes, by the company he chooses, and..." *The Pig Got Up And Slowly Walked Away* ("... Yes the pig got up and slowly walked away, slowly walked away, slowly walked away") - a popular new song by Bert Ambrose and his Orchestra (with Sam Browne on vocals) is banned by the BBC ... Radio Luxembourg plays popular, up tempo tunes - even on a Sunday ... "Peanuts! Peanuts! Fresh roasted, they're nice and hot" - *The Peanut Vendor* by Marius B. Winter and his Dance Orchestra is enjoyed by thousands of wireless listeners ... A London and North Eastern Railway steam locomotive sets a new world speed record of 108 mph, running between London and Newcastle ... 42-year-old Robert Watson-Watt from Brechin is granted a patent for his new invention - a radio device that detects and locates aircraft. (In a few years time, Watson-Watt's wonderful creation will be better known as, 'Radar') ... 45-year-old Percy Shaw's recent invention 'Cats Eyes' are used on English roads for the first time ... The latest Humber *Snipe* luxury motorcar (with running boards, Lucas *King of the Road* headlamps and spare wheel positioned in a recess on the front wing) is favoured by royals and politicians ... The latest Austin *Ten* (with a newly designed radiator grill and improved boot space) is favoured by middle-class families ... *The Modern Boy* magazine features a fantastic new Percy F. Westerman story ... 11-year-old Leslie Phillips from Tottenham in Middlesex plays out with his friends ... Great excitement builds for this year's Football Association Cup final. 28-year-old outside-left Ellis Rimmer scores two late goals to give Billy Walker's Sheffield Wednesday a 4-2 victory over Fred Everiss' West Bromwich Albion, in front of 93,204 spectators. 38-year-old Bert Fogg from Bolton is referee. A ticket for the standing enclosure at the Empire Stadium in Wembley costs 2s/6d. A seat in the North Terrace (uncovered) is 7s/6d ... George Allison's Arsenal are champions of Division One for the third year running. 22-year-old centre-forward Ted Drake has scored forty-two goals in the season. Drake's teammates, Frank Moss, Eddie Hapgood, George Male, Herbie Roberts, Jack

Crayston, Wilf Copping, Pat Beasley, Ray Bowden, Frank Hill, Joe Hulme, Cliff Bastin and 33-year-old Alex James have also played a part in Arsenal's grand achievement ... Johnny Cochrane's Sunderland are runners-up ... Tottenham Hotspur finish bottom of the table, and are relegated to Division Two along with Leicester City ... 46-year-old Thomas Edward Lawrence (aka Lawrence of Arabia) dies following a motorbike accident in Dorset ... German Fuehrer Adolf Hitler introduces compulsory military conscription - in defiance of the Treaty of Versailles ... 42-year-old Hermann Goering announces the creation of the Luftwaffe, as Germany builds up its armed forces ... 67-year-old Stanley Baldwin (Lord President in Ramsay MacDonald's National Government) announces plans to increase Britain's defence spending, and to treble the size of the RAF over the next two years ... 20-year-old Unity Mitford attends a luncheon party in Berlin with Adolf Hitler and Oswald Mosley - leader of the British Union of Fascists ... "Fanlight Fanny, the frowsy nightclub queen" - *Fanlight Fanny* by George Formby from Wigan is a popular song of the day ... 25-year-old John Bridge batters his girlfriend Amelia Nuttall to death in Salford. Police charge Bridge with murder, and six weeks later, after a trial and conviction, he's hanged by the neck until dead at Strangeways ... Street parties take place across the country, as 69-year-old King George V and 67-year-old Queen Mary celebrate their Silver Jubilee - some of the ceremony is recorded in new-fangled 'full-colour' moving pictures ... In a radio speech to the nation - the King says, "In the midst of this day's rejoicing, I grieve to think of the numbers of my people who are still without work. We owe to them, and not least to those who are suffering from any form of disablement, all the sympathy and help that we can give. I hope that during this Jubilee year, all who can, will do their utmost to find them work and bring them hope." ... 47-year-old Boris Karloff from Camberwell and 32-year-old Elsa Lanchester from Lewisham star in *The Bride of Frankenstein* at cinemas ... 31-year-old George Formby and his 33-year-old wife Beryl play the roles of John Willie and Snooky in a new film called, *Boots! Boots!* "So if women like that like men like those…" *Why Don't Women Like Me?* (performed by Formby) is a popular song from the movie ... The gramophone recording of *Lookie, Lookie, Lookie, Here Comes Cookie* by Jay Wilbur and his Band (with Pat O'Malley on vocals) is now available in department stores and electrical shops ... 41-year-old Eric Gillett presents a programme called *Bookshelf* on the wirelesss ... "We're really too utterly utter. As bored as two blighters could be. We always step over the gutter" - *We're Frightfully BBC* is a brand new comedy song, performed by The Western Brothers ... 24-year-old Fred Worrell scores a goal for England's national football team in a 1-0 victory over The Netherlands in Amsterdam ... 15-year-old Tommy Lawton from Farnworth signs for Burnley as a centre-forward ... Posters proclaim there's, '1½ glasses of full cream milk in every ½ lb slab' of *Cadbury's Milk Chocolate.*

Summer 1935... The girl who adores Hitler

The weather is warm and sunny - it's the third hot summer in a row ... Robinson's *Lemon Barley Water* is a refreshing new drink ... 26-year-old Fred Perry from Stockport wins the men's tennis singles championship at Wimbledon for the second consecutive year - defeating Gottfried von Cramm of Germany 6-2, 6-4, 6-4 in the final ... 47-year-old jockey Freddie Cox rides *Bahram* to victory in the Epsom Derby ... South Africa's cricketers win a Test Match in England for the first time - defeating Bob Wyatt's home team by 157 runs at Lord's. 32-year-old Wally Hammond is England's top run scorer. 30-year-old Hedley Verity is the pick of England's bowlers ... Motor racing drivers 27-year-old Johnny Hindmarsh and 22-year-old Luis Fontes win the Le Mans 24 hour race in France, covering a total distance of 1,867 miles at an average speed of 78 mph, in a Lagonda *Rapide* ... Back in England - driving tests are made compulsory, and 'L' plates become a legal requirement for anyone learning to drive ... Advertisements state, 'You buy a car - but you invest in an Austin'. The latest Austin *Ten Cambridge* saloon is £178 'at works' ... A speed limit of 30 mph in built-up areas comes into effect ... Standard grade petrol costs 1s/5d a gallon ... 11-year-old Tony Hancock from Hall Green in Birmingham plays out with his friends ... "The wheel of the wagon is broken, it ain't-a gonna turn no more. My days on the prairie are over, there's weeds round the old ranch door" - *The Wheel Of The Wagon Is Broken* an exciting new Foxtrot from Billy Reid and his Novelty Accordeon Band is a popular gramophone record ... Stanley Baldwin (Conservative) takes over as prime-minister from Ramsay Macdonald (National Labour) in the National Government. Sir John Simon (Liberal) is the new Home

Secretary. Sir Samuel Hoare (Conservative) is the new Foreign Secretary ... 35-year-old movie director Alfred Hitchcock attends the premier of his new 'talkie' film, *The 39 Steps*, in London - Robert Donat (from Manchester) and Madeleine Carroll (from West Bromwich) are the stars ... *Boys Will Be Boys*, a new 'talkie' featuring 46-year-old Will Hay and 16-year-old Jimmy Hanley, is now on general release at cinemas all around the country ... 65-year-old entertainer George Robey (aka the Prime Minister of Mirth) stars in *Accidentally Yours* at the Theatre Royal on New Street in Birmingham ... The Smith family from Chigwell take a short seaside holiday on Canvey Island, and enjoy afternoon tea in the Labworth Café ... 29-year-old Bill Lovell from Birmingham sits on the beach at Barmouth reading *English Journey* - a book by 40-year-old author J. B. Priestley ... 57-year-old convicted murderer Walter Worthington is hanged by the neck until dead at Bedford ... Fourteen people die in a train crash at Welwyn Garden City ... A new cartoon strip called Rupert the Bear is published in *The Daily Express* newspaper ... Big-band swing music is hugely popular ... 38-year-old Bert Ambrose and his Orchestra begin a two-week stint at the Palladium ... 37-year-old Henry Hall directs the BBC Dance Orchestra daily on the wireless ... 42-year-old Jack Hylton and his Orchestra record their own version of the popular song *Anything Goes* ... A new 'Art Deco' *Odeon* cinema opens at Kingstanding in Birmingham ... A new 'Art Deco' independent cinema called 'Towers' opens at Hornchurch in Essex ... 34-year-old Gary Cooper stars in *The Lives of a Bengal Lancer* ... The latest MG *PB* 'sports' motorcar has a 939cc engine and re-designed radiator grill - top speed is 76 mph and 0-60 mph takes 27.4 seconds ... The General Post Office introduces a new Greeting Telegram - charging just 9d for nine words ... The world's longest escalator is now operational at Leicester Square tube station ... 'The Girl Who Adores Hitler' - 20-year-old student Unity Mitford openly supports Nazism, and makes a statement in the press denigrating Jewish people ... "I get no kick from Champagne. Mere alcohol doesn't thrill me at all" - *I Get A Kick Out Of You* by The Radio Three is a popular song ... *Penguin* paperback books are launched. The first ten titles in the affordable new range include Ernest Hemingway's *A Farewell To Arms* and detective novels by Agatha Christie and Dorothy L Sayers. (The books are available now in *Woolworths* for just sixpence each) ... The village of Mardale in the Lake District is flooded, and disappears forever, making way for Manchester Corporation's new Haweswater Reservoir ... Rodney Stephen Hull is born on the Isle of Sheppey in Kent ... 45-year-old Adolf Hitler approves the Swastika as the new official emblem of Germany ... "Red sails in the sunset, way out on the sea. Oh! Carry my loved one home, safely to me" - *Red Sails in the Sunset* by Joe Loss and his Orchestra (with 18-year-old Vera Lynn on vocals) is a wonderful new song - and it's now available as a gramophone recording ... *I Wished On The Moon* ("... for something I never knew") by Ray Noble and his Orchestra (with 37-year-old Al Bowlly on vocals) is also new ... The 1935-1936 football season gets underway ... 23-year-old Ted Drake scores twice as reigning champions Arsenal beat Sunderland 3-1 in front of 66,428 at Highbury ... 22-year-old Fred Howe scores four goals as Liverpool thrash Everton 6-0 in front of 46,082 at Anfield ... 29-year-old Tom 'Pongo' Waring scores for Aston Villa in a 1-2 victory over Middlesbrough in front of 22,421 at Ayresome Park ... 'Well-to-do' young men dash along England's narrow roads on Matchless *Silver Hawk* motorcycles ...

Advertisements say, ‘Combine Health with Pleasure in a glass of OVALTINE COLD - the delightful summer drink’.

Autumn 1935...
Baldwin defeats Attlee at general election

28-year-old Charlie Smirke rides *Bahram* to victory in the St. Ledger at Doncaster - and *Bahram* is the first racehorse to win 'the triple crown' since *Rock Sand* in the year 1903 ... Mortgage rates remain low under Stanley Baldwin's National Government ... House building continues in the South and the Midlands ... Unemployment black spots (mainly in the North) miss out on the housing boom ... Poverty, sickness and squalor are commonplace for tens of thousands of families ... 17-year-old Bill Davies begins work at the U.C.P. (United Cow Products) tripe preparation factory in Bolton earning £1/7s/- a week ... 19-year-old student Edward Heath from Broadstairs goes up to Oxford to read Philosophy, Politics and Economics ... 19-year-old Harold Wilson from Huddersfield begins a second year reading Modern History at Jesus College ... 11-year-old Benny Hill from Southampton plays out with his friends ... *Dandy Dick* - a new 'talkie' film, starring 46-year-old Will Hay and 27-year-old Nancy Burne, is 'now showing' at picture houses ... 42-year-old Stuart Hibberd announces the news on BBC radio ... Allan Grierson murders 63-year-old Louise Gann near Regents Park in London ... A major fire breaks out at the Colonial Wharf in Wapping - and it takes firemen four days to get the blaze under control ... Bud Flanagan, Chesney Allen and 35-year-old Alastair Sim star in new comedy film *A Fire Has Been Arranged* at cinemas ... 37-year-old Gracie Fields from Rochdale stars in *Look Up and Laugh* ... "I'm, puttin' on my top hat, tyin' up my white tie, brushin' off my tails" - Ray Noble and his Orchestra (with Al Bowlly on vocals) perform the title song from a new American musical called *Top Hat* ... Schoolboys collect *Ogden's* cigarette cards with pictures of famous footballers. 'W. R. Dean (Everton)' - the image of 28-year-old Dixie Dean of Everton is much sought after ... 20-year-old outside-right Stanley Matthews of Stoke City scores a hat-trick in a 5-0 win against Birmingham at the Victoria Ground ... Tom 'Pongo' Waring of Aston Villa scores twice in 2-0 victory over Sunderland - and shortly afterwards is transferred to Barnsley without explanation. Dismayed supporters gather outside Villa Park to protest ... A record attendance of 82,905 is at Stamford Bridge to watch Chelsea play against their London rivals, Arsenal. Joseph Bambrick (Chelsea) and Jack Crayston (Arsenal) are the goal scorers in a 1-1 draw ... Three-inch hail stones injure live-stock and cause damage to buildings during a storm in Oxfordshire and Northamptonshire ... 27-year-old convicted murderer Allan Grierson is hanged by the neck until dead at Pentonville ... 76-year-old George Lansbury is ousted as leader of the Labour party and is succeeded by 52-year-old Clement Attlee from Putney ... 68-year-old prime-minister Stanley Baldwin (Conservative) calls a general election and leads the coalition National Government to victory. (Conservative: 386 seats, Labour: 154 seats, Liberal National: 33 seats, Liberal: 21 seats, National Labour: 8 seats, Independent Labour Party: 4 seats) ... Former prime-minister Ramsay MacDonald (National Labour) loses his seat by a margin of 20,000 votes to Manny Shinwell (Labour) ... 30-year-old Labour candidate Jennie Lee (wife of Aneurin Bevan) fails to get elected in North Lanark ... The new RAF Hawker *Hurricane* fighter plane makes its maiden flight ... 50-year-old Sir Malcolm Campbell sets a new land speed record of 301.3337 mph in Bluebird at the Bonneville Salt Flats in America … 53-year-old wireless presenter Major Christopher Stone plays gramophone records 'live' on-air on Radio Luxembourg ... *You're The Top*

("... you're the Colosseum! You're the top! You're the Louver Museum") by 43-year-old Jack Hylton and his Band (with Pat O'Malley and Eve Becke on vocals) is a popular song ... Lunch hour fitness classes keep office workers full of vim and vitality ... *J. Lyons & Co* open a new teashop on Whitefriargate in Hull ... 'A Merry Musical Burlesque' - a new film called *Off the Dole*, starring 31-year-old George Formby from Wigan and his 34-year-old wife Beryl, is now showing at cinemas ... *Gaudy Night* - a new novel by 42-year-old Dorothy L Sayers, featuring the characters Lord Peter Wimsey and Harriet Vane, is now available in book shops ... Thousands of eager spectators flock to the Brooklands motor racing circuit for the International 500 mile event. The 'daring' John Cobb and his co-driver Tim Rose-Richards win the race in a 120 mph Napier-Railton car (number 42) ... A new road sign with the instruction, 'Halt At Major Road Ahead' is ignored by motorists and dozens of accidents occur ... A new public transport system comprising of bright yellow trolley-buses is now operational on the streets of Newcastle-upon-Tyne ... A lorry driver and his wife, Mr. & Mrs. Miles, are proud parents of newborn quadruplets in St Neots - the happy news is reported in the newspapers and well-wishers from all around the country send gifts to the babies: Ann, Ernest, Paul and Michael ... Advertisements say, *Lucozade* is 'tonic food beverage'.

Christmas 1935… We are the Ovaltineys

There's a light covering of snow ... Mr. Victor Farmer enjoys a game of bar-billiards at the Locomotive public house in Ashford, Kent ... 24-year-old petty criminal Billy Hill carries out a smash and grab raid on a jewellery shop in London's West End ... 12-year-old Frankie Fraser from Lambeth plays out with his friends ... "It was on the Isle of Capri that I found her, beneath the shade of an old walnut tree. Oh, I can still see the flowers blooming around her, where we met…" *On The Isle Of Capri* by Ray Noble and his Orchestra (with Al Bowlly on vocals) is a popular gramophone recording ... Women in clogs clip-clop over cobbled paving stones to begin a ten-hour shift in northern factory mills ... High pollution and heavy smog chokes major cities in the week before Christmas ... 1,779 coal mines are operational in Britain - employing 750,000 workers and producing 226 million tonnes per year ... *Blackshirt* - 'the patriotic worker's paper' can be purchased from street vendors for one penny ... "It's behind you!" - Middle-class families enjoy an evening at the Pantomime ... 60-year-old music-hall star Florrie Forde appears in *40 Thieves* at the Lyceum in London ... *Jack and the Beanstalk* is now showing at Drury Lane ... Advances in communication technology are embraced by hundreds of thousands of people ... The number of telephone users is on the increase ... The amount of telegrams being sent is in decline ... The weather turns extremely cold in the week before Christmas, bringing widespread frost and ice ... Christmas arrives ... Schoolboys make a wish for a new *Dinky Toys* model of a motorcar or a lorry ... Lucky young chaps get a *Meccano* construction set on Christmas morning ... 'The Biscuits of the Year - in Christmas Gala Boxes' - Assorted Tea Biscuits from *Huntley & Palmers* are

2s/6d ... A full length 'talkie' version of Scrooge is now showing at cinemas, with 64-year-old Sir Seymour Hicks in the title role ... 24-year-old Jean Harlow (34-25-36) has men flocking to picture-houses to see her latest movie, *Reckless* ... "If there's one thing that I like, it's riding around on a motorbike" - up and coming comedy star George Formby from Wigan plays the role of an Isle of Man TT motorcycle racer in his new film, *No Limit* ... "Sailing home at the end of the day, with the North Star to guide him and light the way" - Charlie Kunz and the Casani Club Orchestra (with 18-year-old Vera Lynn on vocals) perform *Sailing Home With The Tide* ... "We are the Ovaltineys, little girls and boys" - children tune in to Radio Luxembourg every Sunday between 5.30 p.m. and 6.00 p.m. to hear *The Ovaltiney Club* ... "A grand little lad was young Albert, all dressed in his best - quite a swell. With a stick with a horse's head handle - the finest that Woolworths could sell" - 45-year-old Stanley Holloway recites a delightful monologue called *The Lion And Albert* ... British-Pathé newsreels keep cinema audiences up to date with the latest news and sports events ... 55-year-old Foreign Secretary Sir Samuel Hoare makes a mess of the crisis in Abyssinia and is forced to step down. (38-year-old Anthony Eden from County Durham replaces Hoare) ... 32-year-old Charlotte Bryant (a mother of five children) poisons her husband with arsenic at Coombe in Dorset ... George Allison's Arsenal football team thrash Jimmy McMullan's Aston Villa 1-7 at Villa Park, with centre-forward Ted Drake scoring all seven goals! Two weeks later, 59,250 turn out at Roker Park to see league leaders Sunderland beat Arsenal 5-4 with Bert Davis, Patsy Gallacher, Jimmy Connor and 22-year-old Raich Carter (2) scoring the goals for Sunderland ... Second placed Derby County draw 3-3 with Everton at the Baseball Ground ... 24-year-old Bunny Bell scores nine goals as Tranmere Rovers thrash Oldham Athletic 13-4 in Division Three (North) ... 20-year-old outside-right Stanley Matthews plays for England in a 3-0 victory over Germany in front of 54,164 at White Hart Lane - Middlesbrough's George Camsell scores twice and Arsenal's Cliff Bastin gets the third ... "There's a wonderful light in the sky tonight" - *Roll Along, Prairie Moon* by Jack Jackson and his Dorchester Orchestra (with Fred Latham on vocals) is a popular new song ... *Brylcreem* is advertised as 'the perfect hair dressing' ... *Men Only* magazine goes on sale in newsagents and costs one shilling ... There are 77,500 public houses in the UK ... A pint of mild in the Red Lion costs fourpence ... "Believe me, you'll smoke them sooner or later!" - a packet of twenty *Craven 'A'* cigarettes costs one shilling.

New Year 1936... The King is dead. Long live the King

'Rag and bone' men go about their business, buying and selling junk from wooden hand-carts, as they pass through dreary urban streets ... 11-year-old Harry H. Corbett from Wythenshawe in Manchester reads a comic, by torch light, beneath his bed covers ... An exciting new 'Ken King' story begins in *The Modern Boy* magazine ... *The Mickey Mouse Weekly* goes on sale for 2d ... The weather turns cold ... Roads and railways are blocked in the Midlands and the North after heavy snowfalls ... Telephone lines and telegraph poles are brought down ... Author and poet Rudyard Kipling dies from a perforated duodenal ulcer aged 70 ... King George V rejects a trip to the seaside (saying "Bugger Bognor!") and dies also aged 70 ... The mood across Britain and the Commonwealth is somber as images of the King's state funeral are transmitted by Pathé Gazette on cinema screens ... George's son - the dashing, chain smoking, 41-year-old Prince of Wales succeeds his father and becomes King Edward VIII ... "Oh moanin' Minnie, her voice is tinny, but when she starts to wail, it sounds just like a gale at sea" - Jack Hylton and his Band (with 12-year-old Pat Sibley on vocals) perform the popular song *Moanin' Minnie* ... 52-year-old John Maynard Keynes publishes *The General Theory of Employment, Interest and Money* - showing that recessions are caused by insufficient demand in the economy and that increased investment in public works, and the lowering of interest rates, would boost consumer spending ... 32-year-old writer George Orwell lives among the poor mining communities of Wigan, carrying out research for his next book ... Communication technology moves on apace ... The GPO introduces the iconic K6 red telephone boxes, as part of a plan to provide public telephones to every village in England with a post office ... Over six-million radio 'Receiving Licenses' are issued annually ... A Marconi *556* all-wave radio receiver costs 13½ guineas, or can be obtained on hire-purchase for four shillings weekly ... *The ABC Murders* - a new 'whodunit' novel by 45-year-old Agatha Christie is now on sale in book shops ... *Alone* - a new gramophone record by 30-year-old Tommy Dorsey and his Orchestra (with Cliff Weston performing vocals) is on sale in department stores ... In Football League Division One, 23-year-old Ronnie Dix scores twice as Jimmy McMullan's bottom-of-the-table Aston Villa gain a surprise 1-3 away victory over league leaders Sunderland ... In Football League Division Two, 23-year-old Tommy Manley scores four goals, and 32-year-old Henry Rowley scores twice, as Manchester Utd thrash Port Vale 7-2 in front of 22,265 at Old Trafford ... The brand new 'streamlined' London and North Eastern Railway steam locomotive *Silver Jubilee* runs between King's Cross and Newcastle-upon-Tyne in just four hours ... Cedric Hardwicke, Raymond Massey and 33-year-old Ralph Richardson star in H.G. Wells' terrifying new science-fiction film *Things to Come* ... Stylish new 'Art Deco' *Odeon* cinemas are springing up in towns and cities all around the country ... 'Again the jungle trembles to the challenge of his mighty roar!' - 31-year-old Johnny Weissmuller is Tarzan, and 24-year-old Maureen O'Sullivan is Jane, in the new movie *Tarzan Escapes* ... 29-year-old Greta Garbo (36-28-38) stars in *Anna Karenina* ... 32-year-old Bing Crosby and 28-year-old Ethel Merman star in the film version of *Anything Goes* ... "A fine romance, with no kisses. A fine romance, my friend this is" - 36-year-old Harry Roy (aka the King of 'Hot-Cha') and his May Fair Hotel Orchestra perform the popular song *A Fine Romance* ... 25-year-old Dennis Buckley from Bristol purchases a HMV *102* portable gramophone player for £6, after saving up for twelve months. The first record to be played on the new machine is *Nagasaki* by Nat Gonella and his Georgians ... 21-year-old Norman Wisdom completes a five-year stint in the army in India and returns to England ... 'Player's Please' - advertisements for cigarettes say, 'From every point of view... it's the tobacco that counts' ... Advertisements for matches declare, '*Swan Vestas* - The Smokers' Match'.

Spring 1936... Amy 'Johnnie' Johnson takes to the skies

The weather is cold, dull and windy ... Voguish women in London pay to have their ears pierced - a new 'fashion' that's all the rage among the bright young set ... 32-year-old 'Queen of the Sky' Amy Mollison (nee Johnson) flies single-handedly from London to Cape Town - and back again - in just 7 days, 23 hours, 46 minutes ... 31-year-old Captain Joseph 'Mutt' Summers takes the brand new *Spitfire* fighter plane for an initial test flight - and is so impressed with the splendid new aircraft, he tells engineers, "Don't touch anything!" ... The brand new MG *TA* Midget motorcar is launched - with a top speed of 79 mph and capable of reaching 60 mph in 23.5 seconds ... Stanley Baldwin's National Government announces plans to build thirty-eight new warships ... "There may be trouble ahead but while there's moonlight and music, and love and romance..." *Let's Face The Music And Dance* by Billy Cotton and his Band (with Alan Breeze on vocals) is a top selling gramophone record ... 36-year-old Richard Hauptman is convicted of murdering the Lindbergh baby in America and is executed in 'Old Smokey' electric chair on the third of April ... Unemployment in Britain falls to 1.9 million - it's the first time the figure has dipped beneath 2 million in six years ... 32-year-old writer George Orwell moves from Wigan to Sheffield to continue his research into the lives of poor people ... 11-year-old Anthony Wedgwood Benn from Marylebone in London reads books and listens to the wireless ... *Reynoldstown* wins the Grand National for a second year running. The favourite, *Golden Miller*, falls at the eighth ... Cambridge win the Boat Race by five lengths - it's their thirteenth consecutive win ... 36-year-old convicted murderer Dorothy Waddingham is hanged by the neck until dead at Winson Green. (Waddingham had poisoned an elderly woman and her daughter in a Nottingham nursing home last year) ... *Golden Miller* recovers from the fall at Aintree to win the Cheltenham Gold Cup for a fifth successive year ... 22-year-old footballer Joe Payne scores ten goals as Luton Town thrash Bristol Rovers 12-0 in Division Three (South) ... 23-year-old Arsenal centre-forward Ted Drake scores the only goal of the tie in the Football Association Cup final as 'The Gunners' beat Sheffield Utd 1-0. A ticket for the standing enclosure at the Empire Stadium in Wembley costs 2s/6d ... 26-year-old right-half Matt Busby leaves Manchester City and joins Liverpool for £8,000 ... 16-year-old Tommy Lawton makes his first team debut for Burnley as centre-forward ... 17-year-old Bill Nicholson is taken on as a trainee by Tottenham Hotspur ... 28-year-old Bobby Gurney scores four goals as Johnny Cochrane's Sunderland thrash Birmingham 2-7 at St. Andrew's - and Sunderland are the new champions of Division One. Jimmy Thorpe, Jimmy Clark, Jimmy Connor, Sandy McNab, Bert Davis, Len Duns, Patsy Gallacher, Raich Carter, Bobby Gurney, Alex Hall, Alex Hastings, Tom Morrison, Charlie Thompson and 34-year-old Bill Murray have all been outstanding for 'The Black Cats'... Aston Villa and Blackburn Rovers are relegated to Division Two - a massive humiliation to two long established and highly respected football clubs ... 35-year-old Joe Davis is the World's Professional Snooker Champion for a tenth consecutive year - he beats Horace Lindrum from Australia by 34 frames to 27 in the final at Thurston's Hall in Leicester Square ... 46-year-old German Fuehrer Adolf Hitler violates Article 43 of the Treaty of Versailles by moving his troops into the demilitarised zone of the Rhineland ... 38-year-old British Foreign Secretary Anthony Eden appears to turn a blind eye to Hitler's military aggression ... "I'd work for you, I'd slave for you, I'd be a beggar or a knave for you - if that isn't love, it'll have to do..." *Until The Real Thing Comes Along* by Jack Payne and his Band (with Billy Scott-Coomber on vocals) is a popular song ... The British Broadcasting Corporation prepares to transmit new-fangled 'television' to households in London - a two-hundred foot high mast is erected at the Alexandra Palace ... Children purchase Trebor *Refreshers* from the sweet shop ... Mackintosh introduce *Quality Street* - 5lbs tins of individually wrapped chocolate covered sweets, for ten shillings ... Bentley introduce a new 4¼ litre motorcar to replace the 3½ litre model - top speed increases from 90 mph to 96 mph ... Standard grade petrol costs 1s/6d a gallon ... 'Delicious. Economical. Refreshing.' - a 4oz packet of *Ty-Phoo* tea costs 1s/9d ... An exciting, new (small and individually wrapped) chocolate bar from *Mars* costs tuppence.

Summer 1936... New-fangled 'television'

93,267 spectators turn out at the Empire Stadium in Wembley to see England's footballers take on Scotland in the final match of British Home Championship. George Camsell opens the scoring for England but an equalising penalty from Tommy Walker in the 77th minute is sufficient for Scotland to become champions - and England are the runners-up ... 10-year-old Nat Lofthouse from Bolton in Lancashire dreams of one day playing football for his country ... Boys climb trees ... Girls take turns with a skipping rope ... The skies turn grey and there are frequent thunder storms throughout June and July ... 36-year-old Billy Butlin opens his first holiday camp in Skegness. ... Celebrity aviators (and popular 'golden' couple) 32-year-old Amy and 31-year-old Jim Mollison are on hand to perform the opening ceremony for the new out-door swimming pool ... The sun shines in late August and temperatures rise ... Children enjoy *Eiffel Tower* lemonade ... The new swimming pool in Morecambe is the largest open air lido in Europe ... 29-year-old jockey Charlie Smirke rides *Mahmoud* to victory in the Epsom Derby ... The ocean liner *Queen Mary* makes its maiden voyage to New York ... "Hurry to me great liner, for you can make my dream come true, wherever you be, answer my plea..." *Somewhere At Sea* by Henry Hall and the BBC Dance Orchestra (with Dan Donovan on vocals) is a popular song ... 29-year-old inventor Frank Whittle from Coventry dreams of creating a high powered jet engine for aircraft - and forms a new company to develop his idea ... The German airship *Hindenburg* crosses the Atlantic in forty-six hours ... Gatwick airport opens ... Aer Lingus makes its first flight between Ireland and England ... Alfred Hitcock's new 'talkie' film *Secret Agent*, starring 32-year-old John Gielgud and

30-year-old Madeleine Carroll, is now showing at cinemas ... 'What's the use of trying? / Buck up - never say die. We'll get along!' - 47-year-old world-wide movie star Charlie Chaplin plays a factory worker in the silent movie *Modern Times* - the story of a little man trying to survive in the fast moving industrial world ... The number of unemployed people in Britain stands at approximately 1.9 million ... The hated U.A.E. 'means test' confines many families to poverty and hunger ... Frustrated at having no job - Mr. R. Tebbit (father of sweet little 5-year-old Norman) gets on his bicycle and goes looking for work - and keeps looking until he's found it ... 33-year-old Arthur Mitchell and 21-year-old Harold Gimblett stride out together to open the batting for England's cricket team at Lord's against India. England win the series 2-0 with captain Gubby Allen taking 7 wickets for 80 runs and batsman Wally Hammond scoring 217 in the final Test at the Oval ... 27-year-old tennis player Fred Perry from Stockport wins the men's singles championship at Wimbledon for the third consecutive year - beating Gottfried von Cramm of Germany 6-1, 6-1, 6-0 in the final ... 33-year-old convicted murderer (and mother of five) Charlotte Bryant is hanged by the neck until dead at Exeter ... George McMahon pulls out a gun as the dashing, chain smoking King Edward VIII passes by on Constitution Hill. McMahon is overpowered by a policeman and the new King is unharmed ... An exciting new Biggles story begins in *The Modern Boy* magazine ... An explosion at Wharncliffe Woodmoor Colliery in South Yorkshire kills fifty-eight men - and a local schoolroom is set up as a makeshift mortuary as the recovery operation gets underway ... Over in Europe - 22-year-old Jesse Owens wins gold in the 100 metre sprint at the Olympic Games in Berlin. German Fuehrer Adolf Hitler refuses to bestow the medal on the black athlete.

Owens (from Alabama in America) also wins the 200 metre race, the 400 metre relay and the long jump ... Back in England - 44-year-old band leader Jack Hylton records a number of popular songs including *You Turned The Tables On Me* and *You've Got The Wrong Rumba* ... Billy Cotton and his Band record *I Bet You Tell That To All The Girls* ... "Good afternoon ladies and gentlemen. It is with great pleasure that I introduce you to the magic of television" - 30-year-old Leslie Mitchell introduces black and white images of a performing horse called Pogo as the BBC broadcasts moving pictures to television sets at Waterloo Station ... The GPO introduces 'the speaking clock' ... Civil War breaks out in Spain and 33-year-old author George Orwell takes up the cause for the Republicans, fighting against Francisco Franco's Nationalists ... Millions of people flock to the pictures to see lovable entertainer George Formby in his latest film, *Keep Your Seats, Please.* "Now I go cleaning windows to earn an honest bob. For a nosey parker it's an interesting job. Now it's a job that just suits me, a window cleaner you would be, if you can see what I can see…" *When I'm Cleaning Windows* (performed by 32-year-old Formby) is a hugely popular song from the movie ... 23-year-old dwarf Max Haslam robs and murders 74-year-old Ruth Clarkson in Nelson ... 23-year-old Christopher Jackson robs and murders his 62-year-old aunt in Sunderland ... Agatha Christie's latest 'whodunit' novel *Murder in Mesopotamia* is in bookshops priced at 7s/6d ... Author G. K. Chesterton dies of heart failure aged 62 at his home in Beaconsfield ... 42-year-old King Edward VIII and his companion Mrs. Wallis Simpson take a cruise on a luxury yacht in the Aegean. This potentially scandalous affair between the King and a married woman goes unreported in the newspapers ... 61-year-old Winston Churchill MP warns prime-minister Stanley Baldwin that a tougher approach is needed to counter the threat of the German Fuehrer Adolf Hitler and his Nazis ... "I find it difficult to think that once you cared for me at all. I can't believe that you refuse to speak to me each time I call" - Charlie Kunz and his Casani Club Orchestra (with 19-year-old Vera Lynn on vocals) make a gramophone recording of the popular song *Have You Forgotten So Soon* ... *J. Lyons & Co* open a new teashop on the High Street in Chatham ... Men flock to cinemas to see 42-year-old Mae West (38-24-38) in *Klondike Annie* ... The ocean liner *Queen Mary* sets a new speed record - crossing the Atlantic in just four days and twenty-seven minutes ... The BBC broadcasts a television programme showing highlights of a football match between Arsenal and Everton. 34-year-old Alex James scores a goal for Arsenal and 29-year-old Dixie Dean scores for Everton - the result of the match is a 3-2 victory to the Arsenal ... The income of middle-class people has increased over the past couple of years ... 'Modern homes for modern people!' - a contemporary semi-detached house with three bedrooms costs around £650 ... The improved Austin *Seven* motorcar has a new engine with three-bearing crankshaft, more efficient brakes, a new flexible clutch and improved coachwork - the *Ruby* fixed-head saloon has a top speed of 50 mph and costs £125 'at works' ... A shiny new Ariel *Square Four* 600cc motorcycle has a top speed of 77 mph and costs £80 ... Advertisements for *Shredded Wheat* say, 'Britons make it - it makes Britons'.

Autumn 1936... Jarrow March

The Modern Boy magazine runs a feature on the 'wonders of the new television!' ... The BBC begin regular television broadcasts from Alexandra Palace - but only transmitting over a distance of twenty-five miles to the two-hundred or so television receivers in the London area ... A Baird *Televisor* receiving set (with a 12-inch x 9-inch screen) is available for 85 guineas ... 24-year-old Elizabeth Cowell is the first female presenter on BBC television ... 33-year-old Beryl Markham from Rutland flies single-handedly across the Atlantic in twenty-hours - before crash landing in Novia Scotia ... 44-year-old 'Flying' Freddie Dixon from Stockton-on-Tees wins the 500 mile race at Brooklands in a Riley motorcar - in front of two hundred-thousand enthusiastic spectators ... A new film studio opens at Pinewood ... Courting couples enjoy a Friday night out at the cinema ... 34-year-old Marlene Dietrich (36-26-33) stars alongside 35-year-old Gary Cooper in a new film called *Desire* ... Courting couples enjoy a Saturday night out at the dance hall ... 36-year-old Victor Silvester and his Ballroom Orchestra perform *Let's Sing Again* - a popular new (slow) Foxtrot ... 19-year-old student Denis Healey from Keighley in Yorkshire goes up to Oxford to read Literae Humaniores (Greats) ... 11-year-old Margaret Hilda Roberts from Grantham in Lincolnshire sets the rules for skipping games with her friends ... Millionaire businessman Frank Hornby dies aged 73 in Maghull ... 69-year-old prime-minister Stanley Baldwin confronts the dashing, chain smoking King Edward VIII over his relationship with the twice married Mrs. Wallis Simpson ... Newspapers and radio maintain a reporting embargo - and the general public is unaware of the King's love affair ... "When troubles trouble you..." *Sing, Baby*

Sing by Jack Hylton and his Band (with Alice Mann on vocals) is a popular gramophone record ... "Boo-boop-de-do" - Betty Boop stars in the cartoon *Betty Boop and Grampy* ... Heavy smog pollutes the skies over Manchester, Liverpool and Birmingham ... Poverty and hunger prevail in overlooked communities ... 44-year-old 'Red' Ellen Wilkinson MP leads a march of two-hundred unemployed ship workers from Jarrow to London. Prime-minister Stanley Baldwin refuses to meet the crusaders when they arrive in the capital twenty-six days later ... 42-year-old King Edward VIII witnesses thousands of unemployed people on a visit to South Wales and says, "Something must be done." ... Approximately one hundred-thousand people barricade the streets of East London to prevent Oswald Mosley's fascist 'black-shirts' from passing through - at least eighty are injured in violent clashes on Cable Street ... The new 'Art Deco' East Stand at Arsenal's football stadium is opened - it's designed to match the West Stand which was completed in 1932. Arsenal's first match in front of the new stand is a 0-0 draw against Grimsby Town ... 17-year-old Tommy Lawton scores a hat-trick for Burnley in a 3-1 victory over Tottenham Hotspur ... Jimmy Hogan's Aston Villa are top of Division Two after a 5-1 victory over Bradford City ... Gladstone Edwards and his wife Sarah from Dudley in Worcestershire are proud parents of Duncan - their new baby boy ... 38-year-old Jimmy Nervo and 40-year-old Teddy Knox star as two hapless chancers in a grand new comedy film called *It's In The Bag* ... 34-year-old 'Queen of the Sky' Amy Mollison (nee Johnson) announces that she is separating from her husband Jim, amidst rumours of his affair with Beryl Markham ... Band leader Bert Ambrose performs *I've Got You Under My Skin* ("... I've got you deep in the heart of me") - Sam Browne is on vocals ... Young children are encouraged to walk, run, skip and gallop around the room as they listen to *Music and Movement* on BBC radio ... 'Well-to-do' young men with pencil moustaches and a glint in their eye race along England's narrow country roads in sports cars ... The latest Alvis *Speed 20* two-seater drophead tourer has a top speed of 90 mph.

Christmas 1936... Abdication of King Edward VIII

People purchase 10-inch shellac gramophone discs, containing recordings of popular songs, from electrical shops and department stores for 1s/6d ... "A cigarette that bears a lipstick's traces. An airline ticket to romantic places. And still my heart has wings..." *These Foolish Things* ("... remind me of you") by notorious 36-year-old entertainer Leslie 'Hutch' Hutchinson (at the piano) is one of the best selling songs of the day ... Children become excited as Christmas draws near ... Advertisements claim train-sets and dolls-houses in Bakelite make 'better and more durable toys' ... Rowntree's *Dairy Box* chocolates are new ... *Monopoly* (an exciting board game from America) is in demand ... 43-year-old Stuart Hibberd announces the news on the wireless for the BBC ... The 85-year-old Crystal Palace building (constructed of cast iron and plate-glass) is destroyed by fire ... The entire nation is shocked when details of King Edward VIII's relationship with divorcee Mrs. Wallis Simpson are finally reported in the newspapers. A week of turmoil follows before the popular 42-year-old monarch abdicates from the throne - he speaks on the wireless, explaining that he found it impossible to carry the burden of kingship "without the help and support of the woman I love." ... Edward's 41-year-old brother, the Duke of York, becomes King George VI ... *Queen of Hearts*, starring 38-year-old Gracie Fields from Rochdale, is now showing at picture houses ... 48-year-old Wally Patch stars in *Busman's Holiday* ... "Oh, every time it rains, it rains pennies from heaven. Don't you know each cloud contains..." *Pennies From Heaven* is a hugely popular movie from America, starring 33-year-old Bing Crosby ... The selection committee from the Football Association chooses the England team for an international match against

Hungary at Highbury - 24-year-old centre-forward Ted Drake (of the Arsenal) scores a hat-trick as England win 6-2. Cliff Britton (of Everton), Raich Carter (of Sunderland) and Eric 'hot-shot' Brook (of Manchester City) are also on the score-sheet ... 21-year-old outside-right Stanley Matthews scores twice for Stoke City in a 2-2 draw against Bolton Wanderers in Division One ... Schoolboys collect *Godfrey Phillips* cigarette football cards ... Everton sign teenage centre-forward Tommy Lawton from Burnley for £6,500 - hoping he'll become a worthy successor to the legendary Dixie Dean (who's nearing the end of his career) ... 34-year-old Gubby Allen leads England's cricketers in the first Test Match down-under. 28-year-old Don Bradman captains the Australians for the first time - but he's on the losing side as Maurice Leyland knocks 126 runs and England win in Brisbane. Wally Hammond scores an unbeaten 231 in the second Test and England take a 2-0 lead into the new year ... 24-year-old convicted murderer Christopher Jackson is hanged by the neck until dead at Durham ... 25-year-old petty criminal Billy Hill steals from a furrier's shop in London and spends Christmas in prison ... Popular singer 38-year-old Al Bowlly performs vocals for Maurice Winnick and his Sweet Music on the popular new gramophone recording of the song *There's A Gold Mine In The Sky* ("... far away. We will find it, you and I some sweet day") ... Alfred Hitchcock's new thriller *Sabotage* draws crowds of people to cinemas ... 30-year-old John Wayne stars in *The Lawless Frontier* - an American 'Western' film ... A new guide to 'self advancement' called *How To Win Friends and Influence People* by 48-year-old American author Dale Carnegie is now available from a few select bookshops ... 24-year-old Melita Norwood from Bournemouth joins the Communist Party ... 23-year-old Nelly Aldridge from Liverpool is engaged as house-keeper at a mansion on Lancaster Gate in London ... Advertisements say, '*Brasso* - For Beautiful Brass'.

New Year 1937... Life in Metroland

Stanley Baldwin's National Government introduces the Public Order Act banning public demonstrations by political groups wearing uniforms - preventing Oswald Mosley and his British Union of Fascists from wearing their infamous black shirts ... 54-year-old Franklin D. Roosevelt begins a second term as President of America ... Henry and Eliza Bassey from Cardiff are proud parents of newborn daughter Shirley - their sixth child ... 11-year-old Kenneth Williams from Kings Cross in London goes to the cinema to see new comedy film *All That Glitters* - starring 43-year-old Jack Hobbs and 33-year-old Moira Lynd ... *Good Morning, Boys,* starring 48-year-old Will Hay, is also now showing ... Vocalist Al Bowlly sings with Ray Noble and his Band on the popular new song *The Touch Of Your Lips* ("... upon my brow, your lips that are cool and sweet") ... 'If you move, it's rude' - The Windmill theatre in London draws crowds of men to watch notable historic scenes depicted by statuesque nude women ... 23-year-old dwarf and convicted murderer Max Haslam is hanged by the neck until dead at Strangeways ... Australian cricketer Don Bradman scores two double hundreds and a century in the remaining three Test Matches - and the Aussies come back from 2-0 down to retain the Ashes with a 3-2 series win over Gubby Allen's England. T S Worthington, C J Barnett, A E Fagg, W R Hammond, M Leyland, L E G Ames (wk), G O B Allen (cpt), J Hardstaff, R W V Robins, H Verity, W Voce, J M Sims and K Farnes are all downcast by an Ashes defeat ... King George VI receives a Nazi salute from the German Ambassador in London ... Adolf Hitler makes a speech at the Reichstag confirming that Germany no longer acknowledges the Treaty of Versailles ... Bob McGrory's Stoke City thrash Fred

Everiss' West Bromwich Albion 10-3 in front of 8,325 at the Victoria Ground - 20-year-old Freddie Steele scores five of Stoke's goals... 23-year-old Walter Winterbottom plays wing-half for Manchester Utd in a 1-1 draw against the Arsenal ... A snap of cold weather hits the country ... Working men in cloth caps and mufflers shuffle along icy pavements to the local pub ... A bottle of *Whitbread's* pale ale costs 5d ... Deep snow (up to two-feet in places) and severe blizzards lead to transport chaos ... The Austin *Ten* motorcar is updated and redesigned - its top speed is increased to 60 mph ... Safety glass in the windscreens of all road vehicles becomes a mandatory requirement ... 32-year-old Joan Crawford (37-24-37) and 35-year-old Clark Gable star in *Love on the Run* at picture houses ... "I saw the harbour lights, they only told me we were parting" - *Harbour Lights* by Bert Ambrose and his Orchestra (with Sam Browne on vocals) is a popular song of the day ... Working-class families in the North-West eat tripe and sleep three to a bed ... Middle-class families in the South drink *Bantam* instant coffee and grow hollyhocks in the garden ... London's gentlemen business commuters wear long *Baracuta* raincoats and felt fedora hats - and take the Metropolitan Line to grand new houses in Harrow, Northwood and Amersham - aka Metroland.

Spring 1937... The Road to Wigan Pier

The Mass-Observation project (brainchild of Tom Harrisson, Charles Madge and Humphrey Jennings) gets underway - with the thoughts and views of regular, everyday people being solicited on the street ... *Calling All Stars* - a new musical comedy, starring 36-year-old Arthur Askey (and with Carroll Gibbons and Bert Ambrose providing the music), is now showing at cinemas ... Heavy snow returns in March with the North being worst hit ... The Duchess of Bedford takes off in a de Havilland bi-plane from her home at Woburn Abbey and flies north-east towards the Wash. The 71-year-old aviator is never to be seen again ... 10-year-old football supporter Arthur Rowley from Wolverhampton stands on the terrace at the Molineux ground and watches as Major Frank Buckley's Wolverhampton Wanderers thrash Fred Everiss' West Bromwich Albion 5-2 ... 35-year-old Joe Davis is the World's Professional Snooker Champion for the eleventh year in a row - he beats Horace Lindrum from Australia by 32 frames to 29 in the final at Thurston's Hall in Leicester Square ... 62-year-old Winston Churchill MP continues to lead the calls for more investment in Defence to counter the growing threat from Adolf Hitler and his Nazis ... HMS *Ark Royal* - a brand new aircraft carrier is launched on Merseyside ... George Orwell's book *The Road to Wigan Pier* (describing the squalid lives of working-class people in Northern England) is published ... 69-year-old prime-minister Stanley Baldwin raises MP's salaries from £400 per year to £600 ... Millions flock to the pictures to see George Formby in his new film, *Feather Your Nest*. "I'm leaning on a lamp-post at the corner of the street, in case a certain little lady comes by. Oh me. Oh my. I hope the little lady comes by" - *Leaning On A Lamp-post* is a popular song from the movie. The lovable 32-year-old Formby has become such a huge box office attraction - he can now command £20,000 for each film! The 'cheeky' entertainer from Wigan treats himself to a new Rolls-Royce motorcar ... Standard grade petrol costs 1s/6d a gallon ... British-Pathé newsreels keep cinema audiences up to date with the latest news events ... 41-year-old King George VI and 36-year-old Queen Elizabeth attend the Grand National at Aintree - *Royal Mail* ridden by Evan Williams is the winner ... Oxford win the Boat Race for the first time since 1923 ... The River Thames bursts its banks at Richmond and nearby parks and a golf course are flooded ... 24-year-old Leslie Stone murders 23-year-old Ruby Keen at Leighton Buzzard in Bedfordshire ... 30-year-old Philip Davis murders his 33-year-old wife and 15-year-old niece at Camborne in Cornwall ... *Goodnight My Love* ("... the tired old moon is descending. Goodnight my love, my moment with you is now ending") by Charlie Kunz and his Casani Club Orchestra (with 20-year-old Vera Lynn on vocals) is a top selling gramophone record ... 40-year-old Bert Ambrose presents *Up To The Minute Rhythm Music* - a popular programme on Radio Luxembourg ... Multi-talented band leader Billy Cotton wins the Easter Short Handicap motorcar race at Brooklands - driving an MG ... 149,415 spectators turn out at Hampden Park to watch a football match between Scotland and England (with players wearing numbered jerseys for the first time). Young Freddie Steele opens the scoring for England but Scotland go on to win 3-1, with goals from Frank O'Donnell and Bob McPhail (2) ... Advertisements proclaim, '*Scots Porage Oats* - the food of a mighty race!' ... Talented schoolboy footballer 15-year-old Tom Finney is apprenticed as a plumber at Preston in Lancashire ... 23-year-old right-half Bill Shankly is on the losing team as Tommy

Muirhead's Preston North End go down 3-1 (after being in the lead) to Johnny Cochrane's Sunderland in the Football Association Cup final. A ticket for the standing enclosure at the Empire Stadium in Wembley costs 2s/6d. A seat in the South Terrace (uncovered) is five shillings ... Wilf Wild's Manchester City win eight of their last ten league matches in Division One to become champions of England. Bill Dale, Sam Barkas, Bobby Marshall, Jack Percival, Jackie Bray, Ernie Toseland, Alec Herd, Fred Tilson, Eric 'hot-shot' Brook (with twenty goals), Peter Doherty (with thirty goals) and 23-year-old goalkeeper Frank Swift have all been outstanding for City ... Charlton Athletic are runners-up ... Manchester Utd and Sheffield Wednesday are relegated to Division Two ... Thirty-six people die when the Zeppelin airship *Hindenburg* explodes on its approach to Lakehurst in the USA ... *The Golden Gate* suspension bridge opens in San Francisco ... Back in England - souvenir porcelain teacups go on sale in shops to commemorate the Coronation of King George VI and Queen Elizabeth ... People purchase Trebor *Extra Strong Peppermints* from the sweet shop ... London's omnibus drivers and conductors go on strike for four weeks, but return to work when tram drivers and tube train drivers refuse to join them ... 69-year-old Stanley Baldwin (Conservative) stands down as prime-minister and is succeeded by 68-year-old Neville Chamberlain (Conservative) who forms a National Unity government ... Sir John Simon (Liberal) is the new Chancellor of the Exchequer ... Sir Samuel Hoare (Conservative) is the new Home Secretary ... 22-year-old Charles Hawtrey appears alongside 23-year-old Vivien Leigh in *Bats in the Belfry* - a light comedy - at the Ambassadors Theatre on Shaftsbury Avenue ... "In the Blue Ridge Mountains of Virginia, on the trail of the Lonesome Pine" - *Way Out West*, a new film starring Hollywood comedy icons 46-year-old Stan Laurel and 45-year-old Oliver Hardy, is at cinemas ... "You tell me you love me only. Say you're feelin' so lonely. But I know you're lyin', that's why I'm cryin', now…" *Don't Try Your Jive Talk On Me* by 21-year-old Una Mae Carlisle is a top selling gramophone record ... A guide to 'self advancement' called *Think and Grow Rich* by 53-year-old American author Napoleon Hill is now available from a few select bookshops ... 'Well-to-do' middle-class families take a spin in their Austin *Seven* or Ford *Model Y* motorcars ... Approximately two thirds of households now have electricity ... The latest *Hoover Junior* vacuum cleaner costs £10/15s ... Nestle's *Milky Bar* is new - and it's made with white chocolate!

Summer 1937... Dixie Dean's last goal for Everton

It's a mild and dull start to the summer - improving slightly in August when temperatures rise ... 'The Queen of Comedy' - 24-year-old Tessie O'Shea appears in summer season at the Pavillion Theatre in Blackpool ... "Do you play Golf, Miss Gladeye? No - but I know some nice indoor games." - saucy postcards are on sale at seaside resorts ... 11-year-old John Eric Bartholomew from Morecambe in Lancashire makes his friends laugh by telling jokes and 'acting the clown' ... 'Scrumptious!' - Lyons *Pola-Maid* ice-cream is available in vanilla and strawberry flavours ... The London-Midland-Scottish streamlined steam locomotive *Coronation Scot* takes passengers from Euston Station to Glasgow in 6½ hours ... The French ocean liner *Normandie* crosses the Atlantic in record time of 3 days, 23 hours, 2 minutes - and regains the coveted Blue Riband from Britain's *Queen Mary* ... "Lovely you and Blue Hawaii. With all this loveliness there should be love" - *Blue Hawaii* by Roy Fox and his Orchestra (with Denny Dennis from Derby on vocals) is a summer-time gramophone hit ... Popular singer 39-year-old Al Bowlly performs *Smile When You Say Goodbye* ... 31-year-old Lou Preager and his Orchestra play swinging dance tunes at Caproni's Restaurant and Ballroom in Bangor, County Down ... The former King Edward VIII (now the Duke of Windsor) marries Mrs. Simpson in France ... 21-year-old student Edward Heath attends a political rally in Nuremberg and witnesses a speech from 48-year-old Nazi leader Adolf Hitler ... 26-year-old film actress Jean Harlow dies of kidney failure ... Cricketers 34-year-old Jim Parks and 21-year-old Len Hutton (making his international debut) stride out together to open the batting for England against New Zealand at Lord's. Hutton is out for a duck but his team-mates Joe Hardstaff and Wally Hammond both make centuries and the match is drawn. The talented young Hutton comes good in the second Test at Old Trafford and scores 100 runs in a fine victory for England. The third and final Test at the Oval is drawn - and Walter Robins' England have won the summer series by one Test to nil ... 28-year-old Alvar Liddell announces the news on the wireless for the BBC ... Thirty miners die when a fire breaks out at the coal face of Holditch Colliery at Chesterton in Staffordshire ... Fianna Fail (led by 54-year-old Eamon de Valera) defeat Fine Gael (led by 57-year-old William Cosgrave) at a general election in Ireland ... The Irish Free State is now known as Eire ... Men flock to cinemas to see 30-year-old Joan Blondell (37-22-36) in *Gold Diggers of 1937* ... Children attend matinee screenings of American 'Westerns' and cartoons as part of 'The Mickey Mouse Club' in *Odeon* picture houses ... "At the Balalaika, oh, let me linger there 'til the break of day, where hearts are young and balalaikas play" - *At The Balalaika* by Billy Cotton and his Band (with Alan Breeze on vocals) is a top selling gramophone record ... 23-year-old footballer Raich Carter marries his sweetheart Gertrude Rose Marsh at Spondon in Derbyshire ... The Wimbledon tennis tournament is televised for the first time - 29-year-old Dorothy Round from Dudley wins the ladies' singles. 22-year-old Don Budge from California wins the men's singles. (30-year-old Bunny Austin from London is knocked-out by Gottfried von Cramm in the semi-finals) ... Tensions grow in Europe. German Fuehrer Adolf Hitler declares that all German children are to be raised as loyal Nazi Germans ... *The Times* correspondent in Berlin is expelled - in retaliation for the expulsion of three Germans from Britain ... The first gas masks are issued to civilians in England ... Posters outside council buildings appeal for volunteers to help in the event of 'air raids' ... Neville Chamberlain's government orders the production of one-thousand *Spitfire* fighter planes ... The emergency '999' telephone number is set up - initially covering London only ... 30-year-old convicted double murderer Philip Davis is hanged by the neck until dead at Exeter ... 24-year-old convicted murderer Leslie Stone is hanged by the neck until dead at Pentonville ... 10-year-old schoolboy Jimmy Savile from Leeds in Yorkshire plays out with his friends ... The disgraced former Rector of Stiffkey, 62-year-old Harold Davidson, is mauled to death by a lion in front of a crowd of holidaymakers at Skegness ... 37-year-old pilot Alfred Bacon is killed when his Broughton-Blayney *Brawny* aeroplane spins out of control and crashes near Bromley in Kent ... 26-year-old Philip Compton is also killed in an aeroplane crash when his Gloster *Gladiator* strikes the ground at Gawber near Barnsley ... Famous 39-year-old US aviation pioneer Amelia Earhart disappears during a flight over the Pacific Ocean - never to be seen again ... *It Looks Like Rain In Cherry Blossom Lane* by Jack Harris and his Orchestra (with Jack Cooper on vocals) is a popular new gramophone record ... *Did Your Mother Come From Ireland?* ("… 'cause there's something in you Irish. Will you tell me where you got those Irish eyes?") by Henry Hall and his BBC Dance Orchestra is also in demand ... 24-year-old British boxing champion Tommy Farr goes fifteen rounds with world heavy-weight champion Joe Louis in New York - but loses on points ... Back in England - *J. Lyons & Co* open a new teashop on the High Street in Bedford ... 53,856 spectators watch as 30-year-old footballer Dixie Dean scores (what turns out to be) his last goal for Everton in a 1-4 defeat to Arsenal at Goodison Park. (25-year-old Ted Drake scores a hat-trick for 'The Gunners' in the same match) ... 28-year-old George Mills bags a hat-trick for

Chelsea in a 6-1 thrashing of Liverpool in front of 41,553 spectators at Stamford Bridge ... 24-year-old Tommy Manley scores twice in Division Two as Manchester Utd beat Newcastle Utd 3-0 in front of 29,446 spectators at Old Trafford ... 22-year-old John Rodgers from Northwood in Middlesex batters 25-year-old Lilian Maud Chamberlain to death - Rodgers is arrested and charged with murder ... A packet of ten *Craven 'A'* cigarettes costs sixpence ... A pint of mild in the Red Lion is fourpence.

Autumn 1937... White chocolate is all the rage

"Oh what a glorious thing to be. A healthy, grown-up, busy, busy bee" - 37-year-old comedian Arthur Askey sings *The Bee* ... Bert Ambrose and his Orchestra (with Sam Browne on vocals) perform *Sweet Leilani* ("... heavenly flower, nature fashioned roses kissed with dew") ... John Riddoch Rymill and his team of explorers return home after a two-year expedition to Antarctica ... 11-year-old David Attenborough from Isleworth plays out with his friends ... Millions of people enjoy an evening out at the pictures ... 'Back by popular demand' - the lovable 33-year-old entertainer George Formby stars in a re-release of the hit film *Off the Dole* at the Maypole cinema in Birmingham ... 48-year-old Will Hay stars in *Windbag the Sailor* at the Solihull Picture House ... A stylish new *Odeon* cinema opens at Leicester Square - *The Prisoner of Zenda* (starring Ronald Colman and Madeleine Carroll) is the first film to be screened there ... A brand new 'Art Deco' exhibition hall opens at Earls Court - the Chocolate & Confectionary show is the first exhibition to be held there ... White chocolate is all the rage. 'Eat More Milk' - A Nestle's *Milky Bar* costs 2d ... Former prime-minister Ramsay Macdonald dies aged 71 onboard a ship in the Atlantic Ocean ... Back in England - *Death on the Nile*, a new 'whodunit' featuring the fictional detective Hercule Poirot and written by 47-year-old Agatha Christie, is on sale in book shops for 7s/6d ... *The Hobbit*, a new novel by 45-year-old J. R. R. Tolkien, is also available ... 22-year-old convicted murderer John Rodgers is hanged by the neck until dead at Pentonville. (67-year-old hangman Tom Pierrepoint carries out the execution) ... Approximately twelve-thousand television sets have now been sold in the London area ... The BBC broadcasts programmes such as *News Film* - 'from

British Movietonews', *Song and Dance* - 'with music by Spike Hughes', *Picture Page* - 'a magazine programme of general and topical interest' and *Football at the Arsenal* - 'a demonstration by members of the Arsenal team at the Arsenal Stadium, Highbury' ... 37-year-old racing driver 'daring' John Cobb wins the 500 mile race at Brooklands in his Napier-Railton racing car. Charles Dodson is second in a Riley ... A new Humber *Snipe* motorcar costs £345. A new Hillman *Minx* costs £169 - and both cars come with *Triplex* safety glass! ... State-of-the-art Hawker *Hurricane* fighter planes are being tested by the Air Ministry ... 43-year-old Duke of Windsor and his wife (the former Mrs. Simpson) travel to the Berchtesgaden mountain retreat in Bavaria for a meeting with Adolf Hitler. The royal couple offer a Nazi salute as they greet the 48-year-old German Fuehrer ... 28-year-old footballer George Mills of Chelsea bags a hat-trick for England in 1-5 victory over Ireland at Windsor Park in Belfast ... 22-year-old Stanley Matthews of Stoke City scores a goal for England in a 2-1 victory over Wales at Ayresome Park ... 26-year-old Welsh international Les Jones leaves Coventry City and transfers to the Arsenal for £8,000 ... 18-year-old Jack Rowley leaves Bournemouth & Boscombe Athletic and joins Manchester Utd for £3,000 ... Jimmy Seed's Charlton Athletic lead the way in Division One after a 1-0 victory over Middlesbrough ... 18-year-old centre-forward Tommy Lawton scores twice for Everton in a 4-1 victory over Chelsea at Goodison Park ... 22-year-old Frank Broome is on the score-sheet for Second Division Aston Villa in a 2-0 victory over Fulham in front of 42,224 spectators at Villa Park ... 31-year-old Tommy Bamford scores a hat-trick for Second Division Manchester Utd in a 4-1 win against Barnsley in front of 22,394 spectators at Old Trafford ... There's more trouble brewing in Europe ... 56-year-old Viscount Halifax meets Adolf

Hitler and tells him a diplomatic solution must be found to resolve the issue of Germany's claim over territories in neighbouring Austria, Czechoslovakia and Poland ... Back in England - *J. Lyons & Co* open a new teashop on Pride Hill in Shrewsbury.

Christmas 1937... Knock, knock / Who's there?

All around the country, families sit together in small, cramped living rooms ... Tinsel decorations and Christmas crackers (containing paper hats) are all the rage ... "Knock, knock / Who's there?"- 43-year-old comedian Wee Georgie Wood tells 'Knock, Knock' jokes on the wireless ... "It's behind you!" - Middle-class families enjoy an evening out at the Pantomime ... *Jack and the Beanstalk* is showing 'twice nightly' at the Empress Theatre in Brixton ... Schools break up for Christmas ... Boys head for the newsagent's shop ... *The Modern Boy* magazine (2d every Saturday) features the exciting new story of 'Captain Justice's Adventure in Space' ... *The Dandy* is published for the first time - with Desperate Dan as its main character ... Other weekly comics such as *The Wizard*, *The Skipper* and *The Hotspur* are also popular ... 11-year-old Leonard Rossiter from Wavertree in Liverpool plays out with his friends ... 39-year-old Henry Hall and his Band (with Bob Mallin on vocals) perform the hit song *The First Time I Saw You* ... 37-year-old Victor Silvester and his Ballroom Orchestra perform *Can I Forget You* - a popular new (slow) Foxtrot ... 22-year-old footballer Stanley Matthews scores a hat-trick as England beat Czechoslovakia 5-4 at White Hart Lane in front of 45,879 spectators ... 30-year-old Dixie Dean makes his final appearance for Everton in a 1-1 draw against Birmingham ... 42-year-old Jimmy McMullan takes over from 40-year-old Billy Walker as manager of Sheffield Wednesday ... Major Frank Buckley's Wolverhampton Wanderers thrash Portsmouth 5-0 at the Molineux - it's rumoured that the Wolves' players are being injected with monkey glands to give extra strength and stamina ... Snow descends in mid December with the heaviest falls in the North ... The poor weather conditions contribute to two trains colliding at Castlecary in Scotland where thirty-five people are killed and more than one-hundred are injured ... *The First News* bulletin is broadcast on BBC radio's National Programme at 6 p.m. each evening. *The Third News* is transmitted at 9.45 p.m ... 44-year-old convicted child killer Fred Nodder is hanged by the neck until dead at Lincoln. (Nodder strangled 10-year-old Mona Tinsley at Hayton in Nottinghamshire earlier this year) ... Thousands of people flock to the Victoria Palace Theatre in London to see popular new musical *Me and My Girl*. At the end of the show, audiences depart singing *The Sun Has Got His Hat On* ("... hip-hip-hip-hooray!") or humming the catchy new tune of *The Lambeth Walk* ... George Allison's Arsenal football team lose 2-1 away at Blackpool on Christmas Day. 'The Gunners' gain revenge two days later with a 2-1 victory in the return match at Arsenal Stadium ... 244 million tonnes of coal have been mined in Britain this year - up by 12 million tonnes compared to 1936 ... "Holding hands at midnight, 'neath the starry sky. Nice work if you can get it, and you can get it if you try" - *Nice Work If You Can Get It* by Geraldo and his Gaucho Tango Orchestra (with Cyril Grantham on vocals) is a top selling gramophone record ... Pre-sliced bread is becoming more and more popular ... Lyon's *Kut-Bread* has thirty slices 'wrapped and sealed' ... Wireless technology moves on apace ... The latest Philips *Type 747* five-valve radio set (for A.C. mains) costs 12½ guineas ... Motoring technology moves on apace ... The new Alvis *12/70* sports saloon motorcar has adjustable front seats and a top speed of 81 mph ... A *Deluxe Model Y* Ford costs £135 (plus £7/10s/- purchase tax) ... Fog descends on the country in the last week of December, leading to a speight of road accidents ... A Rudge-Whitworth *Roadster No. 78* bicycle costs £6/10s/- including a dynamo lighting set and a bell ... The tense political situation in Europe worsens ... The aggressive policies of 48-year-old German Fuehrer Adolf Hitler and his ruling Nazi party have brought the continent to the brink of war ... Hitler appoints 47-year-old Walther Funk as his new Minister of Economics ... Back in England - the first production Hawker *Hurricane* fighter planes are delivered to RAF Northolt.

New Year 1938... The Lambeth Walk

Severe gales sweep across the country ... Strong winds bring down trees ... Unemployment rises to just under two-million ... Posters for the Trades Union Congress say, 'It Pays To Organise - Join Your Union' ... 47-year-old Harry Pollitt from Droylsden is General Secretary of the Communist Party of Great Britain ... Arthur Scargill is born in Worsbrough Dale ... 12-year-old schoolgirl Margaret Hilda Roberts completes her homework in a room above her father's grocery shop in Grantham ... 11-year-old Ronnie Scott from Aldgate in London listens to gramophone records ... "If your rhythm's been too dreamy, and you like your trumpets screamy, that's when you call to see me, I've got swing for sale! Dad-ee-ah!" - *Swing For Sale!* by Harry Roy (aka the King of 'Hot-Cha') and his Orchestra (with Ray Ellington on vocals) is a hugely popular song ... 36-year-old Roy Fox and his Band perform the latest tunes on BBC television, with singers 24-year-old Denny Dennis from Derby and 17-year-old Mary Lee from Glasgow, providing the vocals ... 21-year-old actress Margaret Lockwood stars at cinemas in *Bank Holiday* - a wonderful new film directed by Carol Reed ... British-Pathé newsreels keep audiences up to date with the latest news events ... Three people are killed and more than forty injured in a train crash at Oakley Junction in Bedfordshire ... Body parts of a man are found in the River Severn at Tewkesbury - the head and hands are missing ... The Nazis continue to persecute Jewish people in Germany - some families flee their homes and head for France and England ... 23-year-old socialite Unity Mitford remains in Germany pleasuring Nazi storm troopers ... The threat of war in Europe grows greater each day ... Plans are made to issue school children with gas masks ... 68-year-old prime-minister Neville Chamberlain advocates a program of appeasement with Germany ... 40-year-old Anthony Eden resigns as Foreign Secretary and Viscount Halifax takes over ... 63-year-old Winston Churchill MP leads the protests against appeasement ... *The Modern Boy* magazine has an exciting new Biggles adventure for its readers ... The Lancaster *De-luxe Roadrider* motorcar is available in showrooms for £330. The sports saloon version comes with independent front wheel springs and costs £375 ... Monkey gland enriched Wolverhampton Wanderers (with Tom Smalley, Dennis Westcott and 21-year-old Stan Cullis) beat Arsenal (with Eddie Hapgood, Ted Drake and 19-year-old Denis Compton) 3-1 in front of 39,383 at the Molineux - but it's Harry Curtis' Brentford who currently lead the way in Division One after a seven match unbeaten run ... 24-year-old Jimmy Dougal scores the only goal of the game as Preston North End gain a 0-1 victory over Arsenal in the fifth round of the Football Association Cup ... "Any time you're Lambeth way, any evening, any day, you'll find us all, doing the Lambeth Walk. Oi!" - 46-year-old Eddie Cantor accompanied by 41-year-old Bert Ambrose and his Orchestra perform the ubiquitous song, *The Lambeth Walk* ... 'Biceps, muscle and brawn' - millions of people flock to the cinema to see the lovable entertainer 33-year-old George Formby in the film *Keep Fit* ... Millions of men flock to the cinema to see the Hollywood beauty 44-year-old Mae West (38-24-38) in *Every Day's a Holiday* ... 21-year-old Leonard Merris and his 17-year-old lover Iris Jones from Dudley in Worcestershire elope together to be married at Gretna Green ... 25-year-old Melita Norwood (a secretary at the highly secretive British Non-Ferrous Metals Research Association) and her husband move to a house at Bexleyheath ... Advertisements for washing powder say, '*Dreft* - for silkier silks'.

Spring 1938... England's footballers give Nazi salute

44-year-old Stuart Hibberd announces the news on the wireless ... 33-year-old convicted murderer Walter Smith is hanged by the neck until dead at Norwich. (67-year-old hangman Tom Pierrepoint carries out the execution) ... 17-year-old American jockey Bruce Hobbs rides *Battleship* to victory in the Grand National at odds of forty to one ... 36-year-old Joe Davis is the World's Professional Snooker Champion for a twelfth consecutive year - he beats 30-year-old Sidney Smith by 37 frames to 24 in the final at Thurston's Hall in Leicester Square ... Dance halls are busy on Saturday nights ... 38-year-old Victor Silvester and his Ballroom Orchestra perform *Jealousy* - a popular new Tango ... 10-year-old schoolboy Bruce Forsyth-Johnson attends dance classes at Brixton in London ... 11-year-old Terry Scott from Watford plays out with his friends ... Nazi troops cross the border into Austria and the Third Reich declares that Austria is now part of Germany ... 69-year-old British prime-minister Neville Chamberlain says he will oppose any further aggression by German forces - including any attempt by the Nazis to occupy the Sudetenland region of Czechoslovakia ... "I've something to sing about now, and I want the world to know just why the moon's aglow, why stars are winking up above. I'm in love" - *Something To Sing About* by 32-year-old Mantovani and his Orchestra (with Al Bowlly on vocals) is a popular song ... Modern young in fifty-five shilling suits (procured from *Burton's* on the 'never-never') escort their sweetheart to the dancehalls on Saturday evenings ... A new public transport system comprising of bright red trolley-buses is now operational on the streets of Manchester ... 26-year-old footballer Bryn Jones leaves Wolverhampton Wanderers and joins Arsenal for a new record transfer fee of £14,500 ... 31-year-old centre-forward Dixie Dean leaves Everton after fourteen years (and having scored 349 goals in 399 matches). Dean joins Notts County of the Third Division (South) for £3,000 ... The race to become champions of Division One goes to the very last day of the season ... Monkey gland enriched Wolverhampton Wanderers lose 1-0 at Sunderland ... Arsenal win 5-0 against Bolton Wanderers - so it's George Allison's Arsenal who are the new champions of England. 26-year-old Cliff Bastin has scored fifteen goals in the season. 25-year-old Ted Drake has scored seventeen. George Swindin and Frank Boulton have shared goalkeeping duties. Eddie Hapgood, George Male, Jack Crayston, Bernard Joy, Les Jones and Alf Kirchen have all been outstanding for 'The Gunners' ... Jimmy Hogan's Aston Villa and Walter Crickmer's Manchester Utd gain promotion from the Second Division ... 25-year-old inside-right George Mutch scores an extra-time penalty to give Preston North End a 1-0 victory over Huddersfield Town in the first televised Football Association Cup final. A ticket for the standing enclosure at the Empire Stadium in Wembley costs 2s/6d ... A *His Master's Voice 901* television set (with 10-inch x 8-inch screen) costs 60 guineas, or is available on HP ... *The Stately Homes Of England* ("... how beautiful they stand, to prove the upper-classes have still the upper hand") by 38-year-old Noel Coward is a popular new song ... England's footballers give a Nazi salute before playing a 'friendly' match against Germany in Berlin ... Members of the Third Reich, Herman Goering, Rudolf Hess and Joseph Goebbels are among the 105,000 spectators who see a 3-6 victory for England - with Cliff Bastin, Frank Broome, John Robinson (2), Len Goulden and 23-year-old Stanley 'wizard of dribble' Matthews scoring the goals ... Back in England - 38-year-old William Graves suffocates his 14-month-old son to death in Dover ... An explosion at Markham Colliery in Derbyshire kills 79 miners ... BBC television broadcasts the latest *British Movietonews* ... German Fuehrer Adolf Hitler meets Italian Duce Benito Mussolini in Rome ... British prime-minister Neville Chamberlain says his government will spend £11 million building new airfields ... 32-year-old Jack Jackson and his Band play swinging dance tunes at the Dorchester Hotel ... Advertisements say, '*Weetabix* - more than a breakfast food'.

Summer 1938... 364 runs for young Len Hutton

It's a wet and thundery summer ... Test cricket is televised for the first time ... 27-year-old Charlie Barnett and 21-year-old Len Hutton stride out together to open the batting for England at Trent Bridge in the first Ashes Test of the summer. Barnett makes 126 and Hutton makes 100 in England's first innings total of 658 Eddie Paynter also contributes with a splendid 216 not out - and 20-year-old Denis Compton makes 102 but the match ends in a draw. The third Test Match at Old Trafford is abandoned without a ball being bowled due to rain. Australia win the fourth Test at Headingley to go 1-0 up in the series. In the final Test at the Oval - England gain a famous victory after making 903 for 7 (including a magnificent record breaking knock of 364 from young Len Hutton). The series is drawn, which means Don Bradman's Australians retain the Ashes. England players C J Barnett, L Hutton, W J Edrich, W R Hammond (cpt), M Leyland, E Paynter, D C S Compton, L E G Ames (wk), W F F Price (wk), A Wood (wk), H Verity, A W Wellard, R A Sinfield, D V P Wright, W E Bowes and K Farnes are all downcast after failing to win the coveted terracotta urn ... "Hi-ho, hi-ho, it's off to work we go" - crowds flock to the cinema to see *Snow White and the Seven Dwarfs* - a wonderful new animated film from Walt Disney ... Lovable entertainer George Formby from Wigan stars in hilarious new comedy *I See Ice*. "We're parted from each other and that's too bad. You're my favourite mother, the best I ever had" - *Mother, What'll I Do Now?* (performed by 34-year-old Formby on his ukulele) is a popular song from the movie ... A children's zoo opens in Regent's Park - it costs sixpence to watch the Chimp's Tea Party ... 31-year-old tennis player Bunny Austin from London makes it through to the men's singles final at

Wimbledon - but is beaten in straight sets by 23-year-old Don Budge from California ... The Smith family from Chigwell take a short seaside holiday on Canvey Island and enjoy afternoon tea in *The Monico* - a gleaming new 'Art Deco' restaurant ... The recently opened *Butlin's* Ocean Hotel in Brighton is now taking bookings ... Thomas Cook organise package holidays to Southern France - eight days for £8/7s/6d ... The gloriously streamlined steam locomotive *Mallard* (of the London and North Eastern Railway) travels at 126 mph between Grantham and Peterborough, setting a new world speed record for steam ... The ocean liner *Queen Mary* crosses the Atlantic in record time of 3 days, 21 hours, 48 minutes - regaining the Blue Riband from French ship *Normandie* ... "A table near the band - a small one. Some cigarettes, a drink - yes a tall one" - *Music, Maestro Please!* is a hit gramophone tune for Carroll Gibbons and the Savoy Hotel Orpheans (with Anne Lenner on vocals) ... The stunning 12-cylinder Lagonda *LG45 Rapide* motorcar has a top speed of 108 mph - and is said to be 'the fastest motorcar in the world' ... Standard grade petrol costs 1s/6d a gallon ... The first ever *Beano* comic is published featuring characters Big Eggo and Lord Snooty ... 82-year-old Sigmund Freud arrives in London - fleeing persecution from the Nazis ... German Fuehrer Adolf Hitler gives a clear indication that his troops will take Sudetenland by force ... Neville Chamberlain's National Unity government orders four-hundred war planes from America and issues thirty-five million gas masks to the people of Britain ... 26-year-old trade union official Jim Callaghan marries his 22-year-old sweetheart Audrey Moulton at Maidstone in Kent ... 3-year-old David Nobbs and his grandfather enjoy listening to the wireless together in the drawing room of the family house at Orpington ... 38-year-old convicted child killer William Graves is hanged by the neck until dead at Wandsworth ... The London Passenger Transport Board introduces new bright red electric tube trains to the Underground ... "Hello operator. Sidcup one-three-five please" - the number of telephone users is growing and it's estimated there are now three-million telephones in the UK ... 11-year-old Don Revie from Middlesbrough plays out with his friends ... The new football season begins. 20-year-old Wilf Mannion scores for Middlesbrough in a 3-1 win over Manchester Utd in Division One ... 26-year-old Bryn Jones scores on his debut for Arsenal in a 2-0 win over Portsmouth ... 19-year-old Tommy Lawton scores for Everton in a 0-2 away win at Blackpool ... 21-year-old Harry Brophy scores for Southampton in a 1-2 defeat against Tottenham Hotspur in Division Two ... 51-year-old Fred Westgarth from South Shields is appointed manager of Bradford City in Division Three (North) - his new team thrash Darlington 6-2 at Valley Parade in their opening game of the season ... *I Let A Song Go Out My Heart* ("... it was the sweetest melody. I know I lost heaven, 'cause you were the song") by Roy Fox and his Orchestra (with Denny Dennis from Derby on vocals) is a gramophone hit ... Popular entertainer George Formby from Wigan purchases a new Rolls-Royce motorcar with the registration plate 'GF 1' ... 29-year-old 'swashbuckling' actor Errol Flynn stars in Technicolor at cinemas in *The Adventures of Robin Hood* ... '90 Minutes of Happiness and Hi-Jinks' - Hollywood comedy icons 48-year-old Stan Laurel and 46-year-old Oliver Hardy star in *Block-Heads*.

Autumn 1938... Peace in our time

The weather is mild, grey and wet ... Police begin searching for the killer of 30-year-old Rose Atkins - whose body was found on a road in Kent. 27-year-old George Brain is caught, arrested and charged with murder ... Bob Mallin sings *Blue Skies Are Just Around The Corner* for Henry Hall and his Orchestra ... "I advertised for a typist, and one girl asked me flat, to take down her particulars, but..." *I Don't Do Things Like That* by upcoming comedian Tommy Trinder is a popular song ... The spy thriller *Cause For Alarm* by 29-year-old author Eric Ambler is published - it's now in bookshops priced at 7s/6d ... The first edition of the *Picture Post* is in newsagents ... Schoolboys buy *Wild West Weekly* - a new comic on sale every Thursday for 2d ... Prime-minister Neville Chamberlain meets with Adolf Hitler at the Berchtesgarten. 49-year-old Hitler maintains his demand for the Sudetenland region of Czechoslovakia. Chamberlain flies to Germany twice more for further meetings with the Fuehrer. The 'Munich Agreement' is eventually signed and Sudetenland is surrendered to Germany. 69-year-old Neville Chamberlain returns to England saying, "It is peace in our time." ... German troops enter Sudetenland ... 63-year-old Winston Churchill MP tells the House of Commons, "England has been offered a choice between war and shame. She has chosen shame, and will get war." ... *Code of the Woosters* by 56-year-old author P.G. Wodehouse is published and features characters Gussie Fink-Nottle, Sir Watkin Bassett, Stiffy Byng, Stinker Pinker and Roderick Spode (the political leader of the 'black-shorts') ... 41-year-old Oswald Mosley and his British Union of Fascists are in favour of a negotiated peace with Germany ... Alfred Hitchcock's *The Lady Vanishes* is at cinemas, starring the beautiful 22-year-old Margaret Lockwood and the handsome 30-year-old Michael Redgrave ... *Sailing Along* is also now showing with 31-year-old wide-eyed actress Jessie Matthews ... "While a cigarette was burning, we loved and laughed and learned, that hearts were made for breaking, while a cigarette burned" - *While A Cigarette Was Burning* is a popular new gramophone song by 40-year-old Al Bowlly ... *The Sweetest Sweetheart Of All* by Billy Reid and his Accordeon Band (with 22-year-old Dorothy Squires from Pontyberem performing vocals) is also a hit ... 11-year-old Roger Moore from Stockwell in London plays out with his friends ... A new eighty-thousand ton luxury ocean liner called *Queen Elizabeth* is launched at Clydebank ... The Humber *Super Snipe* motorcar is introduced - with running boards, a four-litre engine and a top speed of around 80 mph ... 19-year-old footballer Tommy Lawton scores on his international debut for England in a 4-2 defeat to Wales at Ninian Park. (23-year-old Stanley 'wizard of dribble' Matthews also bags a goal for England) ... Major Frank Buckley's Wolverhampton Wanderers lose five out of seven matches in Division One and languish near the bottom of the league table - it comes to light that Wolves' players have stopped taking monkey gland injections ... 23-year-old inside-right Archie MacAulay scores a hat-trick for West Ham Utd in a 6-1 victory over Tranmere Rovers in Division Two ... Schoolboys in grey flannel shorts play Marbles on the playground - small glass marbles have to beat large 'steelies' at a ratio of 'fivey to oncey' to complete a victory ... 17-year-old schoolboy Geoffrey Wellum dreams of becoming a flying-ace in the RAF ... 30-year-old test pilot (and former motor-racing champion) Johnny Hindmarsh is killed when his Hawker *Hurricane* aeroplane crashes into the ground at Brooklands in Surrey ... 23-year-old pilot Bob Tate and his two RAF colleagues are killed when their Bristol *Blenheim* aeroplane crashes at Rugeley in Staffordshire ... Reported sightings of a mad knife 'slasher' on the streets of Halifax in Yorkshire are later revealed to be a hoax ... Everton lead the way in Division One after winning six consecutive football matches - including a 0-3 away victory over Aston Villa, and a 5-1 thrashing of Portsmouth in front of 43,913 spectators at Goodison Park ... 27-year-old convicted murderer George Brain is hanged by the neck until dead at Wandsworth ... German leader Adolf Hitler stakes a claim for the Polish city of Danzig - where there's a majority ethnic German population ... Thirty-five thousand Jews are arrested in Germany ... Synagogues are burned ... Jews are expelled from colleges ... Thousand of shops belonging to Jewish families are attacked and looted ... 29-year-old Joe Loss and his Band perform *I'm Gonna Lock Away My Heart And Throw Away The Key* ("… I'm wise to all those tricks you played on me") - Clem Stevens is on vocals ... Cadbury's *Roses* chocolates are new - a ¼ pound box costs sixpence - including wraps!

Christmas 1938... Hornby-Dublo train sets

"It's behind you!" - Middle-class families enjoy an evening at the Pantomime ... Frank O'Brian stars in *Mother Goose* at the New Theatre in Cardiff ... Fay Compton and Greta Fayne star in *Babes in the Wood* at the Theatre Royal Drury Lane in London ... Schoolboys write to Father Christmas asking for a new Hornby-Dublo (00 gauge) train set - 'the perfect miniature railway' ... *Dinky Toys* Builder Outfits, with prices ranging from 2s/6d to 10s/9d, are on sale in toy shops ... A Claud-Butler *Silver-Arrow* racing bicycle with Reynolds *531* frame and Endrick twenty-six inch wheel rims costs £8/10s/- or is available on easy terms with a sixteen shilling deposit and sixteen monthly payments of 11s/9d ... New-fangled three-speed (pulley type) derailleur gears are available for an additional charge ... 29-year-old Tommy Trinder and 30-year-old Max Wall star in *Save a Little Sunshine* at picture houses ... 29-year-old Alan Breeze performs vocals on *Thanks For The Memory* ("... of rainy afternoons, swinging Harlem tunes") for Billy Cotton and his Band ... Al Bowlly sings for Lew Stone and his Band on *The Girl In The Alice Blue Gown* ... 17-year-old Nora Clarke from Whitechapel works as a 'Nippy' at the *J. Lyons & Co* Corner House restaurant on Coventry Street in London ... Queues form outside bookshops as *Hercule Poirot's Christmas* (the latest 'whodunit' novel from 48-year-old Agatha Christie) goes on sale ... 34-year-old George Formby begins work on a new film, alongside talented young co-star, 21-year-old Googie Withers ... 26-year-old footballer Willie Hall of Tottenham Hotspur scores five goals as England thrash Ireland 7-0 at Old Trafford. (Stanley 'wizard of dribble' Matthews and Tommy Lawton are also on the score-sheet for England) ... George Jobey's Derby County and committee controlled Everton draw 2-2 on Boxing Day in a top-of-the-table Division One clash at Goodison Park - 55,401 spectators look on as Torrance Gillick and Billy Cook score the goals for Everton and Ronnie Dix and Dave McCulloch score for Derby ... 23-year-old Frank Broome scores twice for Aston Villa in a 1-5 victory away at Sunderland ... Football pools are extremely popular - *Littlewoods* open a new 'Art Deco' head office in Liverpool ... Wally Hammond's England cricket team is on tour in South Africa. 38-year-old off-spinner Tom Goddard takes a hat-trick of wickets in a drawn Test Match at Johannesburg ... Hundreds of Jewish school children arrive in Britain as refugees from Germany ... War in Europe looks increasingly likely ... 69-year-old prime-minister Neville Chamberlain promises money to build air raid shelters ... 231 million tonnes of coal have been mined in Britain this year - down by 13 million tonnes compared to 1937 ... An intense cold spell of weather brings snow to much of the country ... Charity soup kitchens give out hot tea and bread and dripping to hundreds of homeless men and women in London on Christmas Eve ... 46-year-old Jack Hylton and his Orchestra make a gramophone recording of *I'm Singing A Song For The Old Folks* ... "While tearing off a game of golf, I may make a play for the caddy. But when I do, I don't follow through, 'cause…" *My Heart Belongs To Daddy* by Bert Ambrose and his Orchestra (with 20-year-old blonde-bombshell Evelyn Dall on vocals) is a smash hit ... 39-year-old John Christie and his 40-year-old wife Ethel move to a ground floor flat at 10 Rillington Place in Notting Hill, London ... Cadbury's chocolate *Selection Box* is advertised as a 'Feast of Flavor & Fun' and costs just 2s/6d ... A special Christmas carton of fifty *Capstan* cigarettes is 2s/5d ... A pint of mild in the Red Lion is fourpence.

New Year 1939... Nescafe instant coffee

It's a cold and wet start to the new year ... Unemployment rises to two-million ... Heavy snow descends on the Midlands in late January - followed by a rapid thaw ... 38-year-old Harry Armstrong strangles and kills his 17-year-old girlfriend Peggy Pentecost at a hotel in Lambeth ... A new Biggles story of 'Air-War' begins in *The Modern Boy* magazine ... BBC television broadcasts the latest *British Movietonews* to a few thousand households in London ... Prime-minister Neville Chamberlain meets the Italian Duce Benito Mussolini in Rome ... Jewish people are banned from driving in Germany ... The German navy launches a new state-of-the-art battleship called *Bismarck* ... Irish terrorist bombs explode at Tottenham Court Road and Leicester Square underground tube stations - thankfully there are no fatalities, but a station worker is seriously injured and requires hospital treatment ... *One Day When We Were Young* ("... one wonderful morning in May. You told me you loved me, when we were young one day") by Geraldo and his Orchestra with Al Bowlly on vocals is a popular song ... 19-year-old convicted murderer John Daymond is hanged by the neck until dead at Durham. (68-year-old hangman Tom Pierrepoint carries out the execution) ... Pope Pius XI dies in Rome aged 81 and is succeeded by Pope Pius XII ... Back in Blighty - *It's In the Air*, a new comedy film starring the lovable entertainer George Formby (as a 'would-be' RAF pilot) is now showing at cinemas. "I'm no wise guy, still I get along. I may not know my left from right but I do know right from wrong" - *They Can't Fool Me* (performed by 34-year-old Formby) is a popular song from the movie ... 19-year-old centre-forward Tommy Lawton scores twice as Everton beat George Kay's Liverpool 0-3 at Anfield in front of 55,994 spectators. (24-year-old Joe Mercer plays at wing-half for Everton and 29-year-old Matt Busby plays at wing-half for Liverpool) ... A week later - 61,315 people pack into Molineux Stadium to see Wolverhampton Wanderers beat Liverpool 4-1 in the fifth round of the Football Association Cup ... *Moonlight Serenade* by 34-year-old Glenn Miller and his Orchestra is heard frequently on the wireless ... *Remember Me* by 36-year-old Billy Reid and his Accordeon Band is also popular ... An Anderson bomb shelter is erected in Islington ... A new-fangled domestic washing machine is on display at the Industries Fair in London ... Major Frank Buckley's Wolverhampton Wanderers win six out of seven matches - including a 4-1 victory over Leeds Utd and a 7-0 thrashing of league leaders Everton. It soon comes to light that Wolves' players have started taking monkey gland injections again ... BBC radio's *National Programme* broadcasts daily from 10.15 a.m. until midnight ... BBC television broadcasts daily from 3 p.m. until around 10.30 p.m. ... Approximately fifteen-thousand households (all in the London area) now have television sets ... Middle-class families drink new *Nescafe* instant coffee ... A packet of ten *Piccadilly* cigarettes costs 4½d.

Spring 1939... Hitler invades Czechoslovakia

Adolf Hitler orders his troops to advance further into Czechoslovakia - breaking his agreement to keep to the Sudetenland region only ... Neville Chamberlain's policy of appeasement has failed ... *Trouble Brewing* with 34-year-old George Formby and 21-year-old Googie Withers is now showing at cinemas ... A film version of the hugely popular *The Lambeth Walk* is also on general release - starring Lupino Lane, Sir Seymour Hicks and 24-year-old Sally Gray ... HMS *Prince of Wales* - a new *V-Class* battleship for the Royal Navy is launched on Merseyside ... *Workman* wins the Grand National at odds of one-hundred to eight ... Cambridge win the Boat Race for the first time in three years ... 37-year-old Joe Davis is the World's Professional Snooker Champion for the thirteenth year in a row - he beats Sidney Smith from Derbyshire by 43 frames to 30 in the final at Thurston's Hall in Leicester Square ... 38-year-old convicted murderer Harry Armstrong is hanged by the neck until dead at Wandsworth ... 66-year-old George Stapleton is beaten to death near Flitwick in Bedfordshire ... 53-year-old Beatrice Baxter has her throat cut by former lover Ralph Smith in Swindon ... 24-year-old Norman Wisdom marries his 19-year-old sweetheart Doreen Brett at Willesden Green ... "Jeepers Creepers, where'd ya get those peepers? Jeepers Creepers, where'd ya get those eyes?" - *Jeepers Creepers* by Bert Ambrose and his Orchestra (with 21-year-old blonde-bombshell Evelyn Dall on vocals) is a smash hit ... 55-year-old Edith Pretty commissions the archaeologist Basil Brown to investigate a burial mound on her land at Sutton Hoo in Suffolk - and a hoard of Anglo Saxon treasure is unearthed including jewellery, silverware and an iron helmet from the seventh century ...

Everton are the new champions of Division One, pipping monkey gland enriched Wolverhampton Wanderers to the league title. Ted Sagar, Billy Cook, Tom Jones, Gordon Watson, John Thomson, Stan Bentham, Torrance Gillick, Wally Boyes, Alex Stevenson, Tommy Lawton (with thirty-four goals) and 24-year-old wing-half Joe Mercer have all been outstanding for 'The Toffees' ... Major Frank Buckley's Wolves also miss out in the Football Association Cup final as Jack Tinn's underdogs Portsmouth cause a shock - by winning 4-1 at Wembley. 19-year-old Dickie Dorsett (aka the 'Brownhills Bomber') scores for favourites Wolves, but goals from Bert Barlow, John Anderson and Cliff Parker (2) ensure a victory for Pompey. A ticket for the standing enclosure at the Empire Stadium costs 2s/6d. A seat in either the North or South Grand Stand is fifteen shillings ... 10-year-old schoolboy Jimmy Hill from Balham in South London plays football with his friends ... "The sun for long it doesn't shine, it's either wet or else it's fine. Last night I said when I went to bed..." *It's Turned Out Nice Again* performed by the lovable 34-year-old George Formby on his ukulele is a popular new song ... 24-year-old racing driver Arthur Dobson from Lodsworth wins at Brooklands driving a Delahaye *135C* ... A new version of the Austin *Ten* is launched - the popular saloon now has a more contemporary appearance, with the floor and body constructed in one piece and a newly designed curved radiator grill ... A 'Pact of Steel' is established between Germany and Italy, as Adolf Hitler and Benito Mussolini sign a Treaty of Alliance ... Back in England - it's announced that men aged 20 and over are to be conscripted for military service ... Farmers are encouraged to plough grassland to increase food production ... "Roll out the barrel. We'll have a barrel of fun" - a gramophone recording of *The Beer Barrel Polka* by George Scott-Wood and his London Piano Accordion Band is now available in shops ... The film *Goodbye Mr. Chips*, starring 34-year-old Robert Donat and 34-year-old Greer Garson, is now showing at cinemas ... The month of May is dry, warm and sunny ... Britain's twisty country roads attract daring young motorcyclists ... The new BSA *Gold Star* motorbike has a top speed of over 100 mph ... Advertisements say, '*Craven 'A'* cigarettes - Will Not Affect Your Throat'.

Summer 1939... There'll always be an England

Pan American Airways begin the first Trans-Atlantic air service, flying a Boeing *314 Yankee Clipper* between Newfoundland and Southampton. A maximum of nineteen passengers (each paying £140) make the journey in 18½ hours ... *South Of The Border* ("... down Mexico Way") by Joe Loss and his Band (with Monte Ray on vocals) is a smash gramophone hit ... 11-year-old Alastair Burnet from Sheffield plays out with his friends ... 15-year-old Nicholas Parsons from Grantham takes a caravanning holiday with his family at Studland Bay in Dorset ... 24-year-old jockey Eph Smith rides *Blue Peter* to victory in the Epsom Derby ... Seventy-nine men drown during testing of a new Royal Navy submarine in the waters of Liverpool Bay ... 42-year-old Oswald Mosley of the British Union addresses fifty-thousand people at Earls Court preaching a message of peace ... 'Some Things You Need To Know If War Should Come' - Neville Chamberlain's government launches a national leaflet campaign ... 33-year-old fascist William Joyce leaves the country and flees to Germany ... Storm clouds gather ... Heavy rain across the central region of the UK leads to a flooded London-Midland-Scottish railway line at Milford in Staffordshire ... 40-year-old convicted murderer Ralph Smith is hanged by the neck until dead at Gloucester ... "Hands, knees and..." *Boomps-A-Daisy* by Joe Loss and his Band with 45-year-old vocalist Annette Mills is a popular gramophone record ... 23-year-old American singer Frank Sinatra cuts his first disc with Harry James - *From The Bottom Of My Heart* ... 39-year-old 'daring' John Cobb sets a new land speed record of 368.85 mph at the Bonneville Salt Flats in America ... Cricketers 23-year-old Len Hutton and 24-year-old Harold Gimblett stride out together to open the batting for England against the West

Indies at Lord's. Hutton scores 196 runs. Denis Compton scores 120. Bowler Bill Copson takes 5 wickets for 85 and England win the match by 8 wickets ... Five people are killed and one-hundred injured by an Irish terrorist bomb in the centre of Coventry. Shortly afterwards, two IRA members are arrested, convicted and hung ... 13-year-old Princess Elizabeth falls in love with 18-year-old Prince Philip of Greece and Denmark. The two young sweet-hearts begin exchanging letters ... *Uncle Fred In The Springtim*e is a new novel from P.G. Wodehouse (and features characters Pongo Twistleton, Polly Pot and the Empress of Blandings - a large, black Berkshire sow pig) ... 46-year-old William Morrison is Minister for Agriculture in Chamberlain's National Government ... 52-year-old Leslie Burgin is Minister for Transport ... The new MG *TB Midget* open-top sports car is launched - with an improved 1,250cc engine developing 45 horse-power. Top speed is around 80 mph and 0-60 mph comes in 17.6 seconds ... Standard grade petrol has risen in price to 1s/9d a gallon ... The new Pye *4044 Teleceiver* set (with a 10-inch x 8-inch screen) costs 75 guineas, or is available on HP ... Mass-Observation invites members of the public to send personal diaries describing their day to day lives ... Dennis Clarke from Sowerby Bridge goes fishing ... Thomas Barclay from Frome sings in the choir at Christ Church ... British-Pathé newsreels keep cinema audiences up to date with the latest news events ... Adolf Hitler signs a twenty year non aggression pact with the USSR and opens the way for a Nazi invasion of Poland ... Prime-minister Neville Chamberlain confirms his support for Poland ... It's announced that British children are to be evacuated from large cities ... "There'll always be an England, and England shall be free, if England means as much to you as England means to me" - Glyn Davies sings the popular new song, *There'll Always Be An England.*

Autumn 1939... It's war!

The BBC Home Service is new on the wireless - broadcasting at 330 metres on the dial ... 46-year-old Stuart Hibberd announces the news ... The evacuation program is well underway as millions of children move from large cities to rural areas ... 11-year-old Bob Monkhouse from Beckenham in Kent plays conkers with his friends ... German troops invade Poland ... 70-year-old prime-minister Neville Chamberlain makes a radio broadcast on the third of September saying - "This morning, the British ambassador in Berlin, handed the German government, the final note, stating that unless we heard from them, by 11 o'clock, that they were prepared at once, to withdraw their troops from Poland, a state of war would exist between us. I have to tell you now, that no such undertaking has been received, and that consequently, this country is at war with Germany." ... *We're Gonna Hang Out The Washing On The Siegfried Line* ("... have you any dirty washing, mother dear?") by Bert Ambrose and his Orchestra (with Jack Cooper on vocals) is a popular tune ... Air raid sirens are heard across London ... Television broadcasts are suspended but radio continues with news broadcasts made every hour - on the hour - throughout the day ... The football league is abandoned - with Joe Smith's Blackpool at the top of Division One and George Martin's Luton Town at the top of Division Two ... Men aged 19 to 41 are conscripted under the government's National Service Bill ... "Keep buckets of water and sand ready on the landing" - Cinemas throughout the country show the public information film *Do It Now* (a re-make of the earlier film *If War Should Come*) ... 25-year-old socialite Unity Mitford shoots herself in the head in Munich - and survives! ... The National Registration Act is passed by Parliament and identity cards are issued to the people of Britain ... 64-year-old Winston Churchill is appointed First Lord of the Admiralty and gets a place in Neville Chamberlain's wartime Cabinet ... 30-year-old convicted murderer Leonard Hucker is hanged by the neck until dead at Wandsworth. (69-year-old hangman Tom Pierrepoint carries out the execution) ... The ocean liner *Athenia* is torpedoed by a German U-boat and sinks with the loss of over a hundred lives ... American President Franklin D. Roosevelt says his country will remain neutral ... Irish Taoiseach Eamon de Valera says his country will remain neutral ... 158,000 troops from the British Expeditionary Force cross the channel to France ... 'And then there were none' - *Ten Little Niggers* a new 'whodunit' from 49-year-old Agatha Christie is on sale in bookshops ... *Come On George*, a new comedy starring the lovable entertainer George Formby (as a stable boy turned jockey), is now showing at cinemas. "Pardon me if I should criticise but you really can't deny, there's a fascinating twinkle in your eye" - *Pardon Me* (performed by 35-year-old Formby) is a popular song from the movie ... Planes from the RAF drop propaganda leaflets over Germany ... Sigmund Freud dies in London aged 83 ... German troops move into Warsaw and occupy the city ... 810 people lose their lives when a German U-boat torpedoes the battleship *Royal Oak* in Scapa Flow ... All Jewish people in Germany are forced to wear the yellow Star of David ... German planes bomb the Shetland Islands ... "Kiss me goodnight Sergeant-Major. Tuck me in my little wooden bed" - 39-year-old comedian Arthur Askey sings *Kiss Me Goodnight Sergeant-Major* ... Newspaper advertisements state, 'Dettol, the modern antiseptic - from all chemists'.

Christmas 1939...
Wish me luck as you wave me goodbye

The weather is mainly dry but extremely cold and foggy at Christmas ... 'Hot Tripe for Cold Days' - a pound of tripe from a *U.C.P* shop (United Cattle Products) in Lancashire is good value for money ... A second mass evacuation takes place ... Thousands of children are relocated from cities to the countryside - the vast majority spending Christmas away from their parents for the very first time ... Public information posters contain the message, 'Leave This To Us Sonny - You Ought To Be Out Of London' ... 8-year-old Lonnie Donegan is evacuated from East Ham in London to Hale Barns in Cheshire ... 4-year-old David Nobbs and his family move from Orpington in Kent to Marlborough in Wiltshire ... Popular singer 41-year-old Al Bowlly performs *Au Revoir But Not Goodbye* ... 39-year-old Victor Silvester and his Ballroom Orchestra perform *Dear Madam* - a popular new Tango ... 44-year-old King George VI addresses the nation on the wireless, saying, "A new year is at hand. We cannot tell what it will bring. If it brings peace, how thankful we shall all be. If it brings us continued struggle, we shall remain undaunted." ... Lucky schoolboys get a Raleigh *Junior* bicycle (priced at £4/16s/6d) on Christmas morning ... The hard-back *Beano* book costs 2s/6d ... The bumper Christmas edition of *The Hotspur* is 2d ... 12-year-old Ken Dodd from Knotty Ash in Liverpool visits his uncle Jack - who's affectionately known as 'the Diddyman' ... Princess Louise the Duchess of Argyll (a daughter of Queen Victoria) dies at Kensington Palace aged 91 ... American President Franklin D. Roosevelt agrees to sell weapons to Britain and France but reaffirms his position - the USA will not join the war ... The Battle of River Plate takes place. Royal Navy ships attack the German battleship *Admiral Graf Spee.* 45-year-old Hans Langsorff - captain of the German vessel - decides to scuttle his ship rather than let her fall into enemy hands and later shoots himself ... "Wish me luck as you wave me goodbye. Cheerio, here I go, on my way" - 41-year-old Gracie Fields from Rochdale stars in *Shipyard Sally* at cinemas ... 'The One, the Only, the Real… Tarzan' - 34-year-old Johnny Weissmuller returns as Tarzan, after three years away from the silver screen, in a new film called *Tarzan Finds a Son* ... The premiere of *Gone With the Wind* takes place in New York - with 26-year-old Vivien Leigh playing Scarlett O'Hara and 38-year-old Clark Gable playing Rhett Butler ... Back in England - 19-year-old centre-forward Cyril Done scores four goals as Liverpool beat New Brighton 6-2 in the wartime Western regional football league ... Jimmy McMullan's Sheffield Wednesday beat Norman Bullock's Chesterfield 2-1 on Boxing Day in the wartime East Midland regional football league ... 235 million tonnes of coal have been mined in Britain this year - up slightly compared to 1938 ... Young men and their sweethearts kiss and cuddle in the back row of the pictures ... "She had to go and lose it at the Astor. She didn't take her mother's good advice" - 39-year-old Harry Roy (aka the King of 'Hot-Cha') and his Band perform *She Had To Go And Lose It At The Astor* ... Conscripted men join up with their new military units - taking just the bare necessities when they leave home ... *Ever-Ready* razor blades are tuppence each from *Woolworths* ... A special Christmas pack of fifty Player's *Medium Navy Cut* cigarettes costs 2s/5d ... A pint of mild in the Red Lion is sixpence.

New Year 1940... Building Spitfires in Brum

The weather is bitterly cold with deep snow covering much of the country ... The River Thames freezes for the first time in more than fifty years ... The evacuation program to get children out of London continues ... 6-year-old twins Reginald and Ronald Kray leave the capital on a train from Liverpool Street Station - heading for Hadleigh in Suffolk ... 70-year-old prime-minister Neville Chamberlain chairs a meeting of his wartime Cabinet ... 46-year-old Leslie Hore-Belisha is sacked as Secretary of State for War and replaced by 43-year-old Oliver Stanley ... 58-year-old Viscount Halifax remains as Foreign Secretary ... 65-year-old Winston Churchill remains First Lord of the Admiralty ... Children take gas masks to school. Germany and Britain are at a 'stand off' in a period of phoney war ... "Germany calling. Germany calling. Germany calling." - 33-year-old traitor Lord Haw-Haw broadcasts Nazi propaganda on the radio from Hamburg ... The BBC launches the Forces Programme - a new radio channel which will be run alongside the established Home Service ... The construction of a new factory at Castle Bromwich in Birmingham is nearing completion - ready to build *Spitfire* fighter planes ... 29-year-old Douglas Bader re-joins the RAF as a pilot - eight years after losing both legs in a flying accident ... 18-year-old Prince Philip of Greece and Denmark is commissioned as a midshipman in the Royal Navy ... 25-year-old Unity Mitford returns to England on a stretcher after a failed suicide attempt ... Food rationing books are issued and purchase quotas put in place for butter, sugar and bacon ... "It may be sticky but I never complain. It's nice to have a nibble at it now and again" - the lovable, crowd-pleasing entertainer 35-year-old George Formby performs his cheeky song *With My Little Stick Of*

Blackpool Rock for Pathé newsreel ... 17-year-old footballer Billy Liddell scores a hat-trick for Liverpool in a 7-3 victory against Manchester City in the wartime Western regional football league ... Charlie Paynter's West Ham Utd beat George Allison's Arsenal 3-0 at the Boleyn Ground in the South 'A' regional league ... Billy Birrell's Chelsea beat Bournemouth & Boscombe Athletic 4-3 in the South 'B' regional league ... Wolverhampton Wanderers' manager Major Frank Buckley encourages his players to join the forces ... 21-year-old Wilf Mannion of Middlesbrough FC is conscripted and sent to fight in France ... Two million men are called up for war service ... *We'll Meet Again* ("… don't know where, don't know when, but I know we'll meet again some sunny day") by 22-year-old Vera Lynn is the best selling gramophone record of the day ... Strong winds and blustery gales blow across the South-East of England ... 85-year-old music-hall song writer Felix McGlennon retrieves his panama hat from a busy street in London ... 54-year-old actor Arthur Lucan stars as *Old Mother Riley* at cinemas ... 51-year-old Will Hay and 25-year-old Charles Hawtrey star in *Where's That Fire?* ... 25-year-old Norman Wisdom (of the Royal Corps of Signals) divorces his wife Doreen after less than a year of marriage ... "Sleepy little eyes in a sleepy little head" - 40-year-old Harry Roy (aka the King of 'Hot-Cha') and his Band perform *Goodnight Children Everywhere.*

Spring 1940... Blood, toil, tears and sweat

38-year-old Joe Davis beats his younger brother Fred in the final of the World's Professional Snooker Championship at Thurston's Hall in Leicester Square - retaining his title for the fourteenth year in succession ... 42-year-old Derek McCulloch is 'Uncle Mac' on BBC's popular wireless programme *Children's Hour* ... Hundreds of thousands of conscripted young men undergo basic military training - and look forward to a few days of 'leave' ... The stylish new Triumph *Tiger 100* motorcycle has a 500cc engine and a top speed of 103 mph ... Newspapers warn people to be vigilant and keep a look out for German spies ... 43-year-old Oswald Mosley and other fascists are rounded up and put in prison ... 17-year-old Philip Larkin from Coventry writes a poem for his school magazine ... 11-year-old Roger Bannister from Harrow pulls on a pair of plimsolls and goes for a run ... Over in Europe, British troops engage with the enemy ... 25-year-old second lieutenant Dicky Annand of the Durham Light Infantry fights off twenty German soldiers single handedly in Belgium ... Lieutenant Ian Scott-Thompson of the Royal Scottish Fusiliers is killed in action near Hollebeke ... "Somewhere over the rainbow, way up high" - 17-year-old Judy Garland sings *Over The Rainbow* ... Nazi forces invade Denmark and Norway ... British troops are forced to retreat from Norway after being out manoeuvred by the enemy ... Royal Navy ships HMS *Gurkha*, HMS *Afridi* and HMS *Curlew* are sunk by German dive bombers with the loss of 126 lives ... HMS *Hunter* is sunk by German destroyers with the loss of 112 lives ... "I'll pray for you while you're away. Each night and day, I'll pray for you. I'll pray for you 'til troubles cease, then you and I will live in peace" - 23-year-old Vera Lynn sings *I'll Pray For You* ... Famous stars from the world of entertainment travel across the English Channel to perform to British servicemen ... 47-year-old Jack Hylton and his Orchestra play in front of soldiers in Paris. (33-year-old Josephine Baker and 51-year-old Maurice Chevalier are also on the bill) ... A few weeks later, the lovable 35-year-old George Formby travels to France and entertains soldiers with cheeky songs played on his ukulele ... Back in England - crowds rush to picture houses to see Hollywood blockbuster *The Wizard of Oz* staring 17-year-old Judy Garland. The spectacular movie captivates audiences, with many returning home at the end of the evening singing, "We're off to see the wizard. The wonderful wizard of Oz." ... 45-year-old comedian Max Miller stars in the hit film *Hoots Mon!* ... *Sad Cypress*, the new novel from 49-year-old author Agatha Christie, is now available in book shops for 8s/3d ... *An Apple For The Teacher*, the latest 78 rpm record from Connie Boswell and Bing Crosby, is on sale in electrical shops and department stores ... 28-year-old PC William Shiell is shot and fatally wounded as he chases two men after a robbery at the Co-op store in Coxhoe, County Durham. Police sweep the nearby countryside and set up road-blocks in search of the killers. 27-year-old William Appleby and 24-year-old Vincent Ostler (both from Bradford) are caught and arrested ... 25-year-old Blackpool footballer George Eastham makes a guest appearance for Birmingham at inside-left. 30-year-old footballer Matt Busby plays right-half for Liverpool in a 1-0 defeat against Walter Crickmer's Manchester Utd ... The BBC Forces Programme broadcasts a *Weekly Newsletter* show on Sunday evenings at 7.20 p.m. ... Holland and Belgium surrender to invading German forces ... Neville Chamberlain warns Adolf Hitler that the opportunity of a peaceful settlement between Britain and Germany has long passed ... *Run Rabbit Run* ("… rabbit, run,

run, run. Bang, bang, bang, bang, goes the farmer's gun") - 43-year-old Bud Flanagan and 46-year-old Chesney Allen perform their popular hit song ... Veteran music-hall star Florrie Forde dies aged 64 in Aberdeen - after performing a show for servicemen ... Taxes on tobacco are increased to help fund the war effort ... A vote at Westminster on Britain's flawed military campaign in Norway leads to a division in the House of Commons. 71-year-old Neville Chamberlain is forced to resign as prime-minister. 65-year-old Winston Churchill takes over and tells parliament, "I have nothing to offer you but blood, toil, tears and sweat." ... Churchill makes 59-year-old Labour stalwart Ernest Bevin his Minister for Labour and National Service ... *In The Mood* by Glenn Miller plays on a gramophone ... A Home Defence Force (made up mostly of older men) is set up ... 51-year-old Adolf Hitler orders the invasion of France ... The period of phoney war comes to an end ... The Andrew Sisters sing *Begin The Beguine*.

Summer 1940... We shall never surrender

Sunny, warm weather gives way to thunderstorms and cooler temperatures ... German forces sweep through France ... Nazi soldiers enter Paris on the fourteenth of June ... A swastika is raised beneath the Arc de Triomphe ... Three hundred-thousand British troops are evacuated from the beaches of Dunkirk in a remarkable operation involving thousands of brave civilians - many piloting their own small boats under instruction from the Royal Navy. Two hundred and thirty-five craft are lost during the operation - including HMS *Havant* and HMS *Keith* ... Middlesbrough FC's inside-right Wilf Mannion is one of the soldiers returning to Blighty ... Manchester Utd's 21-year-old Francis Bertram Carpenter is killed in action ... 58-year-old author (and resident of Le Touquet) P.G Wodehouse is captured by the Nazis and placed under house arrest ... Winston Churchill vows never to surrender to the Germans, telling parliament, "We shall fight on the beaches. We shall fight on the landing grounds. We shall fight in the fields, and in the streets. We shall fight in the hills. We shall never surrender." ... Church bells fall silent - only to toll again to warn of a Nazi invasion of England ... "It's a lovely day tomorrow. Tomorrow is a lovely day. Come and feast your tear dimmed eyes, on tomorrow's clear blue skies" - popular singer 42-year-old Al Bowlly performs *It's A Lovely Day Tomorrow* ... 18-year-old Deanna Durbin sings *Amapola* ... 'Together For The First Time!' - 46-year-old Mae West (38-24-38) and 60-year-old W. C. Fields star at cinemas in *My Little Chickadee* ... Crowds flock to see Hollywood blockbuster *Gone With the Wind* - with Vivien Leigh and Clark Gable ... Ritchie and Elsie Starkey from Liverpool are proud parents of newborn son, Richard (aka Ringo) ... Despite the constant threat of air-raids, thousands of men continue to pack football terraces to cheer on their favourite team ... 28-year-old centre-forward Sam Small scores for Charlie Paynter's West Ham Utd in a 1-0 victory over Bob Crompton's Blackburn Rovers in the Football League War Cup final at the Empire Stadium in Wembley. Radio commentary of the match is given by 32-year-old Raymond Glendenning on the Forces Programme for the BBC ... 25-year-old Stanley 'wizard of dribble' Matthews and 23-year-old Stan Cullis line-up for England in a 1-1 draw against Scotland at Hampden Park ... 24-year-old Len Hutton and 22-year-old Denis Compton star in an England cricketing XI which plays against a West Indian XI at Lord's ... Heavy rain leads to flash floods in mid July ... Convicted murderers William Appleby and Vincent Ostler are hanged by the neck until dead at Durham. (70-year-old hangman Tom Pierrepoint carries out the executions, assisted by his 35-year-old nephew Albert Pierrepoint) ... Troopship *RMS Lancastria* is sunk by the Luftwaffe and four-thousand lives are lost ... 65-year-old Winston Churchill tells parliament the battle of Britain is about to begin - "Let us therefore brace ourselves to our duties and so bear ourselves that if the British Empire and its Commonwealth last for a thousand years, men will still say: This Was Their Finest Hour." ... *Music While You Work* is a new programme on the wireless ... Vera Lynn sings *When You Wish Upon A Star*. Harry Roy (aka the King of 'Hot-Cha') and his Band perform *You Gorgeous Dancing Doll* ... Millions flock to the cinema to see the lovable 36-year-old George Formby land a right hook on Adolf Hitler in a new comedy film called *Let George Do It!* ... The Luftwaffe carries out bombing raids on Cardiff and London ... Operation Sea Lion - Germany's planned invasion of Britain is underway ... Fighter planes from the RAF and the Luftwaffe engage in dog-fights above the English

Channel ... 23-year-old flight lieutenant Eric ‘Nick’ Nicholson is badly injured after coming under attack, but still manages to shoot down an enemy plane before bailing out of his own (burning) Hawker *Hurricane* ... German pilot Oberfeldwebel Beeck crash lands his *Messerschmitt* at East Langdon in Kent and is captured and held as a prisoner of war ... 28-year-old German born scientist Klaus ‘Karl’ Fuchs is interned along with hundreds of his fellow countrymen on the Isle of Man ... After a wet July, the weather is calmer and drier in August ... Britain’s Home Defence Force is now called the Home Guard - but is more commonly referred to as ‘Dad’s Army’ ... 44-year-old Arnold Ridley signs up for the Caterham Home Guard unit ... 43-year-old John Laurie signs up for the Paddington Home Guard unit.

Autumn 1940... Battle of Britain

War rages ... German aircraft cause death and devastation by bombing the city of Birmingham ... British aircraft cause death and devastation by bombing the city of Berlin ... The Channel Islands are now under the control of German forces ... 27-year-old pilot (and former champion racing-driver) Luis Fontes of the Air Transport Auxillary is killed in a aeroplane crash at Llandow in South Wales ... 'Laughs. Excitement. Thrills' - *Night Train To Munich*, starring the beautiful 23-year-old Margaret Lockwood and the handsome 32-year-old Rex Harrison, draws crowds to cinemas ... 'Britain Speaks' - 46-year-old author J. B. Priestley broadcasts his *Postscripts* on BBC radio each evening - and it's estimated that almost half of the nation's population tune-in to listen ... A German U-boat sinks the aircraft carrier HMS *Courageous* in the Atlantic and five hundred and eighteen lives are lost ... The blitz on London begins ... For fifty-seven consecutive nights, swarms of Luftwaffe planes drop their bombs on the capital. Thousands of people are killed and vast quantities of buildings and houses are destroyed ... The Battle of Britain continues to rage over the English Channel. German *Messerschmitts* engage with British *Hurricanes* and *Spitfires*. RAF's Commander-in-Chief Sir Hugh Dowding employs a highly efficient operational system, which enables squadrons to be scrambled at the optimum time to intercept German planes. By the end of September - RAF fighters have gained the upper hand over the Luftwaffe and Hitler is forced to re-think his invasion tactics. Flt. Lt. Phillip 'Pip' Barron and Flt. Lt. Reg Lovatt are among the 1,500 British airmen killed in action. Winston Churchill says, "Never in the field of human conflict was so much owed by so many to so few." ... 37-year-old 'Queen of the Sky' Amy 'Johnnie' Johnson joins the women's section of the Air Transport Auxiliary ... 25-year-old Second Lieutenant Dicky Annand of the Durham Light Infantry is awarded the Victoria Cross by 44-year-old King George VI ... 5-year-old David Nobbs wets himself on his first day at school at Marlborough in Wiltshire ... 34-year-old Leslie Perowne presents *The Gramophone Omnibus* on the wireless ... 36-year-old band leader Geraldo and his Dance Orchestra feature on the popular new show *Music While You Work* ... 78 rpm recordings of Geraldo performing *Tiggerty Boo* and of Bing Crosby singing *April Played The Fiddle* are in demand. (*Woolworths* sell the sheet music versions of the songs - their stores do not stock records) ... Alf and Julia Lennon from Liverpool are proud parents of newborn son, John Winston ... Bill and Nellie Lovell from Birmingham are proud parents of newborn son, David ... Fourteen children are killed by a German bomb in Southampton ... 14-year-old Princess Elizabeth goes on the wireless to address young people of the Empire "at this extremely difficult time." ... 18-year-old student Philip Larkin from Coventry goes up to Oxford to read English ... Former prime-minister Neville Chamberlain dies of bowel cancer at the age of 71 ... Sculptor Eric Gill dies of lung cancer at the age of 58 ... Five-hundred Luftwaffe bombers destroy the city of Coventry - killing more than five-hundred people ... There's also heavy bombing in Bristol - where the *J. Lyons & Co* teashops on Castle Street and Wine Street are severely damaged and forced to close ... 42-year-old Second Lieutenant Sandy Campbell of the Royal Engineers is killed while defusing a German bomb ... The latest news is read in French, Dutch and German (as well as in English) on BBC's Forces Programme on the wireless ... Japan joins the war - signing a Tripartite Pact with Germany and Italy ... German

Junkers and *Heinkels* continue their nightly bombing raids on London ... Thurston's Hall in Leicester Square is one of the many buildings destroyed ... A South regional football league match between Arsenal and Tottenham Hotspur is abandoned after forty-seven minutes because of an air raid warning. Arsenal are leading 3-2 at the time - and the result stands ... 23-year-old RAF flight lieutenant Eric 'Nick' Nicholson is awarded the Victoria Cross by 44-year-old King George VI ... 65-year-old prime-minister Winston Churchill negotiates with 58-year-old US president Franklin D. Roosevelt - and secures fifty old destroyer ships in return for giving the Americans access to military bases in the West Indies and Bermuda ... "Bless you, for being an angel" - The Ink Spots perform the hit song *Bless You* ... "That certain night, the night we met. There was magic abroad in the air. There were angels dining at the Ritz, and a nightingale sang in Berkeley Square" - 23-year-old Vera Lynn sings *A Nightingale Sang In Berkeley Square* ... The Entertainments National Service Association (aka Ensa) organise concerts for British servicemen ... "I thang yaw." - 40-year-old comedian Arthur Askey is one of the stars who takes part in the shows ... Advertisements say, 'When it's No Smoking by order, Rowntree's Fruitgums soothe and refresh.'

Christmas 1940... Bless 'em all

As a wartime security measure, weather forecasts are no longer broadcast on the wireless ... 90 mph winds batter England and Wales ... Posters on walls declare, 'No Sir! I'm not talking about my work' ... A spate of night-time road accidents occur as vehicles are permitted to use side lights only ... 57-year-old retired jockey Freddie Cox dies in a car crash near Abingdon ... Popular singer Al Bowlly performs *The Woodpecker Song* in London music halls ... German bombers blitz the city of Sheffield - Bramall Lane football ground is severely damaged ... Birmingham is blitzed ... Liverpool is blitzed ... Manchester is blitzed and 45-year-old ARP warden Albert Tatlock rescues Ida Barlow and her young baby boy Kenneth Barlow from a collapsed building in Weatherfield ... London is blitzed and a great fire sweeps through the capital ... The bombing is relentless. Night after night, wave after wave of German aircraft drop their explosive shells on London - by the end of the year it's estimated twenty-thousand civilians have been killed and more than one-million homes destroyed ... Hungary, Romania and Slovakia join the war on the side of the Axis Forces ... Prime-minister Winston Churchill speaks to US president Franklin D. Roosevelt on the telephone and asks for more support in fighting the war against Hitler's Nazis ... 38-year-old Marlene Dietrich (36-26-33) sings *Falling In Love Again* ("... never wanted to. What am I to do? Can't help it") ... 31-year-old Joe Loss and his Band perform the *Rumba Medley* ... "It's behind you!" - Despite the threat of German air-raids, 'well-to-do' families still enjoy an evening at the Pantomime ... Lovable entertainer 36-year-old George Formby plays the role of Idle Jack in a production of *Dick Whittington* at the Opera House Theatre in Blackpool ... Jimmy

McMullan's Sheffield Wednesday beat Fred Westgarth's Bradford 2-4 in the North Regional football league ... "When you wish upon a star, makes no difference who you are. Anything your heart desires will come to you" - Walt Disney's *Pinocchio* is at cinemas ... 51-year-old Charlie Chaplin stars in *The Great Dictator* ... 31-year-old comedian Tommy Trinder stars (alongside Claude Hubert and Michael Wilding) in *Sailor's Three* ... 46-year-old Edward Duke of Windsor (the former King of England) is installed as governor of the Bahamas ... Convicted spies 24-year-old Carl Meir and 25-year-old Jose Waldeburg are hanged by the neck until dead at Pentonville ... 26-year-old Desmond Llewelyn of the Royal Welch Fusiliers is captured by the Germans and held as a prisoner of war ... Children look forward to Christmas ... *Bunnikin's Picnic Party* from Ladybird Books is 2s/6d ... *The Beano Book* is three shillings ... A Raleigh *Record Ace* sports bicycle with three-speed Sturmey-Archer gear costs £12/3s/3d - a water bottle container is an optional extra at 11s/6d ... Food rationing means the typical family Christmas dinner is a small chicken with a few slices of ham, followed (if very lucky) by bread pudding ... 11-year-old schoolboy footballer Derek Dooley from Sheffield practices 'keepy-up-ies' in his back yard ... 25-year-old inside-forward Len Carney scores twice as George Kay's Liverpool beat Theo Kelly's Everton 3-1 on Christmas Day ... Wilf Wild's Manchester City draw 2-2 with Burnley at Maine Road ... "Have you ever been embarrassed when you're in a small café and they play a Cuban tempo, is your dancing quite passé?" - 36-year-old Jimmy Dorsey sings *Six Lessons From Madame La Zonga* ... Royal Navy ship HMS *Acheron* strikes a mine off the Isle of White and sinks in minutes with the loss of 196 men ... "Bless 'em all, bless 'em all, the long and the short and the tall" - 36-year-old George Formby sings

Bless 'em All ... 59-year-old Minister for Labour Ernest Bevin devises a plan to maximise coal production. (228 million tonnes have been mined in the past twelve-months - down slightly compared to the previous year) ... Radio reporter Michael Standing interviews people in the crowded air-raid shelters of London's underground railway stations - and broadcasts live on the BBC.

New Year 1941...
Give us the tools and we will finish the job

Much of the country lies under deep snow ... 37-year-old 'Queen of the Sky' Amy 'Johnnie' Johnson loses control of her Airspeed *Oxford* aeroplane and perishes in the Thames estuary ... 53-year-old Home Secretary Herbert Morrison decides to censor the *Daily Worker* newspaper because of its pro-communist views ... 42-year-old German spy Josef Jakobs parachutes into England and is immediately caught and arrested ... Sergeant Billy Flynn of the Pioneer Corps agrees to swap guard duty with a colleague and is killed by a land-mine dropped by the Luftwaffe ... 21-year-old Jon Pertwee is selected for officer training in the Royal Navy and is transferred off the ship HMS *Hood* ... The cruiser HMS *Southampton* is attacked by *Stuka* dive bombers in the Mediterranean and sinks with the loss of 81 lives ... Back in Blighty - it's a dark, cold winter ... Winston Churchill addresses the nation on the wireless, hoping to keep up morale ... The 66-year-old prime-minister appeals to US president Franklin D. Roosevelt, saying, "Give us the tools and we will finish the job." ... "Why do you whisper green grass? Why tell the trees what ain't so?" - The Ink Spots perform the popular song *Whispering Grass (Don't Tell The Trees)* ... 30-year-old Artie Shaw performs *Gloomy Sunday* ... Troops from the Australian and British armies defeat the Italian 10th Army in North Africa and take the city of Tobruk - a strategically important Mediterranean port ... German forces led by Field Marshal Erwin Rommel (aka The Desert Fox) land in Tripoli with the aim of crushing the Allies ... Lord Baden Powell (founder of the Boy Scout movement and hero of the Boer War) dies in Kenya at the age of 83 ... Back in Blighty - 'black-out' conditions have led to an increased number of road accidents ... 50-year-old Percy Shaw from Halifax secures a large contract with the government to supply his revolutionary invention - reflective road studs known as 'Cats Eyes' ... Notorious 40-year-old singer and pianist Leslie 'Hutch' Hutchinson performs his new gramophone tune *All Over The Place* ... Plymouth Argyle's football ground, Home Park, is damaged in an air raid ... Matches continue to take place all across the country despite the threat from German bombs ... Richard Davis scores a hat-trick for Aston Villa in a wartime match against an RAF team from Bridgnorth ... 28-year-old Leslie Compton scores ten goals for Arsenal, and his brother Denis scores twice, in a 15-2 victory over Clapton Orient ... 22-year-old Wilf Mannion of Middlesbrough and 26-year-old Joe Mercer of Everton line up in England's international team against Scotland at St. James' Park. England lose the match 2-3, with 21-year-old Tommy Lawton and 28-year-old Ralph Birkett scoring the goals for England, and Dougie Wallace scoring twice for Scotland ... 36-year-old band leader Geraldo and his Dance Orchestra perform *We'll Go Smiling Along* ... 42-year-old scientist Howard Florey tries out a new medicine called penicillin ... Three nights of German air-raids over South Wales leave hundreds of people dead ... Many spend their nights in Anderson air-raid shelters - taking refuge from the enemy bombers overhead ... 26-year-old Signalman Norman Wisdom (a telephone operator in the Cabinet War Rooms beneath Whitehall) patches an important call through to prime-minister Winston Churchill ... Dozens of prisoners of war (including 26-year-old Peter Butterworth) begin digging an escape tunnel from the Dulag Luft camp near Frankfurt ... Back in Blighty - wireless show *On Parade!* is broadcast each morning on the BBC's Forces Programme - playing popular gramophone records ...

“Won’t someone hear my plea and take a chance with me, because I’m nobody’s baby now” - Flanagan & Allen sing *I’m Nobody’s Baby* ... 23-year-old Vera Lynn sings *I’ll Never Smile Again* ... The Ink Spots perform *Stop Pretending* ... Despite the grim times, large numbers of people continue to spend evenings at the cinema ... A hilarious new comedy called *Gasbags*, starring the ‘Crazy Gang’ (Bud Flanagan, Chesney Allen, Jimmy Nervo, Teddy Knox, Charlie Naughton and 54-year-old Jimmy Gold) makes the nation laugh ... The Entertainments National Service Association (aka Ensa) organises morale boosting stage shows for British soldiers ... “Hello playmates” - 40-year-old comedian Arthur Askey takes to the stage to entertain the troops ... “Turned out nice again!” - the lovable 36-year-old film star George Formby also takes to the stage to entertain the troops ... 47-year-old Stuart Hibberd announces the news on the wireless for the BBC ... 23-year-old convicted murderer Clifford Holmes is hanged by the neck until dead at Strangeways. (Holmes had shot and stabbed his wife in Manchester last October) ... 33-year-old Gene Autry (aka the Singing Cowboy) performs the popular new song *Sierra Sue* (“... I want you only. No-one but you, Sierra Sue”) ... Advertisements say, ‘*Steradent* - cleans and sterilises false teeth’.

Spring 1941... Dried eggs - build you up!

Freezing temperatures and severe frost affect the whole country ... 'Make the Most of the Weather in a Windak' - rain-proof *Windak* sports coats are promoted in the newspapers ... 56-year-old Lord Woolton is appointed Minister of Food by prime-minister Winston Churchill ... 'Your Bread Is Part Of The War' - a loaf of bread costs 8d ... German bombs cause damage at Manchester Utd's Old Trafford stadium ... Hundreds are killed in a blitz on Clydebank ... Hundreds are killed in a blitz on Plymouth ... 22-year-old stoker Kenneth Beresford from Mansfield is killed along with 1,414 shipmates when HMS *Hood* is sunk by the German battleship *Bismarck* ... 23-year-old former Southampton footballer Norman Catlin is killed along with 721 shipmates when HMS *Gloucester* is bombed and sinks off the coast of Crete ... 28-year-old Sergeant Nigel Leakey of the King's African Rifles is killed in action when his battalion engages with Italian tanks in Abyssinia ... "Such a big hotel, a very grand one, right upon the avenue. We could not afford it, but sweet, I just adored it. My very first and only rendezvous, in room five hundred and four" - notorious 41-year-old singer Leslie 'Hutch' Hutchinson performs *Room 504*. A number of other artists record the same song - including Geraldo and Vera Lynn ... 32-year-old Alvar Liddell announces the news on the wireless for the BBC ... German forces invade Yugoslavia ... German forces invade Greece ... Field Marshal Erwin Rommel (aka the Desert Fox) and his troops advance through the deserts in North Africa and encircle Tobruk. The city is successfully defended by Australian, Polish, Indian and British soldiers (aka the Rats of Tobruk) - and the Mediterranean port remains under the control of the Allies ... Back in England - 35-year-old ukulele player George Formby gives a private performance of his cheeky songs to the royal family at Windsor Castle. 73-year-old Queen Mary is much amused and demands a encore of *When I'm Cleaning Windows* ... 15-year-old footballer Nat Lofthouse scores twice on his debut for Bolton Wanderers in a 5-1 win against Bury ... 10-year-old schoolboy Vic Keeble from Colchester plays football with his friends in the park ... 11-year-old schoolboy Douglas Hurd from Marlborough stays in to finish his homework ... 59-year-old writer Virginia Woolf fills her coat pockets with heavy stones and drowns herself in the River Ouse ... "Do I want to be with you, as the years come and go? Only forever, if you care to know" - 37-year-old Bing Crosby sings *Only Forever* ... 26-year-old actress Vivien Leigh wins an Oscar for her role as Scarlett O'Hara in *Gone With the Wind* ... 33-year-old Frank Whittle and his RAF colleagues test a new jet powered engine for use in aircraft ... 26-year-old Peter Butterworth and his fellow prisoners of war make steady progress on their escape tunnel at the Dulag Luft camp near Frankfurt ... The Luftwaffe carry out bombing raids on Birmingham and Belfast, but London remains the prime target for German *Heinkel* bombers ... Popular singer 43-year-old Al Bowlly is killed by a blast in the capital ... The bombing intensifies on Saturday the tenth of May, when the skies above London are darkened by five-hundred Luftwaffe bombers. Shortly after the raid, around fifteen-hundred people lie dead among the ruins of the city ... The House of Commons is badly damaged along with other historic buildings. Remarkably, the dome of St. Paul's Cathedral is unscathed and stands defiant among the smouldering debris all around ... Other British cities are targeted by the Germans. Nearly two-thousand people are killed when Liverpool is blitzed for six days. The BBC attempts to keep morale high by playing popular music on the Forc ..es

Programme ... "But I can't live without buzzin', Pennsylvania six-five-thousand!" - *Pennsylvania 6-5000* by The Andrews Sisters is a smash hit ... German U-boat *110* is forced to surface in the North Atlantic after depth charges are dropped by Royal Navy ships. A boarding party from HMS *Bulldog* recovers a fully operational Enigma cryptography machine - which is sent onto a team of code and cypher experts at Bletchley Park ... 47-year-old Rudolf Hess parachutes into Scotland on a misguided attempt to negotiate peace ... The German battleship *Bismarck* is crippled after engaging with British aircraft carrier HMS *Ark Royal* in the Atlantic. Four other Royal Navy ships close in for the kill, and - after intense shelling - a torpedo fired from HMS *Dorsetshire* sinks the *Bismark*. More than one-thousand crew go down with the mighty German vessel ... Back in England - 15-year-old schoolboy footballer Arthur Rowley plays as a guest for Manchester Utd - lining up in the same team as his 22-year-old brother Jack in a 2-1 defeat ... 19-year-old inside-left Andy McLaren scores all six goals as Preston North End thrash George Kay's Liverpool 6-1 at Deepdale ... Billy Birrell's Chelsea beat George Allison's Arsenal 3-1 at Stamford Bridge ... 52-year-old Will Hay and 26-year-old Charles Hawtrey star in *The Ghost of St. Michaels* at cinemas ... *Spare a Copper*, a new comedy film starring the lovable George Formby (playing the role of a reserve policeman), is also now showing. "Why can't I make love like other guys, flash with me wicked eyes? Why? Because…" *I'm Shy* (performed by 36-year-old Formby) is a popular song from the movie ... Newspaper advertisements issued by the Ministry of Food say, 'Dried Eggs - Build You Up!' ... A pint of mild in the Red Lion costs ninepence ... A packet of ten *Black Cat* cigarettes is sixpence.

Summer 1941... Good morning, nice day

Warm and sunny weather in July turns cool and wet in August ... 11-year-old Bernard Manning from Ancoats in Manchester plays out with his friends - enjoying games of Off-ground tig, Ackee-1-2-3 and Breaking-through ... "Good morning, nice day" - wireless show *It's That Man Again* with 49-year-old Tommy Handley makes the nation smile ... 41-year-old Victor Silvester and his Ballroom Orchestra perform *You're Dancing On My Heart* - a popular new Quick-step ... MPs are currently sitting in the House of Lords as their usual place of work (the chamber at the House of Commons) was destroyed by German incendiary bombs in May ... 38-year-old Richard Austen 'Rab' Butler is appointed Secretary of State for Education - taking over from 54-year-old Herwald Ramsbotham OBE ... Schools put on sports days ... 12-year-old Jeremy Thorpe from South Kensington comes last in the sack race ... 6-year-old Graham Lovell from Sheldon comes second from last in the bean-bag race ... 'V for Victory!' - 66-year-old prime-minister Winston Churchill raises two fingers as he addresses a public meeting in London and the 'V' sign becomes a symbol of defiance against the Nazis ... Sixty thousand people turn out to see the Football League War Cup final at Wembley between Preston North End and Arsenal. 28-year-old Bill Shankly, 19-year-old Andy McLaren and 19-year-old Tom Finney (a recently qualified plumber) line up for Preston. 23-year-old Denis Compton, 28-year-old Leslie Compton and 32-year-old Eddie Hapgood line up for the Arsenal. The match ends in a 1-1 draw. The replay takes place at Ewood Park in Blackburn where Preston win 2-1 with both goals scored by 25-year-old Bobby Beattie ... Clothes rationing begins ... Pleated skirts and turn-ups on trousers are banned ... The

Midlands is targeted by German Luftwaffe bombers and land-mines are dropped on Dudley ... Royal Navy ship HMS *Calcutta* is attacked in the Mediterranean and sinks with the loss of 107 lives ... Millions flock to cinemas to see the lovable entertainer George Formby in his latest film *Turned Out Nice Again*. "Bow down everyone, here I come. Bang that cymbal and hit that drum. Bow down everyone, yes sir, I'm..." - *The Emperor Of Lancashire* (performed by 37-year-old Formby) is a popular song from the movie ... 41-year-old Arthur Askey stars in *The Ghost Train* ... 19-year-old Deborah Kerr and 29-year-old Clifford Evans star in *Love on the Dole* ... Agatha Christie's new novel *Evil Under the Sun* is now on sale in book shops ... Coal goes 'on the ration' ... "I love to climb an apple tree, though apples green are bad for me, and I'll be sick as I can be" - 19-year-old Deanna Durbin sings *It's Foolish But It's Fun* ... The Glenn Miller Orchestra perform *Yes My Darling Daughter* ... British and New Zealand troops are forced to leave Crete after sustained shelling from German guns ... 30-year-old petty officer Alf Sephton is mortally wounded onboard HMS *Coventry* when the vessel comes under attack from German dive bombers in the Mediterranean ... Prime-minister Winston Churchill and US president Franklin D. Roosevelt meet on board the battleship HMS *Prince of Wales* in the North Atlantic Ocean. Churchill lobbies hard but Roosevelt resists - the Americans will still not join the war ... 31-year-old wing commander Douglas Bader is taken prisoner by the Germans after bailing out of his *Spitfire* over France ... 26-year-old Peter Butterworth breaks free from the Dulag Luft prison of war camp near Frankfurt and goes on the run for three days - before being recaptured by a member of the Hitler Youth ... 'Blitzkrieg!' - Adolf Hitler breaks his non-aggression pact with Joseph Stalin and sends one million troops to invade the Soviet Union. (Germany is now fighting the war on two fronts) ... 59-year-old author P.G Wodehouse makes a number of radio broadcasts from Berlin - at the insistence of the Nazis ... Back in Blighty - 29-year-old MI6 double-agent Kim Philby meets his Soviet contact on a bench in Regents Park - and hands over a briefcase full of confidential government papers ... 43-year-old German spy Josef Jakobs is executed by firing squad at the Tower of London ... 12-year-old schoolboy and promising actor Roddy McDowall appears in *This England* at cinemas ... 6-year-old schoolboy David Nobbs and his best friend Michael Ferguson collect tadpoles near Marlborough in Wiltshire ... Food rationing remains in place but people can eat Woolton pie - a pie with no meat ... The health benefits of an adequate intake of vitamins A, B1, B2, C and D is promoted by *Crookes'* Halibut Liver Oil capsules.

Autumn 1941 ... Target for tonight

Royal Navy's flagship HMS *Ark Royal* is hit and sunk by a German U-boat off Gibraltar. The captain and crew have time to abandon ship and get to safety, but later reports show that the initial torpedo strike did take the life of Able Seaman Edward Mitchell ... German forces advance rapidly through the Soviet Union. The Red Army have been caught by surprise ... British prime-minister Winston Churchill reaches an agreement with USSR leader Joseph Stalin to send regular aid convoys ... "What say, let's be buddies? What say let's be pals? What say, let's be buddies, and keep up each other's morales?" - Flanagan & Allen sing *Let's Be Buddies* ... "But this little piggy was a booglie wooglie piggy, and he boogie-woogied all the way home" - The Glenn Miller Orchestra perform *The Booglie Wooglie Piggy* ... Nazis test the deathly gas chambers at Auschwitz ... Field Marshal Erwin Rommel (aka the Desert Fox) and the Axis forces step up their bombardment of Tobruk - but fail to break through the defiant Allied defences - and in particular the brave soldiers of the 9th Australian Division ... 29-year-old Second Lieutenant George Gunn from Neston in Cheshire is one of the eight-hundred or so Allied soldiers killed in action ... Back in England - Newcastle-upon-Tyne is targeted by Luftwaffe bombers. Fifty people are killed and more than two-hundred injured in a raid on the city ... The music played on BBC wireless programme *On Parade!* keeps morale high in difficult times ... 38-year-old Bing Crosby sings *Dolores* ... The Ink Spots perform *Do I Worry?* ... 41-year-old Alastair Sim and 33-year-old John Mills star in *Cottage to Let* at cinemas ... Also 'now showing' at picture houses is a new documentary film called *Target For Tonight* - which follows the crew of an RAF *Wellington* bomber ... The ominous drone of German *Heinkel* bombers continues to put fear into the hearts of millions of British citizens ... Approximately three-hundred thousand people go to sleep each night in a Morrison shelter ... "London Pride has been handed down to us. London Pride is a flower that's free. London Pride means our own dear town to us, and our Pride it forever will be" - 41-year-old Noel Coward sings *London Pride* ... 50-year-old Richard Tauber sings *You Are My Heart's Delight* ... 62-year-old bogus doctor Harold Trevor murders 65-year-old Theodora Greenhill at her flat in West Kensington ... 11-year-old Sean Connery from Edinburgh plays out with his friends ... German soldiers occupy the city of Paris and enforce strict curfews on Parisians. The French Resistance fights back. 51-year-old General Charles De Gaulle (living in exile in London) calls for his fellow countrymen to resist the Nazi invaders ... 6-month-old baby Gordon Kaye from Huddersfield sleeps soundly in his cot ... *Sincerely Yours, Vera Lynn* is a new radio show on BBC's Forces Programme - delivering news from home, songs from 24-year-old Vera and messages from munition girls to their husbands in the Forces ... Football matches continue to take place at grounds around the country ... 20-year-old outside-left Billy 'Cowboy' Goffin scores for Aston Villa in a 3-0 win over RAF Cosford ... 17-year-old Ken Wilkinson scores a hat-trick for Clem Stephenson's Huddersfield Town in a 5-0 win over Stan Seymour's Newcastle Utd ... People flock to cinemas to see Hollywood blockbuster *Gone With the Wind* - with Vivien Leigh and Clark Gable. (The popular film has been showing in Leicester Square for more than a year) ... 48-year-old Stuart Hibberd announces the news on the wireless for the BBC ... The bodies of 6-year-old Kathleen Trendall and 8-year-old Doreen Hearne are found in woodland near Penn in Buckinghamshire - both girls have been stabbed.

26-year-old Private Harold Hill of the Royal Artillery is arrested and charged with murder.

Christmas 1941... Pearl Harbour

Over two-thousand Americans are killed and eighteen ships destroyed in a surprise attack on Pearl Harbour ... The United States declares war on Japan ... British prime-minister Winston Churchill and US president Franklin D. Roosevelt are now allies in a global conflict. Three days after the bombing of Pearl Harbour - British battlecruiser HMS *Repulse* and battleship HMS *Prince of Wales* are attacked by Japanese aircraft in the Pacific and both ships go down with the loss of 840 lives ... HMS *Audacity*, HMS *Neptune*, HMS *Galatea*, HMS *Stanley* and HMS *Kandahar* are among other Royal Navy ships to be sunk in the month of December ... Back in the England - the RAF conduct test flights of a new 200 mph bomber called the *Lancaster* ... 26-year-old outside-right Stanley 'wizard of dribble' Matthews plays for the England football team (and is man-of-the-match) in a 2-1 win over Wales ... 11-year-old Shirley Crabtree from Halifax in Yorkshire plays wrestling games with his friends ... Oscar Deutsch, founder of the *Odeon* cinema chain (with around 250 sites in the UK) dies of cancer aged 48 ... "I am packing my belongings in the shawl my mother used to wear when she went to market" - Walter Pidgeon and Maureen O'Hara star in *How Green Was My Valley* ... 'Rosebud' - 26-year-old Orson Welles stars in *Citizen Kayne* ... "I yi yi yi yi, I like you very much" - 31-year-old Edmundo Ros and his Rumba Band perform *I Yi Yi Yi Yi* ... 33-year-old Nat Gonella and his new Georgians perform *In The Mood* ... Single women in their twenties are called into service to help ease the labour shortage ... Posters on walls urge, 'Women of Britain - Come into the Factories' ... All British men and women between the ages of 18 and 60 are now liable to some form of national service ... 'Lunch-time Entertainment for

Factory Workers, relayed from a factory somewhere in Britain' - *Workers Playtime* is broadcast on the wireless ... Coal production is being squeezed - only 210 million tonnes have been mined in 1941. That's down by 18 million tonnes compared to 1940 ... Allied forces get ready to engage with Field Marshal Erwin Rommel (aka the Desert Fox) in North Africa ... "I would die to be with my Dolores. Aye-aye-aye Dolores" - 37-year-old Geraldo and his Orchestra perform their own version of the hugely popular song, *Dolores* ... 24-year-old Vera Lynn (from East Ham in London) has the best selling gramophone record at Christmas with a song called *Yours (Quiereme Mucho)* ... Rationing is at its height and items such as turkey, gin, sherry, chocolate and fruit are not available ... 'Make Do and Mend' applies to clothes and gifts at Christmas time ... *The Beano Book* is on sale in shops for 3s/6d - Big Eggo is pictured on the front cover and Lord Snooty is on the rear ... 67-year-old prime-minister Winston Churchill travels to America and stands beside his new ally president Franklin D. Roosevelt on the balcony of the White House on Christmas Eve. "Fellow workers for the cause of freedom" - The two leaders address the crowds gathered on the lawns below, urging people to prepare themselves for the struggle that lies ahead, on the path to ultimate victory ... Back in England - Noel Coward's play *Blithe Spirit* enjoys a long run in London's West End ... "Hut-Sut Rawlson on the rillerah and a brawla" - 42-year-old Billy Cotton and his Band perform *The Hut-Sut Song* ... 23-year-old sports 'all-rounder' Denis Compton scores a penalty for an FA XI in a 2-2 draw against an RAF XI at Elland Road ... 22-year-old Cliff Whitelum scores four goals as Bill Murray's Sunderland beat Wilf Gillow's Middlesbrough 6-0 in a League War Cup tie at Roker Park ... Bob McGrory's Stoke City beat Sam Longmore's Walsall 4-1 ... "It shot up like a rocket, 'til it's nearly reached the sky. It's..." *The Biggest Aspidistra In The World* by 43-year-old Gracie Fields is a hugely popular song of the day ... *South American George* is a hugely popular fim of the day - starring the lovable George Formby from Wigan and 29-year-old Linden Travers from Houghton-le-Spring ... "If you asked me would I entertain the lions at the zoo, by sitting in beside them just before their lunch was due. Would I do it? I'd do more..." *I'd Do It With A Smile* (performed by 38-year-old Formby) is a popular song from the movie ... 38-year-old John Snagge announces the news on BBC radio ... Japanese forces now occupy Hong Kong.

New Year 1942... Keep calm and carry on

50-year-old Tommy Handley cheers the nation for thirty minutes on Friday evenings with his wireless show *It's That Man Again* ... Up to two feet of snow falls on the Midlands and Northern England ... Roads are blocked and dozens of factories are without power ... 22-year-old footballer Tommy Lawton scores twice as England beat Scotland 3-0 on a snow covered Wembley pitch ... Luftwaffe bombers wreak havoc on Liverpool ... Vera Lynn sings *I Don't Want To Set The World On Fire* ("... I just want to start a flame in your heart") ... 37-year-old Geraldo and his Orchestra perform *That Lovely Weekend* ... German U-boats target British ships in the Atlantic ... HMS *Belmont* and HMS *Matebele* are hit and sunk with the loss of 374 lives ... HMS *Jupiter* and HMS *Exeter* are sunk in the Java Sea off Indonesia - and the survivors (more than six-hundred men) are taken as prisoners of war by the Japanese ... Back in England - posters in government buildings remind civil servants to, 'Keep Calm and Carry On' ... Posters at railway stations, post offices and on roadside walls tell the public to, 'Dig for Victory - grow your own vegetables' ... People are instructed to bathe in just five inches of water (or, even less) to help the war effort ... 67-year-old prime-minister Winston Churchill remains in the USA until the fourteenth of January, holding crucial meetings with his new wartime ally, 60-year-old president Franklin D. Roosevelt ... American troops are mobilised and head for Europe ... *Instructions for American Servicemen in Britain* - the War Office issues a pamphlet to the thousands of US military men travelling to Blighty. It offers helpful advise and information such as, "NEVER criticize the King or Queen" and "The British don't know how to make a good cup of coffee. You don't know how to make a good cup of tea. It's an even swap" ... 28-year-old Roy Plomley presents *Desert Island Discs* on the BBC Forces Programme. The first 'castaway' on the show is comedian Vic Oliver. The first piece of music chosen is *Chopin's Etude No. 12 in C minor* ... 25-year-old prisoner of war Airey Neave escapes from Colditz by disguising himself as a German soldier and then makes his way to the Swiss border near Singen ... Back in England - soap goes 'on the ration' ... 15-year-old Princess Elizabeth registers for war service ... 11-year-old schoolboy Fred Trueman from Stainton in Yorkshire plays out with his friends ... 21-year-old Betty Driver from Leicester stars in the comedy film *Facing the Music* ... "Rainy days don't worry me. There's a rainbow that I can see, and it's waiting for me, down forget-me-not lane" - Flanagan & Allen perform their popular song *Down Forget-Me-Not Lane* ... Multiple floods occur across the country as the deep snow thaws ... 51-year-old Mr. Justice Asquith dons a black cap and issues a death sentence to murderer Harold Trevor at the Old Bailey ... Private Harold Hill is sentenced to death at Oxford - for the murder of two young girls ... 28-year-old Gordon Cummins (a serviceman with the RAF) embarks on a barbarous killing spree in London - murdering four women in six days ... Morale in Britain is low ... Wireless announcer Lillian Duff reads the weekly news and also reviews the latest films ... Singapore falls to the Japanese ... Walt Disney's new production *Dumbo* is now showing at cinemas ... Crowds of men continue to watch football matches on Saturday afternoons ... 44-year-old Billy Walker of Nottingham Forest makes the final appearance of his playing career in his team's 1-0 defeat away at Chesterfield ... Joe Smith's Blackpool beat Clem Stephenson's Huddersfield Town 4-2 at Bloomfield Road ... Committee controlled Burnley beat Bob Marshall's Stockport County 6-0 at Turf Moor ... Thousands of women throughout the country work long hours in factories ... Mrs. D. Cheatle from Sheffield (wearing a headscarf and overalls) operates a capstan lathe at a munitions factory in Yorkshire ... Posters say, ‘These Women are Doing Their Bit - Learn to Make Munitions’.

Spring 1942... Loose lips might sink ships

Heavy snowfalls return in March ... Many roads are impassable ... RAF bombers destroy the German cities of Lubeck and Rostock ... 52-year-old Adolf Hitler makes a speech at the Reichstag threatening swift retaliation ... *Stage Coach* by 29-year-old Eric Winstone and his Band is released as a gramophone recording by the Regal Zonophone company ... *That Lovely Weekend* by Joe Loss and his Orchestra (with vocals by Chick Henderson) is on His Master's Voice ... 11-year-old Lonnie Donegan from East Ham in London (currently evacuated to Hale Barns in Cheshire) plays guitar in his bedroom ... 13-year-old Bernard Cribbins from Oldham leaves school and begins an apprenticeship - hoping to become a stage actor ... 59-year-old Major Frank Buckley leads Wolverhampton Wanderers to success in the Football League War Cup, beating Bill Murray's Sunderland 6-3 over two legs. 24-year-old centre-forward Dennis Westcott scores three of Wolves' goals. 28-year-old inside-right Raich Carter scores two of Sunderland's goals ... Arsenal goalkeeper Bill Dean dies in action serving with the Royal Navy ... Teddy Davison's Sheffield Utd beat Eric Taylor's Sheffield Wednesday 3-0 in the wartime football league North section ... American soldiers - based in Britain - complain about the warm beer served in pubs ... 60-year-old Chancellor of the Exchequer Sir Kingsley Wood puts tuppence on a pint - to boost funds at the treasury ... "I peaked into the parlour to see what was a-hatchin', in time to hear the hostess suggest a charade / But who was in the pantry a-laughin' an' scratchin'? / Oh, the waiter / And the porter / And the upstairs maid!" - Bing Crosby, Mary Martin and Jack Teargarden and his Orchestra perform *The Waiter And The Porter And The Upstairs Maid* ... 33-year-old Alvar Liddell announces the news on the wireless for the BBC ... Prime-minister Winston Churchill dispatches 52-year-old Sir Stafford Cripps to India to negotiate with political leaders over the controversial and highly sensitive issue of self governance - the mission does not go well ... Back in Blighty - 26-year-old convicted double child murderer Harold Hill is hanged by the neck until dead at Oxford ... 62-year-old convicted murderer Harold Trevor is hanged by the neck until dead at Wandsworth ... The Luftwaffe launches a bombing raid on Exeter, then on Bath, then on Norwich, then on York ... The *Radio Doctor* broadcasts daily on the wireless and advises, "Make sure the bowels are well open." ... Posters on walls remind people, 'Careless Talk Costs Lives' and, 'Loose Lips Might Sink Ships' ... Royal Navy aircraft carrier HMS *Hermes* is attacked by Japanese dive bombers off the coast of Ceylon - and sinks with the loss of 307 lives ... Japanese dive bombers also attack HMS *Dorsetshire* and HMS *Cornwall* - both ships sink with the loss of 424 lives ... The short propaganda film *Listen to Britain* is now showing at cinemas ... Two squadrons of the new RAF *Lancaster* bombers take part in a daytime bombing raid over Germany ... The BBC broadcasts daily news - by Morse code - to the French Resistance ... 41-year-old Conservative Hugh Linstead wins a by-election in Putney following the death of Marcus Samuel MP ... After a murder trial at the Old Bailey lasting just one day, 52-year-old Mr. Justice Asquith dons a black cap and issues a death sentence to four-time killer Gordon Cummins ... American soldiers - based in Britain - step out for a good time on a Saturday night ... "Ma, I miss your apple pie. Ma, I miss your stew. Ma, they're treating me alright, but they can't cook like you" - 43-year-old Billy Cotton and his Band perform the hit song *Ma I Miss Your Apple Pie* ... "Will this be moon love, nothing but moon love? Will you be gone when the dawn comes stealing through?" - The Glenn Miller Orchestra perform *Adios* ... 50-year-old Arthur 'Bomber' Harris sends one-thousand RAF planes to destroy Cologne ... Bing Crosby sings *Do You Care?*

Summer 1942... Women of the Land Army

Tens of thousands of people die as Britain and Germany continue their devastating 'tit-for-tat' bombing raids ... German U-boats continue to target Allied supply-ships in the Atlantic ... HMS *Veteran* goes down with all hands ... 21-year-old Prince Philip of Greece and Denmark is promoted to the rank of lieutenant in the Royal Navy ... Women in the Land Army work fifty hours a week to keep the nation in food... Railings are removed from public parks to be melted down and made into weapons ... Prime-minister Winston Churhill meets Soviet Foreign Minister Vyacheskav Molotov in London and signs the Anglo-Soviet Treaty ... 28-year-old convicted mass murderer Gordon Cummins is hanged by the neck until dead at Wandsworth prison ... Jim and Mary McCartney from Liverpool are proud parents of newborn son, Paul ... 11-year-old schoolboy Norman Tebbit from Ponders End reads books in his bedroom ... "You are my sunshine, my only sunshine. You make me happy when skies are grey" - Ambrose and his Orchestra perform *You Are My Sunshine* ... 25-year-old forces' sweetheart Vera Lynn sings *(There'll Be Blue Birds Over) The White Cliffs Of Dover* ("… tomorrow, just you wait and see") ... The wireless show *Sincerely Yours, Vera Lynn* is broadcast every Sunday night on the BBC Forces Programme ... *Music While You Work* is broadcast each weekday ... The public is warned that only necessary journeys are to be made - driving for pleasure is banned ... The latest Ford *Anglia* motorcar has a top speed of 59 mph and can reach 50 mph in 35 seconds ... A severe hail storm damages buildings in South London ... RAF aircraft release 175,000 fire-bombs over Hamburg in a single night ... 27-year-old Lance Corporal John Whatley of the Oxfordshire and Buckinghamshire Light Infantry is killed in a raid on Dieppe ... 24-year-old *Spitfire* pilot Bill Ash is captured by German soldiers after making a crash landing in France ... 58-year-old General Claude Auchinleck and his Allied forces hold firm against Field Marshal Erwin Rommel (aka the Desert Fox) at El Alamein ... Serving officer and Blackpool FC right-winger Alex Munro is captured by the Germans and held as a prisoner of war ... Royal Navy aircraft carrier HMS *Eagle* is torpedoed by a German U-boat in the Mediterranean - the ship sinks within minutes and 131 men lose their lives ... The cruiser HMS *Manchester* is crippled after engaging with Italian torpedo boats - and Captain Howard Drew decides to scuttle the ship ... Back in England - sweets go 'on the ration' ... 53-year-old Will Hay and 27-year-old Charles Hawtrey star in *The Goose Steps Out* at cinemas ... 37-year-old Anna Neagle stars in *They Flew Alone* - the story of 'Queen of the Sky' Amy 'Johnnie' Johnson ... 7-year-old schoolboy David Nobbs and his mother hurry along to the pictures to watch *Bambi* ... 20-year-old Judy Garland has a hit record with *How About You* ... Harry Roy (aka the King of 'Hot-Cha') and his Band perform *The Sailor With The Navy Blue Eyes* ... Nellie Major, Violet Sloan, Betty Gates, Winnie Boyle, Rita Wright and dozens of other women work shifts at Dicksons factory in Northern Ireland - making munitions for the war ... "I'm the girl that makes the thing, that drills the hole that holds the ring, that drives the rod that turns the knob, that works the thing-ummy bob" - 44-year-old Gracie Fields sings *The Thing-Ummy Bob* ... 30-year-old German born scientist Klaus 'Karl' Fuchs is granted British Citizenship and is able to continue his work as a researcher on Britain's highly secret atomic bomb project ... 67-year-old Winster Churchill flies to Cairo to review war progress in the Middle East ... Churchill dismisses General Auchinleck and appoints General Alexander and Field Marshal

Bernard 'Monty' Montgomery as commanders of the 8th Army ... Churchill then flies onto Moscow to meet Joseph Stalin ... Back in Blighty - 33-year-old full-back Eddie Hapgood captains England's football team in a 1-0 defeat against Wales at Ninian Park ... The sun shines in August and temperatures rise ... American soldiers - based in Britain - spend their leave days whizzing along narrow country roads in MG *TB Midget* open-top sports cars ... People flock to cinemas to see Hollywood blockbuster *Gone With the Wind* - with Vivien Leigh and Clark Gable ... The popular film has been showing in Leicester Square for more than two years ... 'Essentials' remain in short supply ... Half a dozen eggs from *J. Sainsbury* cost 7½d ... A packet of ten *Embassy* cigarettes costs 9d.

Autumn 1942... The end of the beginning

Much Too Shy - a wonderful new comedy film starring the lovable entertainer George Formby (playing George Andy - the 'andyman) is now showing at cinemas. "In the streets just after dawn, when you can't hear a sound, with my milkcart every morn' I go upon my round" - *Delivering The Morning Milk* (performed by 38-year-old Formby) is a hit song from the movie ... "You're a crazy..." *Humpty Dumpty Heart* is a hit gramophone record for 39-year-old Bing Crosby ... 11-year-old Leslie Dawson from Collyhurst in Manchester takes a piano lesson - and plays the wrong notes ... 36-year-old traitor Lord Haw-Haw continues his radio broadcasts from the continent saying, "This is Germany calling." ... Luftwaffe fighters attack the Royal Navy ship HMS *Coventry* in the Mediterranean. The cruiser is badly damaged and the captain decides to scuttle her ... A German U-boat torpedoes the transport ship RMS *Laconia* in the Atlantic. The vessel sinks with the loss of over one-thousand lives ... 54-year-old Field Marshal Bernard 'Monty' Montgomery and his men defeat Field Marshal Erwin Rommel (aka the Desert Fox) at the second battle of El Alamein. Acknowledging such a significant victory, 67-year-old prime-minister Winston Churchill says, "This is not the end. It is not even the beginning of the end, but it is perhaps, the end of the beginning" ... Morale in Britain is boosted ... Crowds flock to cinemas to see Hollywood blockbuster *Mrs. Miniver*, starring 37-year-old Greer Garson as Kay Miniver - a stoic British housewife guiding her family through the difficult days of war ... Public information posters proclaim, 'Walk Short Distances - go by Shanks' pony and leave room for those who have longer journeys' ... 16-year-old Margaret Hilda Roberts is appointed head girl at Kesteven and

Grantham Girls' School ... The milk ration is cut to two and a half pints a week ... A new children's book called *Five On A Treasure Island* by 45-year-old Enid Blyton introduces *The Famous Five* - Julian, Dick, Anne, Georgina and dog Timmy ... "Home, home, sweet, sweet home. There's no place like home. There's no place like home" - 25-year-old forces' sweetheart Vera Lynn sings *Home Sweet Home* ... "How my heart is singing, while the band is swinging" - 20-year-old Judy Garland sings *Stompin' At The Savoy* ... American soldiers - based in Britain - chew gum, smoke *Lucky Strike* cigarettes and 'turn the heads' of English women ... Sweethearts spend their evenings at the cinema ... A ticket in the stalls costs around a shilling ... A ticket in the circle is 1s/6d ... 49-year-old Leslie Howard and 32-year-old David Niven star in new film *The First of the Few* - the story of the Battle of Britain ... 35-year-old Reserve Police Officer Ernie 'Mush' Callaghan is awarded the British Empire Medal for bravery during an air-raid on Birmingham ... Stolen military supplies find their way onto the black market where they're sold to members of the public by 'spivs' wearing pin-striped suits ... 21-year-old convicted murderer William Collins is hanged by the neck until dead at Durham. (72-year-old hangman Tom Pierrepoint carries out the execution) ... 27-year-old footballer Jack Smith scores a hat-trick as Walter Crickmer's Manchester Utd beat Blackburn Rovers 5-2 in a wartime league match ... 42-year-old Victor Silvester and his Ballroom Orchestra perform *Green Eyes* - a popular new Quick-step ... Evil Adolf Hitler and his Third Reich carry out their (so called) final solution. In just one day, 935 people are sent to their deaths in the gas chambers at Auschwitz ... Joseph Stalin's Red Army begin a large scale counter attack against German forces in the Soviet Union. The fighting in and around the city of Stalingrad is particularly fierce and bloody ... Back in Blighty - schoolboys play conkers, girls play pat-a-cake and the Church of England relaxes its rule stating women must wear hats in church.

Christmas 1942... Over paid, over sexed and over here!

The weather is unsettled - brief storms are interspersed with dry, mild spells ... 30-year-old MI6 double-agent Kim Philby meets his Soviet contact on a bench in Regents Park - and hands over a briefcase full of confidential government papers ... 11-year-old David Cornwell (aka John Le Carre) from Poole in Dorset writes stories in his bedroom ... Thousands of families listen to the wireless behind black-out curtains ... 41-year-old Donald McCullough is chairman on *The Brains Trust* ... 29-year-old Richard Dimbleby reads the *War Report* ... Royal Navy destroyer HMS *Penylan* sinks after being torpedoed by a German E-boat in the English Channel - its crew of 117 hands are rescued ... Operation Torch is underway as Allied troops advance through the deserts of North Africa ... 20-year-old Tom Finney of Preston North End (aka the 'Preston Plumber') does his bit serving under Field Marshal Bernard 'Monty' Montgomery in the 8th Army ... 20-year-old Raymond Baxter from Ilford does his bit serving as a *Spitfire* pilot in No. 93 Squadron ... Operation Frankton gets underway as 28-year-old Major Herbert 'Blondie' Hasler leads eleven Royal Marines in a daring raid - paddling seventy miles in canoes along the River Gironde in occupied France - to blow up German ships in the harbour at Bordeaux. The mission is a success, but does cost the lives of eight of the Marines ... 'Perfect Coffee, Instantly Made!' - Back in England - 'well-to-do' families enjoy a cup of *Nescafe* (which costs 1s/3d a tin from leading grocers) ... The Ink Spots sing *Someone's Rocking My Dreamboat* ("... someone's invading my dream. We were sailing along, so peaceful and calm, suddenly, something went wrong") ... Bing Crosby sings *Be Careful It's My Heart* ("... it's not my watch your holding, it's my heart") ... Footballer Johnny Spuhler scores a hat-trick and Harry Potts scores twice as Bill Murray's Sunderland thrash Middlesbrough 2-7 at Ayresome Park ... Cyril Done scores a hat-trick and Dickie Dorsett aka the 'Brownhills Bomber' (a guest player from Wolves) scores twice as George Kay's Liverpool thrash Burnley 9-2 at Anfield ... HMS *Achates* is shelled and sunk while escorting a convoy in the Barents Sea - 113 men lose their lives ... "Here's looking at you, kid" - the premiere of a new film called *Casablanca*, starring 42-year-old Humphrey Bogart and 27-year-old Ingrid Bergman, takes place in the USA ... *Went The Day Well?* with 32-year-old Elizabeth Allan and 31-year-old Thora Hird is now showing at UK cinemas ... Coal production is at its lowest level since 1926 - only 207 million tonnes have been mined this year ... 68-year-old prime-minister Winston Churchill and his wife Clementine attend the annual festive Songs Night at Harrow ... "Away in a manger, no crib for His bed, the little Lord Jesus lay down His sweet head" - On the streets of Brighton, children go carol singing, despite the black-out restrictions. 11-year-old David Knowles and his sister sing Yuletide harmonies and receive sweets and coins for their endeavours ... "I'm dreaming of a white Christmas, just like the ones we used to know" - *White Christmas* by Bing Crosby is the best selling gramophone record of the festive season ... Overpaid, over-sexed and over here - the American G.I.s spend Christmas in London, lavishing chocolate and nylons on British women ... 'Careful, You Can't Tell Who Has It!' - a campaign to halt the spread of venereal disease begins ... 48-year-old comedian Max Miller stars in the hit film *Asking For Trouble* ... 46-year-old convicted spy Johannes Dronkers is hanged by the neck until dead at Wandsworth. (37-year-old hangman Albert Pierrepoint carries out the execution) ... 62-year-old William Beveridge publishes a report giving solutions to the five giant evils in

British society: squalor, ignorance, want, idleness and disease ... In just one day, 1,558 people are sent to their deaths in the gas chambers at Auschwitz.

New Year 1943...
William Beveridge reports to Parliament

68-year-old British prime-minister Winston Churchill and 61-year-old US president Franklin D. Roosevelt meet at Casablanca. The two leaders discuss ongoing military strategy for Allied forces. USSR leader Joseph Stalin does not attend the meeting - he remains at home where his Red Army is engaged in a fierce and bloody battle for the city of Stalingrad ... Back in England - it's a wet January with heavy rainfall across much of the country ... 20-year-old Dutch resistance fighter George Behar joins his family in London and changes his name to George Blake ... "I can't dance. (I can't dance). Got ants in my pants. (Got ants in my pants). Boy, I can't dance. (I can't dance). Got ants in my pants. (Got ants in my pants)" - *I Can't Dance* by Harry Parry and his Radio Rhythm Club Sextet plays in dance halls ... *By The Sleepy Lagoon* (the theme tune from *Desert Island Discs*) plays on the wireless ... 82-year-old Ann Wade is murdered by 19-year-old William Henry Turner in Colchester ... Wartime football matches continue to take place with enemy aircraft 'spotters' on top of the stands ... Wolverhampton Wanderers' 23-year-old inside-left Dickie Dorsett (aka the 'Brownhills Bomber') scores as a guest player for Liverpool in a 0-1 victory over Wrexham ... Lovells Athletic thrash Bristol City 8-0 ... Newcastle Utd thrash Middlesbrough 7-3 ... The House of Commons votes to accept the proposals in William Beveridge's report - and to eradicate the five giant evils in British society; squalor, ignorance, want, idleness and disease. The single most important step will be the creation of a new 'Welfare State' ... 11-year-old Dennis Skinner from Clay Cross in Derbyshire reads *Europe, Russia and the Future* by G. D. H. Cole - a publication from the Left Book Club

... Radio presenter Lillian Duff announces the weekly news on the wireless ... Fighting continues in North Africa ... Battles intensify between Monty's 'Desert Rats' led by 55-year-old Field Marshal Bernard Montgomery and German soldiers led by 51-year-old Erwin 'Desert Fox' Rommel ... In Stalingrad - Soviet troops overpower the Nazi invaders and the Germans are forced to retreat and eventually surrender ... Adolf Hitler orders Joseph Goebbels to make a radio broadcast, informing the German people that they are now fighting a defensive war ... Morale in Berlin is at its lowest point ... Allied leaders decide to turn the screw on the enemy ... The RAF sends high-speed *Mosquito* bombers to make daylight raids on the city ... "Who wouldn't love you, who wouldn't care. You're so enchanting, people must stare" - *Who Wouldn't Love You* by The Ink Spots is the top selling gramophone record ... 39-year-old Bing Crosby sings *Moonlight Becomes You* ... 40-year-old Nazi spy Franciscus Winter is hanged by the neck until dead at Wandsworth ... The rationing of food, clothes and fuel has become a long standing inconvenience ... Young people keep their spirits up by going to the pictures or attending dance halls on a Saturday night ... Nylon stockings remain in short supply. Women apply gravy browning to their legs before going out ... "We'll meet again, don't know where, don't know when, but I know we'll meet again some sunny day" - 25-year-old forces' sweetheart Vera Lynn stars in *We'll Meet Again* at cinemas ... 17-year-old George Cole stars in *Those Kids From Town* - a propaganda film featuring evacuated children ... Wartime posters ask, 'Is Your Journey Really Necessary?' Cars (both new and second hand) are in short supply and almost impossible to buy. Any that do become available are reserved for doctors and government officials ... An Austin *Eight* has a top speed of 59 mph and accelerates from 0-50 mph in 31.7

seconds ... Harold and Louise Harrison from Wavertree in Liverpool are proud parents of newborn son, George ... 33-year-old movie star Errol Flynn is acquitted on three rape charges in Los Angeles ... 42-year-old Heinrich Himmler orders his German SS officers to liquidate the forty-thousand Jews living in Warsaw.

Spring 1943... Desert Rats

Allied forces make three notable military break-throughs. Firstly, Monty and his Desert Rats are successful in North Africa - German and Italian forces are swept aside and forced into surrender. Secondly, nineteen Lancaster bombers take part in a bombing raid on river dams in the Ruhr valley of Germany. The Mohne and Eder Dams are successfully breached when 'bouncing bombs' (designed by 55-year-old Barnes Wallis) are used. Thirdly, the Nazi high-command is fooled by Operation Mincemeat - when false military information is discovered on the body of a dead tramp dressed in the uniform of an RAF officer ... "I got a gal in Kalamazoo. Don't want to boast but I know she's the toast of Kalamazoo" - 43-year-old Harry Roy (aka the King of 'Hot-Cha') and his Band perform *I've Got A Girl In Kalamazoo* ... Aberdeen is severely damaged by German bombs ... Birmingham is severely damaged by German bombs ... More than one-hundred people die from asphyxiation when a large crowd rushes for shelter from falling bombs in Bethnal Green tube station ... 19-year-old convicted murderer William Henry Turner is hanged by the neck until dead at Pentonville ... *Fires Were Started* a film depicting real London firemen is now showing at cinemas ... 43-year-old James Cagney wins an Oscar for his role in *Yankee Doodle Dandy* ... 28-year-old Hedy Lamarr (36-25-35) stars in *White Cargo* ... 8-year-old schoolboy David Nobbs reads a *Biggles* book (written by Captain W. E. Johns) and listens to the wireless at his home in Marlborough ... German U-boats continue to attack British supply ships in the Atlantic ocean ... Royal Navy destroyers HMS *Harvester* and HMS *Beverley* are sunk with the loss of 284 lives ... German E-boats continue to attack British troop ships in the Mediterranean ... Royal Navy destroyer HMS *Lightning* is on escort duty when she's torpedoed and sunk ... HMS *Amethyst* - a new anti-submarine vessel - is launched on the River Clyde ... 68-year-old prime-minister Winston Churchill travels to Washington for a meeting with US president Franklin D. Roosevelt ... 47-year-old King George VI and 42-year-old Queen Elizabeth are guests at an international football match in London. The royal couple watch as 25-year-old Dennis Westcott of Wolverhampton Wanderers scores a hat-trick for England in a 5-3 victory over Wales at the Empire Stadium in Wembley ... 28-year-old outside-right Stanley 'wizard of dribble' Matthews is a guest player for Blackpool in a 4-2 victory over Arsenal in the Football League War Cup final at Stamford Bridge. (24-year-old Denis Compton scores Arsenal's second goal) ... "You were never lovelier, you were never so fair. Dreams were never lovelier, pardon me if I stare" - 29-year-old singer Denny Dennis from Derby performs (with Ambrose and his Orchestra) at dance halls ... 'George joins the Home Guard and saves the day with his secret weapon!' - Millions of people flock to the cinema to see *Get Cracking* a wonderful new comedy starring the lovable entertainer George Formby. "On sentry go in the night. If it's wet the water trickles down your neck to where it tickles, and the raindrops ooze through your socks and shoes. If you're feeling on the black side with the wind around your earholes, then you'll get those..." *Home Guard Blues* (performed by 39-year-old Formby) is a popular song from the movie ... 11-year-old Des O'Connor from Stepney in East London plays out with his friends ... *Five Little Pigs* - the new crime thriller by Agatha Christie (featuring detective Hercule Poirot) is on sale in bookshops for eight shillings ... Posters in public places say, 'On Her Their Lives Depend. Women Munition Workers. Enrol at Once' ... 46-year-old Mrs. T Wilkinson breaks down fuses at the

Royal Ordnance Factory at Aycliffe near Darlington ... 52-year-old William Quayle sexually assaults and murders 8-year-old Vera Clarke in Birmingham.

Summer 1943... Allies invade Sicily

The weather is mostly unsettled and dull, with a few days of sunshine at the end of July ... Hundreds are killed in Grimsby and Cleethorpes by German 'butterfly' bombs - a new type of explosive device, some of which are fitted with delay fuses designed to maximise damage and destruction ... "Play it, Sam" - the Hollywood blockbuster, *Casablanca*, starring 43-year-old Humphrey Bogart and 27-year-old Ingrid Bergman, is now showing at British cinemas ... "Said Mr. Wu, 'What shall I do?' and Mr. Wu's a window cleaner now" - 39-year-old George Formby sings *Mister Wu's A Window Cleaner Now* ... 27-year-old Dinah Shore sings *You'd Be So Nice To Come Home To* ... Prime-minister Winston Churchill addresses British soldiers at the Roman amphitheatre in Carthage, Tunisia ... Allied forces invade Sicily ... 29-year-old actor Alec Guinness commands a landing craft ... 25-year-old footballer Wilf Mannion is caught up in crossfire, and survives ... 38-year-old cricketer Hedley Verity is hit in chest, and dies ... 21-year-old *Spitfire* pilot Raymond Baxter of RAF's No. 93 Squadron is mentioned in despatches - for brave action during Operation Torch ... Benito Mussolini and his fascists are ousted in Italy. Marshal Pietro Badoglio takes over as prime-minister and signs an Armistice with the Allies ... 'Operation Gomorrah' gets underway as 51-year-old Air Chief Marshal Arthur 'Bomber' Harris orders RAF aircraft to cause havoc and devastation on Hamburg ... 50-year-old actor Leslie Howard is one of seventeen people killed when the *BOAC* aeroplane he's travelling on crashes into the Bay of Biscay after being attacked by German war planes ... The Entertainments National Service Association (aka Ensa) organises morale boosting stage shows for soldiers posted overseas ... Lovable entertainer 39-year-old George Formby travels around the Mediterranean performing cheeky songs on his ukulele for Allied troops in Sicily, Malta, Gibraltar, Libya, Tunisia and Egypt ... Back in England - 44-year-old John Christie murders Ruth Fuerst at 10 Rillington Place ... 22-year-old Terence Casey murders Bridget Mitton at 8 Gwendolen Street in Putney ... 26-year-old Thomas James murders Gwendoline Sweeney at 4 Kitchen Street in Liverpool ... 21-year-old Philip Larkin from Coventry fails an interview with the British Intelligence Service at Bletchley Park - and decides to become a librarian instead ... Geraldo and his Orchestra perform the hit song *Keep An Eye On Your Heart* ... Joe Loss and his Orchestra perform *I'm Gonna Get Lit Up (When The Lights Go Up In London)* ... Joe and Eva Jagger from Dartford in Kent are proud parents of newborn son, Michael (aka Mick) ... 19-year-old footballer Jackie Milburn makes his debut for Newcastle Utd in the wartime league ... 37-year-old cricketer Les Ames scores 133 runs at Lord's for an England XI against the Dominions ... 25-year-old all-round sportsman Denis Compton plays for England's national team at both football and cricket ... 22-year-old southpaw boxer Jackie Paterson from Scotland is the new world fly-weight champion - Paterson beats Peter Kane of England in a title fight held at Hampden Park ... Royal Navy cruiser HMS *Charybdis* is attacked by German torpedo boats in the English Channel (off the coast of France) and sinks with the loss of over four-hundred lives ... "Who's building the ship, who's flying the plane, who's manning the tank and the gun? It's the Smiths and the Jones, and the Kellys and Cohens" - Flanagan & Allen perform the hit song *The Smiths And The Jones* ... 21-year-old amateur actress Hattie Jacques does her bit for the war effort - working shifts as a welder in a London factory ... Crowds flock to the cinema to see *In Which*

We Serve - an inspirational film telling the wartime story of Royal Navy destroyer HMS *Torrin* - 43-year-old Noel Coward, 35-year-old John Mills, 35-year-old Bernard Miles and 34-year-old Celia Johnson are the stars ... "Daughter! Daughter!" - 58-year-old Arthur Lucan returns as the ever popular character *Old Mother Riley* ... 52-year-old convicted child murderer William Quayle is hanged by the neck until dead at Birmingham ... *That Old Black Magic* ("... has me in its spell. That old black magic that you weave so well") by 20-year-old Judy Garland is a popular song on the radio ... *You Made Me Love You (I Didn't Want To Do It)* ("... I didn't want to do it. You made me want you, and all the time you knew it. I guess you always knew it") by Harry James and his Band (with Helen Forrest on vocals) is also popular ... Winston Churchill attends a conference in Quebec along with his friend and ally US president Franklin D. Roosevelt ... Back in England - *The Man in Grey* - a new film starring Stewart Granger, James Mason and the beautiful 26-year-old Margaret Lockwood - is now showing at picture houses around the country ... 38-year-old Albert Pierrepoint marries his sweetheart Annie Fletcher in Manchester ... Meat, milk, cheese, butter, sugar and dry fruit are all now 'on the ration' ... A pint of mild in the Red Lion is 10d.

Autumn 1943... Allies invade Italy

55-year-old Field Marshal Bernard 'Monty' Montgomery leads the 8th Army as the Allies invade Italy. Having already signed an Armistice with the Allies, Italy now declares war on Germany ... 61-year-old author P.G. Wodehouse moves from Berlin to Paris under supervision of the Nazis ... Back in England - 11-year-old Reginald Bosanquet from Chertsey in Surrey plays conkers with his friends ... 11-year-old Sally Clarke from Epsom in Surrey practices singing in front of a bedroom mirror ... Residents of Imber in Wiltshire are told to leave their homes to make way for military manoeuvres ... Chancellor of the Exchequer Sir Howard Kingsley Wood dies suddenly aged 62 in London ... "Save the Home Coming Waltz for me, we will dance when the world is free" - Kay Yorston is vocalist for Ivy Benson and her All Girl Band on *The Home Coming Waltz* ... 21-year-old acting Flight Lieutenant William Reid is severely injured by enemy fire as he flies his RAF *Lancaster* bomber on a raid over Dusseldorf ... Royal Navy destroyer HMS *Dulverton* is attacked by German aircraft off the Greek island of Kos - the ship goes down with the loss of 78 lives ... Captain the Reverend Alfred Cecil Parr dies in a prisoner of war camp in Thailand ... Back in England - 33-year-old Ernest Digby batters his 3-week-old daughter Dawn to death in woodlands near Milborne Port in Somerset ... 18-year-old student Margaret Hilda Roberts goes up to Oxford to read Chemistry ... "Don't know why there's no sun up in the sky..." *Stormy Weather* by 26-year-old Lena Horne is a popular new gramophone tune ... "She has to wear a what-do-ya-call-it tied round her chest. She hung it on a clothes line and a tramp said 'I'm blessed, that's a lovely hammock, I'll climb in for a rest.' 'Cause Bunty's such a big girl now" - 39-year-old George

Formby performs his cheeky little song *Bunty's A Big Girl Now* ... People flock to cinemas to see Vivien Leigh and Clark Gable in Hollywood blockbuster, *Gone With the Wind.* The popular movie has been showing in Leicester Square for more than three years ... Manchester Utd's 24-year-old centre-forward Jack 'cannonball' Rowley scores twice as a guest player for Tottenham Hotspur in a 5-1 victory over Chelsea ... 32-year-old Don Welsh and 27-year-old guest-player Bobby Beattie both score hat-tricks as George Kay's Liverpool thrash Southport 9-0 in a North region wartime league match ... Bill Camkin's Birmingham are now called Birmingham City - they beat local rivals Aston Villa 2-1 in a North region wartime league match ... England thrash Scotland 8-0 at Maine Road, with 24-year-old Tommy Lawton notching four goals and 28-year-old Stanley 'wizard of dribble' Matthews also on the score-sheet ... Popular radio show *Music While You Work* continues to keep the nation entertained ... "Where ever you wander, on land or on sea, if you really love me..." *Be Honest With Me* by Bing Crosby is a top selling gramophone record ... 22-year-old convicted murderer Terence Casey is hanged by the neck until dead at Wandsworth ... Winston Churchill attends a conference in Cairo along with his friend and ally US president Franklin D. Roosevelt ... HMS *Tyndale* is torpedoed by German U-boat *593* in the Mediterranean and sinks with the loss of 73 lives. HMS *Holcombe* goes in search of U-boat *593*, but is also torpedoed and sinks with the loss of 81 lives. The following day, HMS *Calpe* and USS *Wainwright* (of the US Navy) track down U-boat *593* and drop a depth charge on her.

Christmas 1943 ... Music while you work

War continues to rage ... The distinctive and eerie wail of a siren fills the air as enemy bombers approach ... 'In a raid - do not rush, take cover quietly, then others will do the same' ... Allied generals and senior politicians plan the next phase of the war - the invasion of Europe ... Residents of Tyneham in Dorset are told to leave their homes to make way for military manoeuvres ... "You'll never know just how much I miss you. You'll never know just how much I care" - *You'll Never Know* by 26-year-old forces' sweetheart Vera Lynn is a popular tune ... Herbert and Doris Richards from Dartford in Kent are proud parents of newborn son, Keith ... 'The Big Three' - British prime-minister Winston Churchill, US president Franklin D. Roosevelt and USSR general secretary Joseph Stalin meet together for the first time at a conference in Tehran ... Back in Britain - Bevin Boys go to work in the coal mines ... 17-year-old Jimmy Savile from Leeds is one of the young men conscripted to work down a pit ... 202 million tonnes of coal have been mined this year in Britain ... 47-year-old fascist Oswald Mosley is released from prison on the grounds of ill health ... 34-year-old Harry Goslin a Bolton Wanderers footballer dies after being wounded in Italy ... 21-year-old acting Flight Lieutenant William Reid of the RAF receives the Victoria Cross in recognition of most conspicuous bravery during a bombing raid on Dusseldorf ... 69-year-old Winston Churchill contracts pneumonia on his visit to Tunisia and is treated with penicillin ... *Silver Wings In The Moonlight* ("... flying high above, while I'm patiently waiting, please take care of my love") by 20-year-old Anne Shelton from Dulwich is a popular new tune ... 26-year-old convicted murderer Thomas James is hanged by the neck until dead at Liverpool ... *The Life and Death of Colonel Blimp*, starring 23-year-old Deborah Kerr, is at cinemas ... 22-year-old Jane Russell (38-24-36) sizzles on the big screen in *The Outlaw* ... "And, can I do yer now sir? Can I do yer now? If you don't want doing, we'll have a pow-wow" - Mrs. Mopp (a character from popular radio show *It's That Man Again*) sings *Can I Do Yer Now Sir* ... Veteran music-hall song writer Felix McGlennon dies aged 88 in London ... 11-year-old schoolboy Ray Reardon from Tredegar in Monmouthshire beats his best friend in a game of snooker ... 27-year-old 'guest' football player Bobby Beattie and 23-year-old Cyril Done both score hat-tricks as George Kay's Liverpool thrash Tranmere Rovers 2-9 in a wartime league match at Prenton Park ... Billy Birrell's Chelsea draw 3-3 with Charlie Paynter's West Ham Utd at Stamford Bridge ... Stan Seymour's Newcastle Utd beat Bill Murray's Sunderland 4-2 at St. James' Park ... *Music While You Work* and *Forces Favourites* ('a programme in which you hear music played at the request of Forces overseas for their relatives at home') are on the wireless ... "I'd rather have a paper doll to call my own" - *Paper Doll* by The Mills Brothers is the best selling 78 rpm gramophone record ... *When Can I Have A Banana Again* by Harry Roy (aka the King of 'Hot-Cha') and his Band is also popular ... On Christmas Eve - Royal Navy ship HMS *Hurricane* is torpedoed by a German U-boat in the Atlantic ... Three of *Hurricane's* crewman are killed ... Prime-minister Winston Churchill convalesces in Marrakesh - after his recent bout of pneumonia ... Back in England - it's almost impossible to get a turkey for Christmas ... Families play *Totopoly* and listen to the wireless ... On Boxing Day - German battleship *Sharnhorst* is attacked and sunk by HMS *Duke of York* and other Allied ships ... Around two-thousand lives are lost ... "When the Fuehrer says, 'We is the master-race.' We heil! heil! Right in the Fuehrer's face" - 34-year-old British comedian Tommy Trinder sings *Der Fuehrer's Face.*

New Year 1944... The Wizard of Dribble

Heavy snowfall (up to sixteen inches in places) disrupts traffic across much of the country ... The Luftwaffe launch a fresh series of bombing raids on London ... RAF *Mosquito* fighter planes are scrambled to intercept the German *Junkers*, *Dorniers*, *Heinkels* and *Focke-Wulfs* ... 33-year-old Chelsea goalkeeper Vic Woodley keeps the Arsenal strikers at bay as his team win 2-0 at Stamford Bridge ... Stan Cullis, Joe Mercer and Stanley 'wizard of dribble' Matthews line up for England at Wembley against a Scottish team which includes Matt Busby, Archie Macaulay and Jock Dodds ... England win the match 6-2 with 24-year-old Tommy Lawton of Everton and 26-year-old Jimmy Hagan of Derby County on the score-sheet ... Commentary of the second half is broadcast live on BBC radio followed by *Andrew Fenner at the Theatre Organ* ... 'He's All At Sea!' - Millions flock to cinemas to see lovable entertainer George Formby in *Bell Bottom George*. "Swim little fish, swim on. Swim little fish, swim on. We're two ambitious fishes, you and I. We'll get our wishes if we try, try, try" - *Swim Little Fish* (performed by 39-year-old Formby) is a popular song from the movie. 39-year-old convicted murderer John H Waters is hanged by the neck until dead at Shepton Mallet. (Waters shot dead his lover Doris Staples last summer). German forces target Allied convoys heading for the Soviet Union ... Royal Navy destroyer HMS *Mahratta* is on escort duty when she's hit and sunk off the coast of Norway - two-hundred and twenty lives are lost ... "Pedro the fisherman was always whistling such a merry call" - 46-year-old Gracie Fields sings *Pedro The Fisherman* ... 40-year-old Bing Crosby sings *If I Had My Way* ... 61-year-old Chancellor of the Exchequer Sir John Anderson addresses parliament - a new tax system called Pay As

You Earn is soon to be introduced ... 41-year-old Secretary of State for Education Richard Austen 'Rab' Butler addresses parliament - and announces a radical new bill to make free secondary education available to all children through a two-tier system of grammar and secondary modern schools ... It's also proposed that the school leaving age be raised to 15 ... The bill wins the support of the House and Butler's Education Act 1944 passes into law. War continues to rage around the world - but the Allies have gained the upper hand ... 69-year-old prime-minister Winston Churchill meets 53-year-old General Charles de Gaulle in Marrakesh and reassures the French leader that he will get his country back soon ... 29-year-old private Bernard Youens from Hove is seriously injured during fighting at Anzio in Italy. Back in England - 18-year-old Nat Lofthouse completes an eight hour shift down the pit as a Bevin Boy and then plays centre-forward for Bolton Wanderers on the same day - 'The Trotters' beat Blackburn Rovers 4-1 at Burnden Park ... 11-year-old Bobby Robson from County Durham plays football in the street with his friends ... Rationing remains in place and good food is scarce ... Bread and dripping is an oft' eaten meal ... Music cheers the nation ... The Buddy Featherstonhaugh RAF Sextet perform *Soft Winds* ("... whisper sweet words to my love") ... 41-year-old Ted Heath and his Music perform *I've Got Sixpence* ("... jolly, jolly sixpence. I've got sixpence to last me all my life") ... "After you Claude / No, after you Cecil" - wireless show *It's That Man Again* (now commonly known by the acronym *Itma*), with 52-year-old Tommy Handley, continues to make people smile.

Spring 1944... A great escape

Allied forces bomb railway lines and bridges in France ahead of a European invasion ... 50-year-old Stuart Hibberd announces the news on the wireless ... Chancellor of the Exchequer Sir John Anderson delivers his first Budget ... The country's finances are in a desperate state ... Rationing is to be retained for some years to come ... Advertisements for National Savings advise everyone to 'Save at least a bob in the pound' ... 51-year-old Basil Rathbone is Sherlock Holmes in *The Scarlet Claw* at cinemas ... 55-year-old actor Wally Patch appears on the bill at the Collins Music Hall in London... 34-year-old baby killer Ernest Digby is hanged by the neck until dead at Bristol. 34-year-old prisoner of war Douglas Bader antagonises his guards at Colditz castle ... Seventy-six Allied prisoners tunnel their way out of Stalag Luft III - some are duly re-captured and shot by the Germans ... 41-year-old Bing Crosby from Tacoma in Washington sings *Sunday, Monday Or Always* ... 20-year-old Anne Shelton from Dulwich sings *Hold Back The Dawn* ... A quiet sense of optimism is building - the Allied forces are in the ascendancy ... People in Britain continue to work hard - but manage to enjoy themselves as well ... 38,540 spectators turn out at Stamford Bridge for the Football League War Cup final between Charlton Athletic and Aston Villa ... 24-year-old Charlie Revell scores for 'The Addicks' and 33-year-old Eric Houghton equalises for 'The Villa' in a 1-1 draw - and the cup is shared ... Crowds flock to the cinema to see 12-year-old Elizabeth Taylor from London starring as Priscilla in *Lassie Come Home* at cinemas ... *Fanny by Gaslight*, with 29-year-old Phyllis Calvert, 30-year-old Stewart Granger and 34-year-old James Mason, is also now showing ... 11-year-old Michael Heseltine from Swansea in South Wales shares sweets with his friends ... A bar of Cadbury's chocolate costs around tenpence on the black market ... "Shoo-shoo-shoo baby. Shoo-shoo-shoo baby. Bye-bye-bye baby. Do-dah do-day. Your papa's off to the seven seas" - *Shoo Shoo Baby* by The Andrews Sisters is a popular gramophone record ... "Oh, mairzy doats and dozy doats and liddle lamzy divey" - The Merry Macs perform *Mairzy Doats* ... Heavy rain causes severe flooding in West Yorkshire ... RAF officer Frederick Shand is killed in an aircraft accident over Ceylon ... 24-year-old footballer Tommy Lawton scores two goals as England beat Scotland 3-2 in a wartime international football match ... 54-year-old Ted Vizard takes over from 61-year-old Major Frank Buckley as manager of Wolverhampton Wanderers ... Wolves beat Stoke City 2-1 in their final game of the season in the North region wartime league (second championship) ... 26-year-old James Galbraith murders radio-operator James Percey on-board a merchant ship at Salford Docks ... 19-year-old John Gordon Davidson strangles and kills 27-year-old Gladys Appleton at St. Helens ... Brum Martin and his Dance Orchestra perform popular tunes on the wireless from the Plaza Ballroom in Derby.

Summer 1944... D Day

Operation Neptune - thousands of troops cross the English Channel and the D Day landings begin ... Sergeant Arthur John Bradley of the Royal Marines is one of two hundred-thousand Allied casualties in the bloody battle for Normandy ... 69-year-old prime-minister Winston Churchill visits Northern France on the twelfth of June and addresses the brave fighting men ... The D Day landings have been a success. Operation Overlord commences as Allied forces begin their advance across Europe ... Troops push on through France. The city of Paris is liberated on the twenty-fifth of August ... 53-year-old General Charles de Gaulle addresses thousands of cheering Parisians on the Rue Saint-Dominique ... 44-year-old Victor Silvester and his Ballroom Orchestra perform *Reconciliation* - a popular new Waltz ... Soviet forces continue their advance from the East - making progress into Poland, Romania and East Prussia as the shattered Germans retreat ... Back in England - it's dull and rainy ... 37-year-old Frank Whittle from Coventry succeeds in his mission to build a jet powered fighter plane - the 600 mph Gloster *Meteor F1* enters service with the RAF ... German V-1 rockets kill thousands of civilians in London. The V-1s (aka 'doodlebugs') continue to wreak havoc over the summer months ... 9-year-old schoolboy David Nobbs dives for cover outside Orpington Library when he hears the drone of a flying bomb overhead ... 11-year-old Michael Caine from Rotherhithe spends the night in an air-raid shelter ... 27-year-old Frank Sinatra sings *A Lovely Way To Spend An Evening* ... "My Lili of the lamplight, my own Lili Marlene" - 20-year-old Anne Shelton from Dulwich sings *Lili Marlene* ... The Gestapo capture 15-year-old Anne Frank and her family in Amsterdam ... MI5 investigate the wartime activities of 62-year-old author P.G. Wodehouse and find no evidence of pro-Nazi behaviour ... 19-year-old convicted murderer John Gordon Davidson is hanged by the neck until dead at Liverpool ... 26-year-old convicted murderer James Galbraith is hanged by the neck until dead at Strangeways ... The Summer Olympics (due to be held in London) are cancelled because of the war ... 37-year-old cricketer Laurie Fishlock scores 108 runs and 41-year-old Wally Hammond is out for a duck as England take on the Dominions at Lord's ... 69-year-old Prime-minister Winston Churchill travels to Algiers to visit the Italian front and meet Allied soldiers ... 40-year-old lovable entertainer George Formby travels to Normandy to perform cheeky songs on his ukulele for the troops ... Back in Blighty - 44-year-old Humphrey Bogart stars at cinemas as Sam Spade in *The Maltese Falcon* ... 35-year-old James Mason stars as Peter Vadassy in *Hotel Reserve* ... 53-year-old Stanley Holloway and 36-year-old John Mills star in David Lean's new movie *This Happy Breed* - and it's in Technicolor! ... 30-year-old Ivy Benson and her All Girl Band perform *How Sweet You Are* ("... how sweet you are, how dear your tenderly smiling face") ... 27-year-old Forces' sweetheart Vera Lynn sings *It's Like Old Times* ("... holding you so close again. Like old times, kissing every now and then. What a kick to do the town like we did before, and to hear you say that you are mine once more") ... 30-year-old footballer Raich 'Silver Fox' Carter tricks opposing half-backs with his 'dribbling' skills ... 31-year-old cricketer Jack Young bowls left arm 'occasionals' for Middlesex ... Royal Navy ship HMS *Boadicea* is attacked by German aircraft off Portland Bill and sinks with the loss of 170 lives ... A pint of mild in the Red Lion costs 11d.

Autumn 1944... Doodle-bugs

Allied forces liberate Brussels ... Soviet forces continue their push towards Germany from the East. Operation Market Garden takes place in Holland and the British Army captures key river bridges at Eindhoven and Nijmegen, but fails to secure a bridge at Arnhem - where Captain Brian 'Basher' Brownscombe of the Royal Army Medical Corps is just one of the soldiers to be taken prisoner and shot ... 69-year-old Winston Churchill meets 65-year-old Joseph Stalin in Moscow. The two leaders discuss how the countries of Europe should be structured after the war ... Optimism is building in Britain. Momentum lies with the Allied forces and German soldiers are being forced back towards Berlin ... Black-out restrictions in London are relaxed ... People enjoy an evening out at the cinema ... 35-year-old Tommy Trinder stars alongside 53-year-old Stanley Holloway and 36-year-old Betty Warren in *Champagne Charlie* - a new comedy film made at Ealing Studios ... RAF *Lancaster* bombers are sent to Norway to sink the German battleship *Tirpitz* - the mission is a success and the ship goes down with the loss of one-thousand lives ... Field Marshal Erwin Rommel (aka the Desert Fox) commits suicide in Germany ... Back in England - schoolboys play conkers in the corner of the playground ... 11-year-old twins Reginald and Ronald Kray from Bethnal Green pick fights with other boys on East End streets - and then go home to their mum ... 35-year-old John Haigh murders William McSwan and disposes of the body in a 45-gallon drum containing sulphuric acid ... 45-year-old John Christie murders Muriel Eady at 10 Rillington Place ... "Why do I do, just as you say? Why must I just give you your way?" - 49-year-old Cliff Edwards performs *It Had To Be You* under his stage name Ukulele Ike ... 40-year-old Geraldo and his Orchestra perform *Milkman Keep Those Bottles Quiet* ("... can't use that jive on my milk diet") ... 37-year-old Laurence Olivier stars in *Henry V* at cinemas ... Crowds flock to see Hollywood blockbuster *Double Indemnity*, starring 36-year-old Fred MacMurray and 37-year-old Barbara Stanwyck ... "She's the sweetest rose of colour a cowboy ever knew. Her eyes are bright as diamonds, they sparkle like the dew" - 33-year-old Roy Rogers stars with his horse Trigger in *The Yellow Rose of Texas* ... Convicted rapist Madison Thomas (a US serviceman) is hanged by the neck until dead at Shepton Mallet ... 32-year-old Flight Lieutenant Ted Drake leads the forward line for Arsenal in the wartime football league (South) division ... Liverpool's Matt Busby lines up alongside Stoke City's Stanley 'wizard of dribble' Matthews for a Combined Services XI against an Ireland XI at Windsor Park - the Combined Services win the match 4-8 ... England take on Scotland at the Empire Stadium in Wembley with 29-year-old Joe Mercer (captain) and 30-year-old Frank Swift (goalkeeper) in the line-up - 90,000 people see 25-year-old centre-forward Tommy Lawton bag a hat-trick as the home team wins 6-2 ... "Oh, I'm packing my grip and I'm leav-in' today, 'cause I'm takin' a trip Cal-i-for-nia way" - 41-year-old Bing Crosby sings *San Fernando Valley* ... "I'll be seeing you in all the old familiar places, that this heart of mine embraces, all day through" - 21-year-old Anne Shelton from Dulwich sings *I'll Be Seeing You* ... Prime-minister Winston Churchill receives rapturous applause as he visits the city of Paris and meets with 53-year-old Charles de Gaulle ... HMS *Rockingham* sinks in the Atlantic after colliding with a mine ... Germany launches its fearsome V-2 rockets on London. A direct hit on *Woolworths* in New Cross claims the lives of 168 people.

Christmas 1944... In a shady nook, by a babbling brook

Allied troops continue to make progress across mainland Europe - heading towards Berlin ... Back in Blighty - the Home Guard (Dad's Army) stands down ... Thick smog engulfs much of the country and air hangs heavy over towns and cities ... *Forces Favourites* is on the wireless - a popular programme playing records chosen by British servicemen overseas ... "In a shady nook, by a babbling brook, that's where I fell in love with you" - *In A Shady Nook (By A Babbling Brook)* by 36-year-old Donald Peers is a popular song ... "I'll have to ask me dad" - 42-year-old Jack Train plays the character Mark Time in the ever popular radio show *It's That Man Again* (aka *Itma*) ... Tom Cragg and Raymond Glendenning commentate on the second half of football matches for the BBC on Saturday afternoons ... 34-year-old Eric Houghton bags a hat-trick as Aston Villa beat Tom Bromilow's Leicester City 5-0 in the Football League North ... 26-year-old Cyril Brown and 27-year-old Len Townshend both score twice as Brentford thrash Jack Tinn's Portsmouth 7-1 in th Football League South ... 45-year-old David Jack (former inside-forward for Arsenal and England) is the new manager of Middlesbrough FC ... 38-year-old Harry Hibbs (former goalkeeper for Birmingham City and England) is new at Walsall ... 11-year-old Dennis Viollet from Fallowfield in Manchester plays football in the park with his friends ... Crowds queue outside cinemas - eager to see the latest films ... 'Up to his tricks in politics!' - lovable entertainer George Formby stars in *He Snoops to Conquer*. "When I'm tired of the saddle, I get off the horse and paddle. Then I get a cheap return and catch the train. I'm Hill Billy Willie from the Cowheel Range, ridin' across the Wigan Plain!" - *Hill Billy Willie* (performed by 40-year-old

Formby) is a popular song from the movie ... 30-year-old silver-screen beauty Hedy Lamarr (36-25-35) stars in *The Conspirators* ... 22-year-old Judy Garland (33-22-34) stars in *Meet Me In St. Louis* ... Allied war planes bomb the city of Leipzig as ground troops continue their push towards Berlin ... The Entertainments National Service Association (aka Ensa) organises musical variety shows for soldiers stationed overseas. Famous stars are encouraged to take part ... Glenn Miller takes off on a US Army plane bound for Paris - the single engine aircraft goes missing over the English Channel and the 40-year-old band leader is never seen again ... 70-year-old prime-minister Winston Churchill spends the festive season in Athens conducting meetings with Greece's political leaders ... Back in England - convicted murderer Private Benjamin Pyegate (a US serviceman) is executed by firing squad at Shepton Mallet ... The 'call up' of young men continues, with one in ten new war recruits being conscripted to work as a Bevin Boy in the coal mines ... Coal production this year has fallen below 200 million tonnes ... Advertisements in post offices around the country advise people to, 'Post Early This Christmas' ... *The Cornish Rhapsody* by 49-year-old pianist Harriet Cohen is the best selling 78 rpm gramophone record ... *White Christmas* by 41-year-old Bing Crosby is also popular ... Young boys ask Father Christmas for a farmyard set ... Young girls ask Father Christmas for a pull-a-long walking dog ... 55-year-old German Fuehrer Adolf Hitler orders a last-ditch effort to halt the advancing Allied soldiers and the Battle of the Bulge begins across Belgium, France and Luxembourg ... "When that man is dead and gone, we'll go dancing down the street, kissing everyone we meet, when that man is dead and gone. What a day to wake upon, what a way to greet the dawn. Some fine day the news will flash, Satan with a small moustache is asleep beneath the lawn" - the late Al Bowlly features on a gramophone recording of *When That Man Is Dead And Gone*.

New Year 1945... Battle of the Bulge

Japanese Kamikaze pilots attack US and Allied ships ... Deadly V-2 rockets continue to wreak havoc on southern England ... Allied leaders 70-year-old Winston Churchill, 62-year-old Franklin D. Roosevelt and 66-year-old Joseph Stalin meet at Yalta - with the aim of establishing a post war arrangement to ensure a long-lasting peace in Europe ... 33-year-old Captain John Ravenhill Sweeting is killed in action in Burma ... Twenty-thousand die (many of them burnt alive) as RAF bombers destroy the city of Dresden ... 45-year-old Noel Coward sings *Don't Let's Be Beastly To The Germans* ... Over twenty-thousand Allied soldiers are killed in fierce and bloody fighting during the Battle of the Bulge. The German army is eventually over-powered and forced to retreat ... "We must keep on watching, we're going to win you bet. Though luxuries are scarcer and may be hard to get" - *Spotting On The Top Of Blackpool Tower* by George Formby is a gramophone hit. The lovable 40-year-old ukulele player travels to Burma, India and Ceylon where he performs cheeky songs for the troops as part of a tour organised by The Entertainments National Service Association (aka Ensa) ... Back in Britain - severe swirling snowstorms cause chaos on the roads ... Lorries become stranded on the A59 near Skipton ... "I only arsked" - 11-year-old Bernard Bresslaw from Stepney in London gets into trouble at school ... 28-year-old convicted murderer Horace Gordon is hanged by the neck until dead at Wandsworth. (39-year-old hangman Albert Pierrepoint carries out the execution) ... 21-year-old Anne Shelton from Dulwich performs vocals with Ambrose and his Orchestra on *I'll Walk Alone* ("... because to tell you the truth, I've been lonely") ... 31-year-old footballer Sid Rawlings scores twice as Theo Kelly's Everton beat George

Kay's Liverpool 4-1 at Goodison Park ... 23-year-old Stan Mortensen scores twice as England beat Scotland 3-2 at Villa Park ... 32-year-old Willie Hall (of Tottenham Hotspur and England) has not played football for a year due to injury - and may now have to have his right leg amputated ... 48-year-old Ambrose and his Orchestra perform *The White Cliffs Of Dover* with 31-year-old Denny Dennis from Derby on vocals ... 74-year-old Charles Walton is murdered in Warwickshire - his body is found under a hedgerow with a pitch-fork driven through his neck ... Soviet forces advance towards Berlin from the east and liberate the Stalag Luft III prisoner of war camp ... Allied forces advance towards Berlin from the west fighting against a shattered and demoralised German army ... Security news black-outs temper the mood of the British people - but a real sense of optimism is building and victory now seems close ... 70-year-old prime-minister Winston Churchill meets the Emporer of Ethiopia, the King of Egypt and the president of Syria at a conference in Alexandria, Egypt ... Back in Blighty - crowds flock to the cinema to see 12-year-old Elizabeth Taylor from London starring alongside 24-year-old Mickey Rooney in the Hollywood blockbuster *National Velvet* ... Millions also enjoy a new British film called *Madonna of the Seven Moons*, starring Phyllis Calvert, Stewart Granger and 29-year-old Patricia Roc ... Schoolboys stay at home and play *Stumpz* - an exciting new board game with a cricketing theme ... Old men smoke pipes and read newspapers ... Advertisements say, 'Get rid of mice. Clear them out in three days by sprinkling two or three packets of *SCRAM* - Harmless to children and pets. 1/- from Boots, Timothy Whites & Taylors'.

Spring 1945... Knees Up, Mother Brown!

There's warm sunshine in March and April, but the weather turns cooler and damper in May ... Former prime-minister David Lloyd-George dies aged 82 in Caernarfonshire ... 28-year-old RAF wing commander Eric 'Nick' Nicholson VC dies in a plane crash in the Bay of Bengal ... A German V-2 rocket strikes a crowded market at Farringdon in London and more than one-hundred people are killed ... Allied forces advance rapidly towards Berlin ... 32-year-old Brian Johnston and his battalion cross the Rhine in armoured tanks ... The city of Cologne is captured from the Nazis ... The Bergen-Belsen concentration camp is liberated - and Allied soldiers come face to face with the harrowing site of thousands of emaciated prisoners, most of whom are close to death. The skeletal corpses of those recently perished are piled high in open railway trucks. 420 miles away, in the south of Germany, inmates at the work camp at Dachau are freed by soldiers of the U.S. 7th Army - and the sickening horrors of the Holocaust slowly come to be known to people of the world ... The Soviet Red Army enters the city of Berlin - brushing aside the last of Germany's defences ... 56-year-old Adolf Hitler commits suicide in his bunker beneath the Reich Chancellery ... "Too-ra-loo-ra-loo-ral, too-ra-loo-ra-li. Too-ra-loo-ra-loo-ral, hush now, don't you cry. Too-ra-loo-ra-loo-ral, too-ra-loo-ra-li. Too-ra-loo-ra-loo-ral, that's..." *An Irish Lullaby* by Bing Crosby is a hugely popular gramophone record ... "Goodman, Kyser and Miller, help to make things bright. Mixin' hot licks with vanilla..." *Juke Box Saturday Night* by The Glenn Miller Orchestra is also in demand ... 35-year-old footballer Matt Busby plays right-half for Liverpool in a 3-0 win against his former club Manchester City ... U.S. president Franklin D. Roosevelt dies suddenly at the age of 63 and is succeeded by 60-year-old Harry S. Truman ... Back in Britain - 37-year-old Howard Grossley shoots dead his girlfriend Lily Griffiths in a secluded lane at Porthcawl ... 27-year-old Jack Tratsart shoots dead his father and sister, and injures his brother, at a family gathering at the *J. Lyons & Co* Corner House restaurant on Oxford Street in London ... 27-year-old Thomas Eric Richardson batters David Walker to death at a house on Beeston Road in Leeds ... 36-year-old Rex Harrison stars in Noel Coward's *Blithe Spirit* at cinemas ... 29-year-old Ingrid Bergman wins an Oscar for her role in *Gaslight*. "Drinkin' rum and Coca-Cola, go down Point Koomahnah, both mother and daughter, working for the Yankee doll-arrhh. Oh, beat it man, beat it" - The Andrews Sisters sing *Rum And Coca-Cola* ... "How d'ya like those guys!?" - 52-year-old comedian Jimmy Durante sings *Inka Dinka Doo* ... 70-year-old prime-minister Winston Churchill announces a permanent cease-fire across Europe and broadcasts to the nation saying, "The German war is therefore at an end. We may allow ourselves a brief period of rejoicing." ... All across the kingdom, revellers take to the streets in glee and jubilation ... 30-year-old Cynthia Jones and her friends dance in the fountain at Trafalgar Square ... 23-year-old Humphrey Lyttleton plays his trumpet for the crowds gathered outside Buckingham Palace ... 49-year-old King George VI waves from the balcony as he stands beside his wife Queen Elizabeth, and daughters 19-year-old Princess Elizabeth and 14-year-old Princess Margaret. A beaming Churchill gives his famous 'V' for victory hand gesture and tells his people, "This is your victory." ... The licensing laws are suspended for one night and thousands of people drink, dance and do what comes naturally ... A pint of mild in the Red Lion costs 12d ... A re-usable French letter costs 4s/6d from chemists ... "Oh knees up

Mother Brown. Knees up Mother Brown. Knees up, knees up, never let the breeze up. Knees up Mother Brown" - Elsie and Doris Waters sing *Knees Up Mother Brown*.

Summer 1945 ... Labour for prosperity

The weather is unsettled for much of the summer ... 'Victory' celebration dances are held in town and village halls. Home-made flags and bunting flutter high-up between lamp-posts in the street ... Schools put on sports days and jamborees ... 10-year-old David Nobbs comes second from last in the sack race ... Footballers Bert 'the cat' Williams (aged 25), Neil Franklin (aged 23), Joe Mercer (aged 30), Stanley 'wizard of dribble' Matthews (aged 30), Raich 'Silver Fox' Carter (aged 31) and Tommy Lawton (aged 25) star for England in a specially arranged 'Victory' football international against France at the Empire Stadium in Wembley. The match ends in a 2-2 draw ... A 'German Guilt' exhibition opens in Wolverhampton and thousands of people attend to see photographic evidence of Nazi war atrocities ... Campaigning gets underway for a general election ... Posters on walls advise, 'Labour for Prosperity' and 'Labour for Homes' ... Prime-minister Winston Churchill warns that if Labour are elected, a Gestapo will be employed to enforce socialist ideals ... "Oh give me land, lots of land under starry skies above..." *Don't Fence Me In* by 36-year-old Joe Loss and his Orchestra is a popular new gramophone record ... "Here am I and there you are, dear, miles and miles apart" - *Coming Home* by 30-year-old Dorothy Squires is also in demand ... With great expectations - people go to the polls on the fifth of July to vote in the general election. The results are announced three weeks later - after overseas servicemen have also cast their votes. It's a landslide victory for Labour and 62-year-old Clement Attlee is the new prime-minister. (Labour: 393 seats, Conservatives: 197 seats, Liberals: 12 seats). 32-year-old Michael Foot is the new Labour MP for Plymouth Devonport. 29-year-old Harold Wilson is the new Labour MP for Ormskirk. 57-year-old Hugh 'Comrade' Dalton becomes Chancellor of the Exchequer. 53-year-old 'Red' Ellen Wilkinson is Education Secretary. 64-year-old Ernest Bevin is Foreign Secretary and 60-year-old Manny Shinwell is Minister for Fuel and Power ... Petrol remains 'on the ration' and costs two shillings a gallon ... 11-year-old schoolboy John Surtees from Tatsfield in Surrey dreams of one day owning a new BSA *B31* motorcycle - with its 348cc single cylinder, four stroke engine and a top speed of around 75 mph ... John Snagge announces the news on BBC radio ... A two-week conference at Potsdam takes place - with Winston Churchill making way for Clement Attlee after the general election ... 39-year-old traitor William Joyce (aka Lord Haw-Haw) is captured in woodland in Germany. Joyce attempts to escape, but is shot in the leg and taken into custody ... Back in England - 19-year-old footballer Nat Lofthouse plays for Bolton Wanderers in a 2-1 victory over Chelsea in the final of the Football League War Cup at Stamford Bridge ... The new Labour government introduces a radical Family Allowances Act - which will come into effect next year ... 'All animals are equal' - *Animal Farm* by 42-year-old George Orwell is published. 45-year-old Harry Roy (aka the King of 'Hot-Cha') and his Band perform *Candy* ("... I call my sugar, Candy, because I'm sweet on Candy, and Candy's sweet on me") ... BBC's Light Programme is now broadcasting on the wireless ... "I don't mind if I do" - 42-year-old Jack Train plays the character Colonel Chinstrap in the ever popular show, *It's That Man Again* (aka *Itma*) ... 37-year-old convicted murderer Howard Grossley is hanged by the neck until dead at Cardiff ... 30-year-old James McNicol shoots dead Donald Kirkaldie at Thorpe Bay in Essex ... John Haigh murders an elderly couple in London and disposes of their bodies in a drum of sulphuric acid ... The cities of Hiroshima and Nagasaki are annihilated by American atomic bombs ... Prime-minister Clement Attlee speaks on the wireless - and announces to the people of Britain and the Empire that Japan has surrendered and World War II has ended ... Celebration parties are held across the country ... People dance and sing in the street ... Posters on walls proclaim, ‘Drink *Coca-Cola* Ice Cold’.

Autumn 1945... VJ Day

62-year-old prime-minister Clement Attlee and his new Labour government begin a radical program to modernise Britain ... There's to be public ownership of fuel and power; transport, iron and steel, as well as the creation of a new welfare state ... In the meantime, life remains hard for most people ... The country's finances are in a terrible state and there's a shortage of food and other essential goods ... Forty-thousand dock workers go on strike - and the nationwide shortages become even worse ... 58-year-old Chancellor of the Exchequer Hugh 'Comrade' Dalton delivers his first Budget - and begins tackling the nation's war debt of £24 billion ... "We'll gather lilacs in the Spring again, and walk together down an English lane, until our hearts have learned to sing again, when you come home once more" - 55-year-old Richard Tauber sings *We'll Gather Lilacs* ... 24-year-old Betty Hutton sings *Doctor, Lawyer, Indian Chief* ... 27-year-old convicted murderer Thomas Eric Richardson is hanged by the neck until dead at Leeds. (75-year-old hangman Tom Pierrepoint carries out the execution) ... 27-year-old convicted murderer Jack Tratsart is declared insane and sent to Broadmoor ... 10-year-old David Nobbs attends Bickley Hall school near Chislehurst ... 10-year-old Brian Clough fails his 11-Plus examination and will be sent to Marton Grove Secondary Modern in Middlesbrough ... 11-year-old Johnny Haynes from Kentish Town stands on the terrace at Craven Cottage football ground. Jack Peart's Fulham team beat George Martin's Luton Town 4-1 ... A gramophone recording of Clive Richardson's *London Fantasia* (performed by the London Concert Orchestra) is in demand at shops ... *Chewing A Piece Of Straw* by Jack Payne and his Orchestra is also popular ... 36-year-old Matt Busby is the new football manager of

Manchester Utd - where goalkeeper Jack Crompton, full-back (and captain) Johnny Carey, centre-half Allenby Chilton, wing-half Jack Warner, outside-left Billy Wrigglesworth, inside-right Johnny Hanlon and 26-year-old centre-forward Jack 'cannonball' Rowley are the star players of his new team ... 26-year-old Tommy Lawton transfers from Theo Kelly's Everton to Billy Birrell's Chelsea for £14,000 ... 31-year-old England goalkeeper Frank Swift keeps a clean sheet in a match against Northern Ireland ... "As we enjoy a cigarette, to some exquisite chansonette, two hands are sure to slyly meet beneath a serviette, with..." *Cocktails For Two* by 33-year-old Spike Jones is now available as a gramophone record ... The body of an 11-day-old baby girl is found washed up on a bank of the River Thames. 41-year-old Arthur Clegg (the girl's grandfather) is arrested on suspicion of murder ... 39-year-old traitor William Joyce (aka Lord Haw-Haw) is found guilty of high treason and sentenced to death ... The Nuremberg war trials get underway ... 51-year-old Rudolf Hess, 42-year-old Ernst Kaltenbrunner and 52-year-old Hermann Goering are just three of the twenty-four Third Reich leaders being tried ... 'Fearless highwayman... Shameless beauty' - the dashing 36-year-old James Mason stars alongside the beautiful 29-year-old Margaret Lockwood in *The Wicked Lady* at cinemas ... "Bonjour le Monde, ici Radio Luxembourg" - Radio Luxembourg is back on air - after being suspended for the war ... Frank Sinatra sings *She's Funny That Way* ... 26-year-old Vic Lewis and his Jazzmen perform "Wonderful, wonderful ..." *Copenhagen*. Will Hay, Tommy Trinder and Wilson, Keppel and Betty appear at the Royal Variety Show in front of 49-year-old King George VI ... *Coronation Scot* by The Queen's Light Hall Orchestra is a top selling gramophone record ... The first few 'de-mobbed' soldiers return home to their families after six years of war ... People of England forge ahead with their lives ... Housewives queue outside grim little shops on the high street ... A two-ounce jar of *Marmite* costs tenpence ... Men sit at home reading newspapers ... The *Daily Sketch* costs one penny ... People smoke ... A packet of twenty *Churchman* cigarettes costs 2s/6d.

Christmas 1945... A brief encounter

Times remain hard ... The economy is in an awful state and the country is on the verge of bankruptcy ... Prime-minister Clement Attlee sends his treasury advisor John Maynard Keynes across the Atlantic to negotiate a multi billion-dollar loan with America and Canada. Keynes secures a loan of $5 billion with an interest rate of 2%. (It'll be more than sixty years before the loan is paid off) ... Back in England - posters on walls depict ex-serviceman with the tagline, 'Help Them Finish Their Job - Give Them Homes and Work!' ... Plans are put in place to construct 500,000 temporary prefabricated houses for returning soldiers and their families ... Life is slow ... People rely heavily on public transport ... Private motorcars are extremely rare and almost impossible to acquire ... A new two-door Ford *Anglia* has a top speed of 56 mph ... The latest four-door Austin *Sixteen* has a top speed of 75 mph and accelerates from 0-60 mph in 19.5 seconds ... Young men take their sweethearts to the dance hall on Saturday evenings ... 45-year-old Victor Silvester and his Ballroom Orchestra perform *The More I See You* - a popular new Quick-step ... Families gather together at Christmas and make festive decorations to put up in the home ... Lucky children get an orange (and not much more) on Christmas morning ... *Family Favourites* is on the wireless - broadcasting simultaneously in London and Germany, playing song requests for those unable to be together at Christmas ... Cartoon characters Tom & Jerry star in a new animated movie called *The Night Before Christmas* ... Sweethearts enjoy a night out at the cinema ... "I love you. I love your wide eyes, the way you smile, your shyness, and the way you laugh at my jokes / Please don't" - 32-year-old Trevor Howard and 37-year-old Celia Johnson star in *Brief Encounter* ...

“Once in a competition to elect a bathing Miss, it didn’t take the judges long to see she’s simply whizz. Their voting was unanimous, the explanation is (hee-hee!), she’s got two of everything” - 41-year-old George Formby sings his cheeky little song *She’s Got Two Of Everything* ... 30-year-old Norman Wisdom makes his first appearance on stage - performing a comedy mime act at Collins Music Hall in London ... 61-year-old Minister for Fuel and Power Manny Shinwell meets with 58-year-old Chancellor of the Exchequer Hugh ‘Comrade’ Dalton to discuss funding for energy ... 186 million tonnes of coal have been mined in Britain this year - down by 10 million tonnes compared to 1944 ... *I’ll Close My Eyes* by 30-year-old Dorothy Squires from Pontyberem is a popular new song ... League football is underway with a transitional season that sees the country’s top clubs split into two regional divisions ... 23-year-old Billy Liddell scores twice as Liverpool beat Huddersfield Town 4-1 in League North ... 27-year-old George Edwards scores four goals as Aston Villa beat Arsenal 5-1 in League South ... Centre-forward Albert Stubbins of Newcastle Utd and goalkeeper Bert ‘the cat’ Williams of Wolverhampton Wanderers are called up to the England team for a match against Wales - England lose 0-1 to a goal scored by 27-year-old Aubrey Powell from Cwmtwrch ... 32-year-old Raich ‘Silver Fox’ Carter transfers from Sunderland to Derby County for £8,000 ... “Manana. Manana. Manana, is soon enough for me” - 45-year-old Harry Roy (aka the King of ‘Hot-Cha’) and his Band perform *Manana* ... 36-year-old Joe Loss and his Orchestra (with vocals by Elizabeth Batey) perform *Let Him Go, Let Him Tarry* (“… let him sink or let him swim. He doesn’t care for me, and I don’t care for him. He can go and get another that I hope he will enjoy, for I’m going to marry a far nicer boy”) ... 30-year-old convicted murderer James McNicol is hanged by the neck until dead at Pentonville. (40-year-old hangman Albert Pierrepoint carries out the execution) ... The *Dandy* and *Beano* comics are published on alternate weeks only - due to paper being in short supply ... 11-year-old schoolboy Ronnie Clayton from Preston listens to the wireless ... Radio Luxembourg presenter 37-year-old Stephen Williams plays popular tunes of the day ... *White Christmas* by Bing Crosby is a top selling gramophone record ... 32-year-old Denny Dennis from Derby sings *There Must Be A Way* with the Stanley Black Orchestra ... 41-year-old Geraldo and his Orchestra perform *Skyliner* ... Dance halls are full on New Year's Eve ... The Jitterbug is all the craze.

New Year 1946... Traitor Haw-Haw hanged

The weather consists of heavy frosts and light snow ... Clement Attlee's Labour government pushes ahead with its plan to modernise Britain ... Chancellor of the Exchequer Hugh 'Comrade' Dalton and Minister for Social Insurance Jim Griffiths draw up plans for a new welfare payment for families ... "With someone like you, a pal good and true, I'd like to leave it all behind and go and find, some place that's known to God alone. Just a spot, to call our own" - 27-year-old Dick Haymes from Argentina performs the popular song *Let The Rest Of The World Go By* ... A converted *Lancaster* bomber takes off from London Airport carrying passengers on a flight to Buenos Aires. "This aeroplane, with its beautiful name 'Star Light', is a symbol of the determination of our country to regain our place in the markets of the world, and to use the air as a means of cultivating peace" - Labour's 60-year-old Minister of Civil Aviation Reginal Fletcher (aka Lord Winster) addresses the crowd gathered on the runway at Heathrow ... 37-year-old Alvar Liddell announces the news on the wireless for the BBC ... A passenger train pulled by a London-Midland-Scottish steam locomotive is involved in a collision at Lichfield Trent Valley station and twenty people are killed ... A maternity grant of £4 for every child born is introduced ... The Bank of England is nationalised ... 39-year-old traitor William Joyce (aka Lord Haw-Haw) is hanged by the neck until dead at Wandsworth. (40-year-old hangman Albert Pierrepoint carries out the execution in eight seconds) ... 67-year-old Soviet Union leader Joseph Stalin takes issue with the international reparation program for Germany - and the political rift widens between powers in the East and the West ... 71-year-old Winston Churchill makes a speech stating, "From Stettin in the Baltic to Trieste in the Adriatic, an iron curtain has descended across the Continent." ... 37-year-old actor Michael Redgrave plays a crazed ventriloquist in the horror film *Dead of Night* ... 33-year-old Brian Johnston joins the BBC as an Announcer after being decommissioned from the army ... Millions of people tune-in and listen to radio sets in the parlour. The price of a Wireless Receiving License increases from ten shillings to twenty shillings a year ... A limited allocation of Bush *DAC90* Bakelite wireless-sets is available in electrical shops. The retail price is £11/11s/- (plus purchase tax) ... Most small luxury goods are still difficult to come by ... 10-year-old schoolboy David Nobbs sits at home listening to radio comedy, *Much Binding in the Marsh* - featuring Kenneth Horne, Richard 'Stinker' Murdoch and Sam Costa ... 10-year-old Barry Cryer from Leeds listens to *It's That Man Again* (aka *Itma*) - featuring 54-year-old Tommy Handley ... "I said you can't send me home, not like this. Then I finally got my kiss" - 30-year-old Frank Sinatra sings *I Begged Her* ... 26-year-old Vic Lewis and his Jazzmen perform *Round About Eight* ... Men hurry along to support their local football team from the terraces on Saturday afternoons ... Tradgedy strikes at Burnden Park when thirty-three fans are crushed to death, and around four-hundred injured during an FA Cup tie between Walter Rowley's Bolton Wanderers and Bob McGrory's Stoke City. Many of the players on the pitch, including Stoke's outside-right 31-year-old Stanley 'wizard of dribble' Matthews and Bolton's inside-left 33-year-old Ray Westwood, are in a state of shock after witnessing such an horrific event ... 76,588 spectators cram into Villa Park to see a match between Alex Massie's Aston Villa and Stuart McMillan's Derby County - 'The Rams' win 3-4 with Peter Doherty (2), Sammy Crooks and 32-year-old inside-right Raich 'Silver Fox' Carter on the score-sheet ... *Pink String and*

Sealing Wax (starring 46-year-old Mervyn Johns, 28-year-old Googie Withers and 22-year-old Gordon Jackson) is now showing at cinemas ... Young men stare longingly at the the silver screen as the image of 28-year-old blonde-bombshell Evelyn Dall appears (in a bikini) in a Pathé newsreel feature ... Dance halls are full on Saturday evenings ... The raucous sound of *Not So Quiet Please* by 43-year-old Ted Heath and his Music (featuring 25-year-old Kenny Baker on trumpet) is popular with jiving young couples ... "I like my riding just like you do, along the Chattanooga choo-choo" - *Thanks For The Boogie Ride* by 37-year-old Nat Gonella also gets people gyrating ... *R. White's 'Old Style'* ginger beer is a refreshing drink.

Spring 1946... Derby County for the cup

Queues form outside fruit and veg shops as bananas become available for the first time since the war ... Many other foodstuffs are still in short supply and rationing remains in place ... 63-year-old Labour prime-minister Clement Attlee authorises a multi-million pound project to grow groundnuts in Tanganyika ... Back in England - Ferguson introduce the *TE20* tractor - a farm machine that will soon become known as 'the little grey Fergie' ... Alvis launches its new *Fourteen* motorcar - it has a top speed of 76 mph and accelerates from 0-60 mph in 22.2 seconds ... Singer relaunches its (pre war) *Super Ten* saloon - it has a top speed of 62 mph ... The publication *John Bull* comes out every Thursday and costs thruppence - it now has a new look 'full-colour' front cover ... Nylons and chocolate remain in high demand on the black market ... *Brylcreem* sells well at chemists as more and more men choose to 'style' their hair before venturing outside - *without* a hat! ... 'There's a lovely sandy bottom here; you ought to see it!' - saucy postcards by Donald McGill are displayed at seaside shops ... 22-year-old Walter Clayton strangles his girlfriend Joyce Jacques on the seafront at Morecambe ... 11-year-old Brian Clough from Middlesbrough plays football with his friends in the park ... Derby County beat Birmingham City 4-0 in an FA Cup semi-final replay at Main Road in front of 80,407 spectators ... *Lovely Cottage* (ridden by 34-year-old Captain Robert Petre) wins the Grand National at odds of twenty-five to one ... Oxford win the Boat Race, beating Cambridge by three lengths ... Bing Crosby sings *June Comes Around Every Year* ... Frank Sinatra sings *Nancy.* 24-year-old Deborah Kerr stars alongside 32-year-old Trevor Howard in *I See a Dark Stranger* at cinemas ... London Airport opens officially and regular international flights are now being made ... *Let Bygones Be Bygones* ("... and start all over again. Let us forget our sorrow, we must live for tomorrow") by 36-year-old Joe Loss and his Orchestra is a popular song ... People peruse window displays in high street shops ... Small luxury goods remain in short supply ... Electrical appliances are particularly difficult to obtain - *Collaro* portable gramophone players and *GEC* radio sets are rare ... Great excitement builds for this year's FA Cup final - the first to be played since the war. Around one-hundred thousand spectators converge on Wembley - with a few wearing home-made rosettes fabricated from paper and ribbon. 27-year-old Jackie Stamps scores twice as Stuart McMillan's Derby County beat Jimmy Seed's Charlton Athletic 4-1, after extra-time. (36-year-old Bert Turner scores Charlton's goal and also has the misfortune of scoring an own goal). A ticket for the standing enclosure at the Empire Stadium costs 3s/6d ... The first full football season since the war comes to an end ... Teddy Davison's Sheffield Utd draw 1-1 with Bradford to become champions of League North. Everton are runners-up ... Harry Storer's Birmingham City beat Luton Town 0-3 to become champions of League South. Aston Villa are runners-up ... Matt Busby's Manchester Utd beat Bob McGrory's Stoke City 2-1 in their final league match of the season ... Dickie and Anne Best of Belfast are proud parents of newborn son, Georgie ... 34-year-old ex-footballer Willie Hall has his right leg amputated after developing thrombosis ... 45-year-old Joe Davis from Derbyshire beats Horace Lindrum from Australia in the final of the World's Professional Snooker Championship. The match is played at the Royal Horticultural Hall in Westminster - and lasts for two weeks! (The irrepressible Davis has now won all fifteen of the world finals held since the year 1927) ... 41-year-old John

Snagge announces the news on BBC radio ... 42-year-old convicted baby killer Arthur Clegg is hanged by the neck until dead at Wandsworth ... The Labour government's ambitious new groundnut scheme at Tanganyika in Africa is scheduled to begin next year. The project will cost millions of pounds, but prime-minister Clement Attlee is convinced it'll prove to be money well spent ... Renowned Economist and advisor to the Treasury John Maynard Keynes dies aged 62 in Sussex - just months after negotiating Britain's long-term financial loan with the USA and Canada ... The Nuremberg war trials are well underway ... 53-year-old Nazi Hermann Goering is called to the dock to give evidence ... Back in England - Big-band swing music remains as popular as ever ... 32-year-old Ivy Benson and her (all-female) Orchestra tour the country, playing to packed dance halls ... 'Single' 78 rpm gramophone records (costing 4s/6d) are in short supply at shops ... Popular new songs sell out fast ... "Bollika, wollika, can't you see? Chickery Chick is me" - Alan Dean provides vocals on a catchy new tune called *Chickery Chick*, performed by 49-year-old Ambrose and his Orchestra ... 42-year-old Bing Crosby sings *On The Atchison, Topeka And The Santa Fe* ... 30-year-old Frank Sinatra sings *Someone To Watch Over Me* ... The weekly periodical *Melody Maker* hails an exciting new sound called BE-BOP - an experimental style of jazz emanating from America, performed by artists such as Dizzy Gillespie (trumpeter), Charlie Parker (saxophonist) and Thelonius Monk (pianist) ... Schoolboys loiter outside sweet-shops ... Rationing remains in place with people restricted to one small bar of chocolate a week ... Advertisements say, 'Mars are marvellous' - A *Mars* bar costs 3d.

Summer 1946... Compton, Hutton and Bedser at Lord's

The weather is unsettled, wet and dull - apart from a few weeks in July when the sun breaks through the clouds ... Thousands of people flock to *Butlin's* holiday camps in Clacton, Filey and Skegness - where teams of Redcoats keep the holiday makers entertained ... *Pontin's* opens its first site at Brean Sands in Somerset - where a team of Bluecoats keep the holiday makers entertained ... The new Bedford 'single-decker' charabanc bus has capacity for twenty-eight passengers ... 41-year-old Reginald Dixon plays the organ at the Tower Ballroom in Blackpool ... 31-year-old comedian Norman Wisdom appears on stage at theatres around England - as part of a touring variety revue ... 29-year-old comedian Frankie Howerd also tours the country - as part of the cast in a new show called *For the Fun of It* ... 42-year-old lovable entertainer George Formby stars in the film *George In Civvy Street* at cinemas. "We sit in the pictures, as warm as a glove. In the back row of the circle above. Two bobs' worth of dark and a basin of love, and I don't need a license for that" - *You Don't Need A License For That* (performed by Formby on his ukulele) is a popular song from the movie ... 63-year-old prime-minister Clement Attlee and his Labour government take a significant step towards establishing a new welfare state ... Jim Griffiths (Minister for Social Insurance) issues the first Family Allowance payments - based on five shillings for every child after the eldest ... 'Red' Ellen Wilkinson (Minister for Education) persuades Parliament to pass the School Milk Act - providing free milk to all school children ... 20-year-old student Margaret Hilda Roberts helps out during the summer months in her father's grocery shop in Grantham ... The grey, wet weather continues ... The latest edition of the *John Bull* publication has a full-colour front cover, depicting an elderly gentleman relaxing on a deck-chair at the beach ... 57-year-old actor Will Hay suffers a severe stroke while on holiday - and is not expected to make a full recovery ... The gramophone recording of *Money Is The Root Of All Evil (Take It Away, Take It Away, Take It Away)* by The Andrews Sisters is a best seller ... *Eager Beaver* by Geraldo and his Orchestra is also popular ... 23-year-old John Mathieson strangles and kills 46-year-old Mona Vanderstay at Holloway in London ... 44-year-old Arthur Boyce shoots dead his lover Elizabeth McLindon in Belgravia ... BBC television resumes transmission ... F. Streeter presents *In Our Garden* ... A. B. Campbell presents *For The Children* ... The puppet *Muffin the Mule* is seen for the first time ... An EKCO *TS46* Television Receiver (with 9-inch tube) costs 58 guineas (plus £13/2s/- purchase tax) ... 34-year-old German born scientist Klaus 'Karl' Fuchs is promoted to Head of Theoretical Physics at the highly secret Atomic Energy Research Establishment at Harwell in Oxfordshire ... There appears to be little, or no, improvement in the economy - and life remains hard for most people ... Working men dream of one day owning a motorcar ... The Alvis *12/70* is advertised as 'the car of distinction' with a top speed of 75 mph ... Young boys dream of one day playing cricket for England ... 29-year-old Len Hutton scores 82 runs and 27-year-old Denis Compton is out for a duck as an England XI play against 'The Rest' in a three-day trial Test Match at Lord's ... Ten days later, 27-year-old Alec Bedser makes his full Test Match debut for England and takes 7 wickets for 49 runs against India ... 34-year-old Brian Johnston commentates on the match for BBC radio ... People queue outside cinemas eager to see *Going My Way* - a new film starring 43-year-old Bing Crosby ... 11-year-old schoolboy David Nobbs spends a day at the cricket - and watches in awe as his hero Len

Hutton completes a century for Yorkshire in a match against Surrey at the Oval ... 22-year-old convicted murderer Walter Clayton is hanged by the neck until dead at Liverpool ... 43-year-old Issy Bonn records his own version of the song *Let Bygones Be Bygones* - and it's a huge hit ... A new season of League football begins with one national top division made up of twenty-two teams ... Hundreds of thousands of supporters pay a few shillings to go through the turnstiles at their local football ground on Saturday afternoons ... 62,850 turn out at Stamford Bridge to see 26-year-old Tommy Lawton score twice for Billy Birrell's Chelsea in a 4-3 win over Bolton Wanderers. (21-year-old Nat Lofthouse also scores two goals in the same match - for Bolton) ... 50,845 turn out at the Molineux to see 26-year-old Jesse Pye bag a hat-trick and 29-year-old Dennis Wescott score twice for Ted Vizard's Wolverhampton Wanderers in a 6-1 demolition of Arsenal ... 41,025 turn out at Maine Road to see 27-year-old Jack 'cannonball' Rowley and 25-year-old Charlie Mitten score for Matt Busby's Manchester Utd in a 2-1 win over Grimsby Town ... 31-year-old Len Carney scores a late winner for George Kay's Liverpool in a 0-1 victory over Sheffield Utd in front of 28,296 spectators at Bramall Lane ... 27-year-old Albert Stubbins is on the score-sheet for Newcastle Utd in a 1-4 victory over Millwall in Division Two in front of 39,287 spectators at The Den ... 33-year-old wing commander Walter Winterbottom (from Oldham) is appointed manager of the England football team ... 49-year-old Stuart McMillan is the new manager of Derby County - taking over from 55-year-old Ted Magner ... 23-year-old Ivor Broadis is appointed player-manager of Carlisle Utd ... 26-year-old inside-left Dickie Dorsett (aka the 'Brownhills Bomber') transfers from Wolverhampton Wanderers to Aston Villa ... Jack and Leah Holder of 31½ Newhall Street in Walsall are proud parents of newborn son, Neville. (In a few years time, young Neville Holder will aquire the nickname 'Noddy') ... "When I'm calling you, oo-oo-oo-ooh, oo-oo-oo-ooh" - *Indian Love Call* by The Harry Parry Sextet is a popular tune ... "Think how the raindrops miss you. They hurry down to kiss you and hope for a sigh. By the way..." *So Would I* by 44-year-old band leader Ted Heath and his Music (with Paul Carpenter on vocals) is also in demand ... 45-year-old world snooker champion Joe Davis announces his retirement from the sport ... Prime-minister Clement Attlee seeks to address the chronic housing shortage ... Only 160,000 homes have been built this year ... Plans are unveiled to build a modern New Town at Stevenage in Hertfordshire ... 50-year-old King George VI awards the popular entertainer George Formby with an OBE in his Birthday Honours List ... H.G. Wells dies in London aged 79 ... Bread goes 'on the ration' - even though war has ended.

Autumn 1946... Dick Barton on the wireless

The nation tunes-in to hear the thrilling *Dick Barton Special Agent* on the wireless - *The Devil's Galop* theme tune intensifies the listeners' excitement ... 11-year-old schoolboy Lester Piggott from Wantage in Berkshire dreams of one day being a jockey ... 34-year-old test pilot Teddy Donaldson sets a new air-speed world record, flying a jet powered Gloster *Meteor F4* at 615 mph above Littlehampton ... Schoolboys around the country learn the name Frank Whittle - the highly revered inventor of the jet engine ... A revolutionary new type of ink pen (known as the Biro) is now available - it doesn't blot, smudge or need to be refilled ... Families gather around the table to eat dinner. *Batchelor's* canned English Garden Peas are said to be, 'The Pick of the Crop' ... 'Ooh...Look!" - chocolate blanc-mange (costing one shilling a packet) is a popular pudding ... 23-year-old MI6 officer George Blake interrogates ex-Nazi officers in Hamburg ... The war trials continue at Nuremberg, and twelve former leaders of the Third Reich (including Hermann Goering) are sentenced to death by hanging ... Back in England - 14-year-old actress Elizabeth Taylor stars as Katherine Merrick in *The Courage of Lassie* at cinemas ... 32-year-old Winifred Atwell from Trinidad studies piano at the Royal Academy of Music in London ... 47-year-old Billy Cotton and his Band (with Alan Breeze on vocals) perform the song *Carolina* - a popular new Foxtrot ... The National Coal Board is set up as part of Clement Attlee's plans to nationalise the coal industry ... The average weekly wage for a miner currently stands at £6/3s/2d ... Thousands flock to the Victoria & Albert Museum in London to see the 'Britain Can Make It' exhibition. Admission costs one shilling and the show runs from the twenty-fourth of September to the thirty-first of

October ... 53-year-old former Nazi Hermann Goering commits suicide by swallowing a cyanide pill on the night before he is due to be hanged ... 31-year-old Dorothy Squires from Pontyberem sings *It's A Pity To Say Goodnight* ("... because I never saw stars so bright. But if you gotta go home, you gotta go home. Give me a goodnight kiss") ... 18-year-old Roger Moore from Stockwell is commissioned into the army as a second lieutenant ... 28-year-old Wilf Mannion from Middlesbrough scores a hat-trick for wing commander Winterbottom's England football team in a 7-2 victory over Northern Ireland. (24-year-old Tom Finney (aka the 'Preston Plumber') makes his international debut in the same match - and scores a second-half goal) ... The gramophone recording of *Sioux City Sue* by Bing Crosby and the Jesters is a big hit ... *Hawaiian War Chant (Ta-Hu-Wa-Hu-Wai)* by Spike Jones is also popular ... 31-year-old footballer Stanley 'wizard of dribble' Matthews is on the score-sheet for Bob McGrory's Stoke City in a 2-1 win against Theo Kelly's Everton at the Victoria Ground ... Matt Busby's Manchester Utd are top of Division One after beating George Kay's Liverpool 5-0 - with goals from Jack 'cannonball' Rowley, Charlie Mitten and a hat-trick from 27-year-old inside-left Stan Pearson ... Joe Smith's Blackpool are second after a 4-3 victory over Portsmouth ... 34-year-old Cliff Bastin makes his final appearance for George Allison's Arsenal ... "Are the stars out tonight? I don't know if it's cloudy or bright, 'cause I only have eyes for you" - 30-year-old Frank Sinatra sings *I Only Have Eyes For You* ... Popular entertainers Jimmy Jewel, Arthur Askey and Tessie O'Shea appear in front of 50-year-old King George VI at the London Palladium ... "I say! What a smasher!" - 32-year-old comedian 'Cheerful' Charlie Chester is on the wireless ... "I'll take you home again Kathleen, across the ocean wild and wide, to where your heart has ever been, since first you were my bonny bride" - 43-year-old Bing Crosby sings *I'll Take You Home Again Kathleen* ... A small number of 'well-to-do' families take a spin in their motorcars on Sunday afternoons ... The Standard *Flying Eight* costs £314, has a top speed of 61 mph and can reach 50 mph in 26.2 seconds ... The news is transmitted in sound only at ten o'clock each evening on BBC television ... 45-year-old convicted murderer Arthur Boyce is hanged by the neck until dead at Pentonville ... *Bless You (For Being An Angel)* by The Ink Spots is currently the best selling gramophone record - some six years after it was first released ... 24-year-old footballer Len Shackleton scores six goals as Stan Seymour's Newcastle Utd thrash Newport County 13-0 is Division Two - 24-year-old Charlie Wayman (4) and 22-year-old Jackie Milburn (2) are also on the score-sheet for 'The Toon' ... A spate of violent crime is reported in the news ... 40-year-old Olive Balchin is beaten to death in Manchester ... 26-year-old Margaret Cook is shot dead outside the *Blue Lagoon* nightclub in London ... Ambitious businessman advertise exciting new products in newspapers and magazines ... 'War-time science discovers Benergy makes a stimulating drink, more appetising than beef-tea'. - An 8oz pack of *Benergy* costs 1s/6d and is now available at grocers and chemists.

Christmas 1946...
Stubbins to Liverpool. Mercer to the Arsenal

Clement Attlee's Labour government continues its radical program of modernising Britain ... MPs vote to nationalise the railways and 59-year-old Minister of Transport Alfred Barnes, from Woolwich, is tasked with setting up a new Transport Commission to operate the country's trains under state ownership ... 21-year-old student Anthony Wedgwood-Benn reads Philosophy, Politics and Economics at Oxford University ... Coal production in Britain has increased slightly to 193 million tonnes - but the number of working miners is at its lowest level for five years ... England's football team - with Frank Swift, Billy Wright, Neil Franklin, Tom Finney (aka the 'Preston Plumber'), Raich 'Silver Fox' Carter, Tommy Lawton and Wilf Mannion in the line-up - thrash the Netherlands 8-2 at Huddersfield. 27-year-old Tommy Lawton scores four goals and Carter (2), Mannion and Finney are also on the score-sheet ... "It's behind you!" - Middle-class families enjoy an evening at the Pantomime ... 31-year-old comedian Norman Wisdom appears in *Robison Crusoe* at the Grand Theatre in Brighton ... 42-year-old George Formby appears in *Dick Whittington* at the Grand Theatre in Leeds ... 39-year-old Charlie Parsons plays Simple Simon in *Jack and the Beanstalk* at the Theatre Royal in Hanley ... 31-year-old American singer Frank Sinatra performs *Some Other Time* ("… I could resist you. Yes, some other time, not now") ... 39-year-old Walter Rowland is found guilty of the murder of Olive Balchin in Manchester ... The killer of Margaret Cook remains at large ... Popular fictional detective Hercule Poirot features in *The Hollow* - an exciting new novel (on sale in bookshops for 8s/6d) from 56-year-old author Agatha Christie ... The first episode of

Pinwright's Progress is on BBC television ... 62-year-old political cartoonist J. F. Horrabin illustrates news stories in the *Empire* journal ... Prime-minister Clement Attlee appoints Albert Victor Alexander as Minister of Defence - with responsibility for the Royal Navy, the Royal Air Force and the Army ... 23-year-old convicted murderer John Mathieson is hanged by the neck until dead at Pentonville ... *Down Your Way* (presented by Stewart MacPherson) is new on BBC Home Service radio ... The *John Bull* weekly paper has a colour picture on the front cover showing a family erecting a Christmas tree and hanging brightly coloured paper streamers from the ceiling as festive decorations ... "Chestnuts roasting on an open fire, Jack Frost nipping at your nose. Yuletide carols being sung by a choir, and folks dressed up like Eskimos" - The King Cole Trio (with 27-year-old Nat 'King' Cole) perform *The Christmas Song (Merry Christmas To You)* ... A new illustrated children's book called *Thomas the Tank Engine*, by Reverend W Awdry, is now on sale ... 38-year-old cricketer Donald Bradman scores 187 runs in Brisbane as Australia beat England in the first Ashes Test Match for eight years ... 32-year-old Perry Como from Pennsylvania sings *Blue Skies* ... Ted Vizard's Wolverhampton Wanderers football team are the new leaders in Division One after a 5-0 victory over Bolton Wanderers in front of 37,775 spectators at the Molineux ... 24-year-old Billy Liddell scores for George Kay's Liverpool in a 1-4 win against Bill Murray's Sunderland at Roker Park ... 23-year-old Irish footballer Con Martin turns down an offer to join Matt Busby's Manchester Utd and signs for Major Frank Buckley's Leeds Utd instead ... On the toss of a coin - 27-year-old Newcastle Utd centre-forward Albert Stubbins chooses to join Liverpool instead of Everton - the transfer fee is £12,500 ... 32-year-old wing-half Joe Mercer leaves Everton and joins the

Arsenal for £7,000 ... 36-year-old actor David Niven stars in *A Matter of Life and Death* at cinemas ... "I'm dreaming of a..." *White Christmas* ("... just like the ones we used to know") by 43-year-old Bing Crosby is the best selling gramophone record ... "One-zy, two-zy, I'll kiss you-zy. Two-zy, three-zy, you kiss me-zy. Three-zy, four-zy, kiss some more-zy" - *One-zy, Two-zy (I Love You-zy)* by The Squadronaires (directed by Jimmy Miller) is also popular ... 11-year-old Fred Heath (aka Johnny Kidd) from Willesden places a patch over one eye, and plays 'pirates' with his friends ... 'Well to do' families watch television in the front room ... '3 for a bull's eye' - 37-year-old Lionel Hale presents *Quiz with Hale* on Saturday nights on BBC television ... The weekly wireless adventures of Dick Barton, Snowy and Jock continue to captivate schoolboys - and their fathers!

New Year 1947... Deep snow, freezing temperatures

"It's turned out nice again!" - 42-year-old entertainer George Formby performs a two-week run at the London Palladium ... Clement Attlee's Labour government nationalises the coal industry ... Around two thirds of the country's 1,500 collieries are now under the control of the National Coal Board ... Deep snow brings the country to a standstill ... Cities and towns are cut off for days on end ... School children go sledging and throw snowballs ... Roads remain blocked ... Buses and trains are caught in sudden drifts ... 11-year-old schoolboy David Nobbs from Orpington waits three hours in deep snow for the delayed 8.14 train to Chislehurst ... A *BOAC Douglas C47* passenger aeroplane crashes in Kent killing five people. (The number of dead eventually rises to eight) ... The freezing cold weather continues ... Just weeks after the nationalisation of coal mines, the country's coal reserve is running low ... 62-year-old Minister for Fuel and Power Manny Shinwell is heavily criticised in the newspapers ... The nationwide fuel shortage leads to the suspension of BBC television. 55-year-old Education minister 'Red' Ellen Wilkinson dies of pneumonia in London - Prime-minister Clement Attlee appoints George Tomlinson as her successor ... Mrs. Jean Mann MP describes popular comedian Tommy Handley as a 'twerp' for telling risqué jokes ... "The crowd sees me out dancing, carefree and romancing, happy with my someone new. I'm laughing on the outside" - Dorothy Squires sings *Laughing On The Outside* ... Edmundo Ros and his Rumba Band perform *Come Closer To Me* ... 11-year-old John Inman from Preston plays out with his friends ... 30-year-old cricketer Len Hutton scores 122 runs in the fifth Test in Australia, but England lose the match and the series. L Hutton, C

Washbrook, W J Edrich, D C S Compton, W R Hammond (cpt), L B Fishlock, J T Ikin, N W D Yardley, T P B Smith, J Hardstaff, P A Gibb (wk), T G Evans (wk), W Voce, D V P Wright and A V Bedser are all downcast by an Ashes defeat ... 43-year-old Wally Hammond retires as England's captain and 31-year-old Norman Yardley takes over ... Ted Vizard's Wolverhampton Wanderers continue to lead the way in Division One of the football league ... Preston North End (with Andy Beattie, Bill Shankly and 24-year-old Tom Finney - aka the 'Preston Plumber') are second ... Stoke City (with Neil Franklin, Freddie Steele and 32-year-old Stanley 'wizard of dribble' Matthews) are third ... 26-year-old Cyril Done scores a hat-trick as George Kay's Liverpool beat Charlie Spencer's Grimsby Town 5-0 at Anfield ... 26-year-old Reg Lewis and 35-year-old Ronnie Rooke each score twice as Arsenal beat Sunderland 1-4 at Roker Park ... 23-year-old centre-forward 'Terrible' Trevor Ford transfers from Swansea City to Aston Villa for £12,000 ... Listeners to Radio Luxembourg tune-in each day to hear presenter Geoffrey Everitt playing popular tunes ... *Zip-A-Dee-Doo-Dah* ("… Zip-a-dee-ay. My-oh-my what a wonderful day") by Geraldo and his Orchestra (with 19-year-old Carole Carr on vocals) is a top selling gramophone record ... *Five Minutes More* by 44-year-old Carroll Gibbons and the Savoy Hotel Orpheans (with Harry Kaye on lead vocals) is also a hit ... Freezing temperatures prevail across the country ... Roads remain clogged by snow and ice ... February has been the coldest month on record for fifty years ... 42-year-old John Snagge announces the news on BBC radio ... 46-year-old Lord Louis Mountbatten is appointed Viceroy of India ... 51-year-old Edward Cavendish, the Duke of Devonshire and his wife Mary help out as their family home at Chatsworth is made ready to be opened to the public ... 39-year-old convicted murderer Walter Rowland is hanged by the neck until dead at Strangeways ... 32-year-old comedian Norman Wisdom purchases a shiny new AJS motorcycle for £35 - it has a 350cc engine and a top speed of 78 mph ... Men go to the pub ... A pint of mild in the Red Lion costs 11d ... *Three Nuns* pipe tobacco is 2s/7d per ounce ... Women go shopping ... Advertisments for face cream declare, 'Skin needs *Nivea*.'

Spring 1947... Nuts from Tanganyika

The long spell of cold weather comes to an end ... Thawing snow and heavy rain lead to severe flooding in the Thames Valley ... 11-year-old Albert Finney from Salford in Lancashire goes to the cinema with his friends ... "Oh, how I loathe adventurous minded boys" - Alastair Sim, Jack Warner, Valerie White and 20-year-old Harry Fowler star in *Hue and Cry* - a wonderful new film made at Ealing Studios ... Joan Griffiths is the new presenter of *Woman's Hour* on BBC's Home Service ... *Woman's Own* journal is published every Friday and costs thruppence ... The school leaving age is raised from 14 to 15 - as set out in the Education Act of 1944 ... 53-year-old Stuart Hibberd announces the news on BBC radio ... 37-year-old Bill Smedley strangles and kills 27-year-old Edith Simmonite on Bridge Street in Sheffield ... Prime-minister Clement Attlee's exciting Tanganyika groundnut scheme is underway, with three million acres of land being cultivated in East Africa ... Back in Britain - the faltering 'Economic Situation' is the main topic for two party political broadcasts on the wireless. 64-year-old prime-minister Attlee speaks for Labour. 49-year-old Mr. Anthony Eden speaks for the Conservative opposition ... 59-year-old Chancellor of the Exchequer Hugh 'Comrade' Dalton presents his Budget - and doubles the duty on tobacco ... Income tax remains high at nine shillings in the pound ... "What's on the table, Mabel?" - 42-year-old Wilfred Pickles hosts the hugely popular BBC radio show *Have A Go* ... The final episode of *Pinwright's Progress* is broadcast on BBC television ... Epic new film, *The Courtneys of Curzon Street*, starring 42-year-old Anna Neagle and 34-year-old Michael Wilding, is now showing at cinemas ... Novelty song *Hi-Jig-A-Jig, Hi-Jig-A-Gig (Follow The Band)* by 41-year-old Lou

Preager and his Orchestra is a popular tune ... Hollywood movie stars Stan Laurel and Oliver Hardy are headline acts at the Victoria Palace in London - 32-year-old comedian Norman Wisdom is also on the bill ... *Caughoo* wins the Grand National at odds of one hundred to one ... Cambridge win the Boat Race - beating Oxford by ten lengths ... There's bright sunshine on the twenty-sixth of April - the day of the FA Cup final. Jimmy Seed's Charlton Athletic beat Cliff Britton's Burnley 1-0 (after extra-time). 28-year-old outside-left Chris Duffy scores the only goal in the dying minutes of the match. A ticket for the standing enclosure at the Empire Stadium in Wembley costs three shillings ... With just a few matches remaining before the end of the football season, 32-year-old outside-right Stanley 'wizard of dribble' Matthews makes a controversial move from Stoke City to Blackpool for a transfer fee of £11,500. Thousands of Stoke supporters gather to protest outside the Victoria Ground - sensing Stoke have thrown away their chance of finishing top of Division One ... George Kay's Liverpool beat Wolverhampton Wanderers 1-2 on the thirty-first of May and 'The Reds' from Anfield are the new champions of England ... Cyril Sidlow, Laurie Hughes, Ray Lambert, Phil Taylor, Harry Eastham, Billy Liddell, Cyril Done and 28-year-old wing-half Bob Paisley have all been outstanding for the Anfield club. Jack Balmer and Albert Stubbins have also been sensational - they're joint top scorers with twenty-four goals each ... Brentford and Leeds Utd are relegated to Division Two ... Manchester City and Burnley are promoted to Division One ... "Swanee! How I love you, how I love you, my dear ol' Swanee!" - the gramophone recording of 61-year-old Al Jolson singing *Swanee* is hugely popular ... England's national football team travel by aeroplane for the first time to take part in an overseas tour. Goalkeeper Frank Swift concedes a goal as England lose 1-0 against Switzerland in Zurich. Centre-forward Tommy Lawton and inside-right Stan Mortensen both score four as England thrash Portugal 10-0 in Lisbon. Outside-left Finney (aka the 'Preston Plumber') and outside-right Matthews (aka the 'Wizard of Dribble') are also on the score-sheet ... 22-year-old Ken Wilkinson leaves David Steele's Huddersfield Town and joins Fred Westgarth's Hartlepools Utd ... 35-year-old ex-footballer Willie Hall has his left leg amputated after developing thrombosis ... 'A Story of Fascinating Adventure in a Strange and Beautiful Land!' - 25-year-old Deborah Kerr and 18-year-old Jean Simmons star in *Black Narcissus* - a film made in Technicolor ... The Standard Motor Company announce the all new *Vanguard* motorcar with a top speed of 78 mph and capable of 0-60 mph in 21.5 seconds ... Advertisements for *Hoover* vacuum cleaners say, 'Beats as it Sweeps as it Cleans' ... "Another bride, another June, another sunny honeymoon. Another season, another reason for makin' whoopee" - 27-year-old Vic Lewis and his Orchestra perform *Making Whoopee* ... Alan Michael Sugar is born at Hackney Hospital in London ... Millionaire retail magnate Harry Gordon Selfridge dies aged 89 in Putney ... 24-year-old John Gartside shoots dead Percy and Alice Baker at Manor House Farm on Saddleworth Moor ... Posters proclaim, 'Cold or Hot - SPAM Hits the Spot!'

Summer 1947... A week at Butlin's

It's a long hot summer ... Temperatures sore to ninety degrees Fahrenheit over the parks, playing fields and bombed-out ruins of England ... Cricketers 30-year-old Len Hutton and 32-year-old Cyril Washbrook stride out together to open the batting for England against South Africa at Trent Bridge ... Families travel to the seaside on trains operated by 'the big four': London-Midland-Scottish (LMS), Great Western Railway (GWR), London and North Eastern Railway (LNER) and Southern Railway (SR) ... Posters at railway stations proclaim, 'Blackpool - Gay and bright, day and night' ... 'From Coast to Coast, the Nation's Host' - *Butlin's* open new luxury holiday camps at Pwllheli and Ayr ... Cinema goers enjoy watching the fictional Huggett family in a new film called *Holiday Camp*, with 51-year-old Jack Warner as Joe Huggett, and 31-year-old Alfie Bass playing the role of a redcoat ... 32-year-old comedian Norman Wisdom travels to Deal in Kent on his AJS motorcycle to find his brother Fred - who he hasn't seen for sixteen years ... "By the waters of the Caribbean, lived a lovely little Latin Queen. In her bathing suit she can be seen" - The Andrews Sisters sing *Her Bathing Suit Never Got Wet* ... Divorce rates reach an all time high ... The Ink Spots sing *To Each His Own* ... Clement Attlee's Labour government calls for improved innovation and greater output from the manufacturing sector ... Robert McArd & Co of Manchester launch a new plastic molded lavatory seat - the *Celmac* ... The Austin Motor Company Ltd. of Longbridge in Birmingham finds new efficiencies and is able to double the number of cars it produces ... The British Empire is diminishing ... India gains its independence after being under British rule for more than two-hundred years ... "Oh, how we danced, on the night we were wed. We vowed our true love, though a word wasn't said" - *The Anniversary Song* by 61-year-old Al Jolson is a top selling 78 rpm gramophone record ... 21-year-old Princess Elizabeth and 26-year-old Prince Philip of Greece and Denmark announce their engagement ... 21-year-old Margaret Hilda Roberts graduates from Oxford University with a degree in Chemistry ... Britain's first atomic reactor is set up at Harwell in Oxfordshire ... 38-year-old convicted murderer Bill Smedley is hanged by the neck until dead at Leeds. One week later - 24-year-old convicted double murderer John Gartside is hanged on the same gallows ... The sun continues to shine and temperatures remain high ... 32-year-old Norman Yardley leads England's cricketers to a series victory over South Africa ... 29-year-old Denis Compton scores a record 3,816 runs in one season for England and Middlesex ... 48-year-old Tom Whittaker takes over from George Allison as manager of Arsenal ... The new football season gets underway and Matt Busby's Manchester Utd defeat reigning champions Liverpool 2-0 in front of 53,610 people at Maine Road ... Alex Massie's Aston Villa draw 1-1 against Manchester City in front of 50,296 people at Villa Park - 27-year-old Dickie Dorsett (aka 'The Brownhills' Bomber') scores Villa's goal ... "I love you, there's nothing to hide. It's better than burning inside" - 35-year-old Vaughn Monroe from Ohio sings *There! I've Said It Again* ... "Whadda they do on a rainy night in Rio? Whadda they do when there is no starry sky?" - 23-year-old Anne Shelton from Dulwich sings *A Rainy Night In Rio* ... The 'killer diller' gramophone recording of Dizzy Gillespie's new tune, *One Bass Hit*, is much sought after by 'hipsters' ... The latest Simon Templar *Saint* novel (by 40-year-old author Leslie Charteris) costs 8s/6d in bookshops ... The country's finances remain in a dire state ... Clement Attlee's Labour government announces wide ranging cuts in public spending.

Autumn 1947...
Princess Elizabeth marries Prince Philip

Children return to school after a six week summer break ... 12-year-old David Nobbs is the new conkers' champion at Bickley Hall School near Chislehurst ... 11-year-old Joey Scragg gets 'six of the best' for insolence at the Brereton Free School in Staffordshire ... 11-year-old Duncan Edwards from Dudley in Worcestershire plays football with his friends in the street ... Matt Busby's Manchester Utd lose 0-1 against Sheffield Utd in front of 50,979 spectators at Maine Road ... 32-year-old comedian Norman Wisdom marries his sweetheart Freda Simpson at Shirley near Croydon ... 60-year-old Chancellor of the Exchequer Hugh 'Comrade' Dalton is forced to resign after leaking details of his emergency Budget to a reporter ... 58-year-old Sir Stafford Cripps takes over at the Treasury ... Austerity prevails in Clement Attlee's Britain ... Rationing remains in place and there's still a shortage of basic household goods and most foods ... Canned Snoek is available (and is relatively cheap to buy), but most people agree - it tastes awful ... *Round Britain Quiz* is broadcast on the wireless ... *Cookery: Stretching the Meat Ration* is broadcast on the television ... Viewers learn how to make curried dishes without rice ... The news is announced at ten o'clock each night ... 21-year-old Princess Elizabeth marries 26-year-old Philip Mountbatten at Westminster Abbey. The young royal couple then spend their honeymoon at the Broadlands country estate in Hampshire ... "They say that falling in love is wonderful" - 56-year-old Richard Tauber sings *They Say It's Wonderful* - a song from American stage musical *Annie, Get Your Gun* ... 32-year-old Dorothy Squires from Pontyberem sings *Danger Ahead* ... Hollywood movie stars 57-year-old Stan Laurel and 55-year-old Oliver Hardy appear at the London Palladium in front of King George VI ... *Dinky Toys* introduce a die-cast model (1:48 scale) of the Riley Saloon motorcar ... 40-year-old Walter Donaldson from Edinburgh defeats Fred Davis in the final of the World's Professional Snooker Championship at Leicester Square in London ... 25-year-old Tom Finney (aka the 'Preston Plumber') scores twice as wing commander Winterbottom's England football team beat Belgium 2-5 in Brussels ... 56-year-old ex-footballer Charles Buchan reports on the match for the *News Chronicle* ... Roy Peskett reports for the *Daily Mail* ... Back in England - Matt Busby's Manchester Utd lose 3-4 at Maine Road to Charlie Spencer's Grimsby Town ... 28-year-old Tommy Lawton stuns the football world by leaving First Division Chelsea and joining Third Division (South) Notts County for a transfer fee of £20,000 ... "Dick-dick-dick, dickory dock. I lost money and my clothes are in hock" - 25-year-old Paul Carpenter is vocalist on *Dickory Dock* a popular new tune played by Ted Heath and his Music ... "Oop Bop Sh' bam, Oop bop!" - the 'killer diller' gramophone recording of Dizzy Gillespie's new tune, *Oop Bop Sh' Bam*, is much sought after by 'hipsters' ... Crowds flock to the cinema to see *The Big Sleep* with Humphrey Bogart and Lauren Bacall ... 23-year-old comedian Benny Hill makes his debut on the wireless ... Prime-minister Clement Attlee sacks Manny Shinwell from the Cabinet ... 41-year-old Hugh Gaitskell from London is the new minister for Fuel and Power - a non Cabinet position ... 'At Your Service' - London Transport runs a poster campaign to recruit new bus drivers ... Construction work begins on a new reservoir at Blithfield near Rugeley in Staffordshire ... 34-year-old Polish staff sergeant Eugeniusz Jurkiewicz murders 76-year-old landlady Emily Bowers at the George Inn public house at Middlezoy in Somerset.

Christmas 1947... But I'm alright now

Dense smog lurks over major towns and cities ... Coal production has increased since the formation of the new National Coal Board - 200 million tonnes have been mined in 1947 ... The total number of coal miners has increased to 707,000 and the average weekly wage has risen from £6/3s/2d to £6/18s/9d ... "It's behind you!" - Middle-class families enjoy an evening at the Pantomime ... 43-year-old George Formby plays the role of Buttons in *Cinderella* at the Empire Theatre in Liverpool ... 20-year-old 'would be' actor Roger Moore auditions for roles in films - with little success ... 32-year-old Dorothy Squires sings, *I'm In The Mood For Love* ... 30-year-old Vera Lynn sings, *How Lucky You Are*. 49-year-old Gracie Fields sings, *How Are Things In Glocca Morra* ... The Labour government's ambitious groundnut scheme at Tanganyika in Africa is not going well. The project has already cost tax-payers millions of pounds and, so far, there has been no return ... Back in Britain - 64-year-old prime-minister Clement Attlee pushes ahead with his modernisation program ... Plans are being finalised to nationalise the railways ... Plans are also being finalised to bring in a new National Health Service. 50-year-old Health Minister Aneurin Bevan will launch the exciting and radical new scheme next year ... Former prime-minister Stanley Baldwin dies aged 80 in Stourport-on-Severn ... Tom Whittaker's Arsenal football team lead the First Division ... Cliff Britton's Burnley are second. 24-year-old centre-forward 'Terrible' Trevor Ford scores for Aston Villa in a 3-3 draw against Liverpool at Anfield ... 26-year-old Stan Mortensen scores a hat-trick as England beat Sweden 4-2 at Highbury ... 32-year-old Stanley 'wizard of dribble' Matthews receives a standing ovation at Stoke City's Victoria Ground when he returns for a match with his new team, Blackpool. (The game ends in a 1-1 draw) ... 27-year-old Michael Henderson commentates for BBC Television on a 'live' broadcast of the first half of the Rugby Football Final Trial between England and 'The Rest' at Twickenham. *The Radio Times* informs readers: 'It is hoped to continue the transmission for part of the second half of the match if light conditions permit' ... Bus driver George Whelpton stands trial for the murder of three people at a house in Doncaster - the 31-year-old is found guilty and sentenced to death ... "Many a year ago in old Sorrento, a certain ditty was quite the thing. Whenever a mother rocked her baby in Sorrento, this little ditty she used to sing..." *Chi-Baba, Chi-Baba (My Bambino Go To Sleep)* by Geraldo and his Orchestra is a popular new song ... "Way down among Brazillians, coffee beans grow by the billions, so they've got to find those extra cups to fill. They've got an awful lot of coffee in Brazil!" - *The Coffee Song (They've Got An Awful Lot Of Coffee In Brazil)* by The Andrews Sisters is also popular ... 34-year-old convicted murderer Eugeniusz Jurkiewicz is hanged by the neck until dead at Bristol ... 35-year-old Melita Norwood from Bexleyheath (secretary to a Civil Servant on Britain's atomic weapons project) takes photographs of secret government documents and passes them on to the Soviets ... 47-year-old Queen consort Elizabeth indulges in a spot of Christmas shopping on Windsor High Street ... 62-year-old actor and comedian Will Fyffe falls from a hotel window in St. Andrews and dies ... "I'm dreaming, of a..." *White Christmas* by 44-year-old Bing Crosby is (yet again) the top selling record over the festive period ... *Bloop Bleep/ I Wonder Who's Kissing Her Now* by 36-year-old Danny Kaye is also popular ... Lucky schoolboys get a *Dinky Toys* die-cast model (1:48 scale) of a Foden eight-wheel lorry on Christmas morning ... "What is it you want Mary?

What do you want? You want the moon?" - James Stewart stars in *It's a Wonderful Life* at cinemas ... "Talk quiet, he's asleep downstairs" - 30-year-old Googie Withers plays an East End housewife sheltering an escaped convict in *It Always Rains on Sunday* - a film noir from Ealing Studios ... "But I'm alright now" - 25-year-old Hattie Jacques plays schoolgirl Sophie Tuckshop in the ever popular wireless show, *It's That Man Again* (aka *Itma*).

New Year 1948... Railways nationalised

It's a foggy start to the new year ... A Vickers *610 Viking 1B* aeroplane operated by British European Airways crashes on its approach to Northolt airport. Captain William Morton is killed along with nine passengers. Eight people survive the crash and are taken to Hillingdon County Hospital ... Clement Attlee's Labour government continues its program of modernisation ... The country's railways are nationalised - and 'the big four' operators (LMS, GWR, LNER and Southern) now come under the control of British Railways ... Pamphlets and posters explain the new National Health Service that's set to begin in the summer ... 'Everyone - rich or poor, man, woman or child - can use it or any part of it. It will relieve your money worries in time of illness' ... Approximately 200,000 houses were built last year, but an overall shortage of housing is still a major issue - and many families are forced to share accommodation with others ... The British Empire is diminishing in size - Burma and Ceylon gain their independence ... "It's not goodbye it's just sweet adieu. Some day I'll sail across the sea to you" - 50-year-old Gracie Fields from Rochdale performs *Now Is The Hour* with Phil Green and his Orchestra ... 43-year-old organist Reginald Dixon from Sheffield performs *Tico-Tico* ... Popular 37-year-old American entertainer Danny Kaye appears in front of a packed house every night for six weeks at the London Palladium ... The nation tunes-in as *Mrs. Dale's Diary*, a fictional new drama, begins on the wireless. People listen attentively as Mrs. Mary Dale (a doctor's wife from Kenton) describes the anxiety of waiting for her son to return home after serving in the army, and also the consternation caused by her daughter's infatuation with Roger Lord - an older man ... The *London Co-operative Society* opens a new supermarket and introduces the modern concept of 'self-service' for shoppers ... 38-year-old John Haigh robs and murders an elderly couple at Crawley before disposing of their bodies in a 45-gallon drum containing sulphuric acid ... "You asked me to make a record of me voice. Well, here it is. What you want me to say is, 'I love you.' Here's the truth. I hate you, you little slut" - 24-year-old Richard 'Dicky' Attenborough stars as Pinkie Brown in *Brighton Rock* at cinemas ... 31-year-old convicted murderer George Whelpton is hanged by the neck until dead at Leeds ... Deep snow causes problems in southern England ... People stay indoors ... The BBC broadcasts the first television newsreel programmes ... Mahatma Gandhi is assassinated in India ... Back in Britain - prime-minister Clement Attlee makes a radio broadcast urging workers to get behind his government's drive for greater productivity ... *Sparky's Magic Piano* by Henry Blair with Ray Turner is released as a 78 rpm gramophone disc ... "Hear my song, Violetta. Hear the song that's in my heart. Please be mine, Violetta. Say that we will never part" - 30-year-old Josef Locke sings *Hear My Song Violetta* ... Football terraces are packed on Saturday afternoons ... 29-year-old Jack 'cannonball' Rowley scores a hat-trick for Matt Busby's Manchester Utd in a 5-0 win against Burnley in Division One ... A new record attendance of 83,260 spectators turn out at Maine Road on the seventeenth of January to watch Utd's match against (top-of-the-table) Arsenal. Jack 'cannonball' Rowley and Reg Lewis are the goal scorers in a 1-1 draw. Utd remain fifth in the league ... 30-year-old Portsmouth centre-forward Duggie 'Thunderboots' Reid breaks the goal-net when he scores a penalty in Pompey's 1-0 win against Manchester City ... 34-year-old inside-right Raich 'Silver Fox' Carter four goals against his old club as Derby County thrash Sunderland 5-1 at the Baseball Ground ... 33-year-old footballer Stanley ‘wizard of dribble’ Matthews dazzles on the wing, and centre-forward Stan Mortensen scores twice in Blackpool’s 5-0 FA Cup fifth round victory over non-league Colchester Utd ... 25-year-old Len Shackleton leaves Newcastle Utd and joins Bill Murray’s Sunderland for a new record transfer fee of £20,500 ... A small number of ‘well-to-do’ men from the upper middle-classes order motorcars from showrooms ... The Standard Motor Company’s new *Vanguard* costs £671 (including taxes) ... Schoolboys peruse the shelves at newsagents ... Biffo the Bear replaces Big Eggo in *The Beano* ... Mackintosh’s *Rolo* chocolate covered sweets are exciting and new - but are also ‘on the ration’ ... Housewives visit the corner shop ... A loaf of bread costs fourpence ... Working men visit their local pub after a hard day at work ... A pint of Watney’s Pale Ale is 1s/5d ... A pint of Watney’s Special is 1s/9d ... Singer Richard Tauber dies in London aged 56 ... Prime-minister Clement Attlee’s expensive groundnut scheme at Tanganyika in Africa has been running for a year - and failed to reap any reward.

Spring 1948... Here come the Huggetts

3-year-old June Anne Devaney is abducted from a children's home in Blackburn. Her body is found the next day - the young girl has been raped and murdered. Police find finger prints at the scene and begin searching for the brutal killer ... 11-year-old James Hanratty from Wembley in London plays out with his friends ... 'For the farmer, the countryman and general industrial use' - the all new, four-wheel-drive *Land Rover* motorcar is unveiled at the Amsterdam Motor Show ... Back in Blighty - economic recovery is slow ... 58-year-old Chancellor of the Exchequer Sir Stafford Cripps presents his first Budget for Clement Attlee's Labour government ... Wages are to be 'frozen' and rationing remains in place ... Austerity prevails ... Most people have yet to see any improvement in their quality of life since the end of the war ... 42-year-old Leslie Mitchell announces the news for BBC Newsreel ... Immigrants from Commonwealth countries are encouraged to come to Britain to help reignite the economy ... 60-year-old Hugh 'Comrade' Dalton returns to the Cabinet as Chancellor of the Duchy of Lancaster ... 59-year-old Sir Percy Sillitoe is Director General of MI5 ... Instances of espionage are going undetected in the offices of some government departments ... 36-year-old German born scientist Klaus 'Karl' Fuchs, of the highly secret Atomic Energy Research Establishment at Harwell in Oxfordshire, passes confidential and classified information onto his Soviet handler ... 48-year-old Victor Silvester and his Ballroom Orchestra perform *The Things I Do For Love* - a popular new Quick-step ... 30-year-old Dizzy Gillespie (aka the trumpet king of Be-Bop), from South Carolina, is forced to cancel a planned visit to Britain, when he's refused a permit by the Ministry of Labour ... "To be, or not to be. That is the question" - 41-year-old actor Sir Laurence Olivier stars in *Hamlet* at cinemas ... 'A Star Is Born' - 33-year-old comedian Norman Wisdom brings the house down at the London Casino and glowing reviews of his performance are printed in the national newspapers ... *Cottage Rake* ridden by Aubrey Brabazon wins the Cheltenham Gold Cup at odds of ten to one ... *Sheila's Cottage* ridden by Arthur Thompson wins the Grand National at fifty to one ... Prize money of £75,000 is paid out to one lucky 'treble chance' winner on the football pools ... One-hundred thousand spectators travel by road and rail to Wembley for the FA Cup final. Matt Busby's Manchester Utd (wearing blue jerseys) beat Joe Smith's Blackpool (wearing white jerseys) by 4 goals to 2. Jack 'cannonball' Rowley (2), Stan Pearson and John Anderson are the goal-scorers for Utd. 33-year-old Stanley 'wizard of dribble' Matthews is on the losing side. A ticket for the standing enclosure at the Empire Stadium costs three shillings. A seat in the South Terrace (uncovered) is 7s/6d ... Centre-forward Ronnie Rooke scores four goals and outside-left Denis Compton scores twice as Tom Whittaker's Arsenal thrash Grimsby Town 8-0 on the last day of the football season - and 'The Gunners' are confirmed as the new champions of Division One. George Swindin, Walley Barnes, Leslie Compton, Laurie Scott, Joe Mercer, Archie MacAulay, Jimmy Logie, Reg Lewis, Denis Compton, Don Roper and 36-year-old Ronnie Rooke have all been outstanding ... Harry Storer's Birmingham City and George Martin's Newcastle Utd are promoted from the Second Division into the First ... 'Just like that!' - 27-year-old comedian Tommy Cooper (in a fez hat) wins a BBC talent show ... 39-year-old Wynford Vaughan-Thomas hosts new radio quiz *Top of the Form* ... "There's a story the gypsies know is true, that when your love wears golden earrings, she belongs to you" - 20-year-old

Carole Carr is vocalist on *Golden Earrings* with Geraldo and his Orchestra ... 24-year-old Anne Shelton from Dulwich sings, *What Did I Do*, with Ted Heath and his Music ... 41-year-old Freddy Martin and his Band perform *Bumble Boogie* ... Columbia introduce a new twelve-inch 33 1/3 rpm long-playing record as alternative to the ten-inch 78 rpm gramophone disc ... Actress Dame May Whitty dies aged 82 in California ... Back in England - 34-year-old Fred Davis beats Walter Donaldson by 84 frames to 61 in the final of the World's Professional Snooker Championship at Leicester Square ... Wireless listeners tune-in to *Mrs. Dale's Diary* on BBC's Light Programme to hear Mrs. Mary Dale's account of her son Bob's argument with his father Jim and of daughter Gwen's continuing infatuation with Roger Lord - an older man ... 'The Lively, Laughing, Lovable Huggetts are Britain's Very Own Family' - crowds flock to cinemas to see 52-year-old Jack Warner starring alongside 55-year-old Kathleen Harrison, 21-year-old Jane Hylton, 18-year-old Susan Shaw and 15-year-old Petula Clark in the hugely popular film, *Here Come The Huggetts* ... "So when there's trouble around your way, just try walking backwards all the day" - young Petula Clark sings, *Walking Backwards* ... Mischievous schoolboys play Knock-Down Ginger ... 13-year-old David Nobbs from Orpington in Kent stays at home reading the adventure story *Pigeon Post* by Arthur Ransome.

Summer 1948... National Health Service - for everyone!

The weather is dull and cool for much of the summer ... Holiday makers in Scarborough flock to the Spa Theatre to see 33-year-old comedian Norman Wisdom appearing in a double-act with 28-year-old conjurer David Nixon ... Darts enthusiasts gather at the Empire Pool in London to see Harry Leadbetter (representing the Windle Labour Club in St. Helens) step up to the ockey, and win the annual *News of the World* darts tournament ... 11-year-old Jim Bowen from Heswall in Cheshire plays out with his friends ... The Labour government's initiative to recruit workers from Commonwealth countries is underway ... Five hundred settlers from Jamaica and Trinidad arrive on the *Empire Windrush* at Tilbury docks. Many head for Clapham Common where temporary accommodation has been set up in an old air-raid shelter ... Clement Attlee's Labour government continues its program of modernisation ... 50-year-old Health Secretary Aneurin Bevan launches the new National Health Service - bringing together hospitals, doctors, nurses, pharmacists, dentists and opticians all under one organisation - and providing services that are 'free for all at the point of use' ... 44-year-old John Snagge announces the news for BBC Newsreel ... The gas industry is nationalised ... A mid-air collision between a Swedish *DC-6* and an RAF transport aeroplane above Northolt Airport kills all passengers and crew - a total of thirty-nine people lose their lives ... 41-year-old Frank Whittle (inventor of the jet engine) is knighted at Buckingham Palace ... Police in Blackburn continue their search for the brutal killer of 3-year-old June Anne Devaney ... British and American aeroplanes deliver food and essential supplies to the people of West Berlin - after the Soviets cut road and rail links to the city ... Back in England - the new wireless programme, *Mrs. Dale's Diary*, continues to captivate listeners. Families sit around the radio set and hear how Mrs. Mary Dale's son, Bob, almost lost his life in a motorcar accident, and how daughter Gwen's quarrel with Roger Lord ended in tears ... 53-year-old ex-cricketer Lionel Marson introduces *Saturday Sport's Review* on the BBC Home Service ... 28-year-old tennis player Tony Mottram from Coventry makes it through to the quarter finals at Wimbledon, but loses to Gardnar Mulloy from America ... "So, bongo, bongo, bongo, I don't want to leave the Congo. Oh-no-no-no-no-no. Bingo, bangle, bungle, I'm so happy in the jungle, I refuse to go" - 39-year-old band-leader Joe Loss and his Orchestra perform *Civilisation (Bongo, Bongo, Bongo)* ... The Luton Girls' Choir perform *Count Your Blessings* ... The grey summer brightens in late July when it becomes extremely hot and sunny ... The London Olympic Games are shown on BBC television ... Emil Zatopek wins four gold medals for Czechoslovakia ... Fanny Blankers-Koen wins four gold medals for the Netherlands ... Britain's 38-year-old Tom Richards wins a silver medal in the marathon ... 21-year-old Dorothy Manley from London wins a silver medal in the 100 metre sprint ... 28-year-old cyclist Reg Harris from Bury wins two silver medals - one in the sprint, and one in the tandem sprint (along with Alan Bannister) ... Cricketers Denis Compton, Alec Bedser, Norman Yardley and 31-year-old Len Hutton line up for England against Australia in the summer Test Match series. Australia's 39-year-old captain Donald Bradman scores 173 not out at Headingley and 26-year-old fast bowler Ray Lindwall takes 6 for 20 at the Oval as the Aussie's win the series 4-0 and retain the Ashes. L Hutton, C Washbrook, W J Edrich, D C S Compton, J G Dewes, G M Emmett, J Hardstaff, H E Dollery, J F Crapp, C J Barnett, N W D Yardley (cpt), T G Evans (wk), A Coxon, J C Laker, A J

Watkins, A V Bedser, K Cranston, R Pollard, J A Young, D V P Wright and W E Hollies are all downcast by an Ashes defeat ... 29-year-old boxer Freddie Mills from Bournemouth is the new light-heavyweight champion of the world ... "If you ever go across the sea to Ireland, then maybe at the closing of your day, you can sit and watch the moon rise over Claddagh, and see the sun go down on…" *Galway Bay* by 45-year-old Bing Crosby is a popular gramophone song ... *How Deep Is The Ocean* by 32-year-old Frank Sinatra is also in demand ... Police in Blackburn arrest 22-year-old Peter Griffiths and charge him with the murder of 3-year-old June Anne Devaney ... 31-year-old Stan Cullis takes over from Ted Vizard as football manager of Wolverhampton Wanderers ... Theo Kelly resigns as Everton's manager and is replaced by 39-year-old Cliff Britton ... 66-year-old Fred Everiss retires as manager of West Bromwich Albion, after being in charge of the Black Country club since the year 1902. (Everiss is succeeded by 36-year-old Jack Smith) ... 24-year-old Jackie Milburn scores a goal for Newcastle Utd, and 24-year-old Roy Bentley scores for Chelsea, in a 2-2 draw at St. James' Park ... 23-year-old Ken Chisholm scores twice as Major Frank Buckley's Leeds Utd beat Dally Duncan's Luton Town 2-0 in Division Two ... 68-year-old Nancy Chadwick is found battered to death at Rawtenstall in Lancashire - 41-year-old Margaret Allen is charged with murder ... "So tired of waiting for you. So tired of longing for you. Tired of waiting, saving my love for you" - Russ Morgan and his Orchestra perform *So Tired* ... "In Dublin's fair city, the girls are so pretty, 'twas there that I first met sweet Molly Malone" - Danny Kaye sings, *Molly Malone* ... 'Well-to-do' young men dash along England's narrow roads on motorcycles ... The new Vincent *Black Shadow* has a top speed of 126 mph ... Food remains 'on the ration' ... A dozen eggs cost 2s/6d ... A nice cup of tea at the *J. Lyons & Co* teashop on Cook Street in Liverpool is 1½d.

Autumn 1948... Morris Minor motorcar

Labour's modernisation plan continues ... The nation's first comprehensive schools are established ... Schoolboys play conkers ... Girls skip and play hopscotch ... Matt Busby's Manchester Utd football team beat George Stephenson's Huddersfield Town 4-1 in front of 60,561 spectators at Maine Road. (29-year-old inside-forward Stan Pearson scores two of Utd's goals) ... 10-year-old Bobby Charlton from Ashington in Northumberland plays football in the street with his friends ... "Toot, toot, Tootsie, don't cry..." *Toot, Toot, Tootsie! (Goodbye)* by 62-year-old Al Jolson is a top selling gramophone record ... 'Big car motoring at small car cost' - the wonderful new Morris *Minor* motorcar (with a top speed of 64 mph, and a price tag of £358/10s/7d) is launched at the Earls Court Motor Show ... Humber introduce an improved *Super Snipe* - retaining the traditional running boards, but with headlamps now integrated into the front wing panels ... Jaguar introduce the sleek new *XK120* Drophead Coupe sports car with a top speed of 124 mph ... 34-year-old Bob Gerard finishes third in the British Grand Prix at Silverstone driving an ERA racing car ... H. R. Walker commentates on the second half of a football match between Wolverhampton Wanderers and Huddersfield Town on BBC radio's Light Programme - and listeners hear details of a grand 7-1 victory for the Wolves! ... More than a thousand deaths are reported after heavy smog in London ... Peter Griffiths is found guilty at Lancaster Assizes of the brutal murder of 3-year-old June Anne Devaney. The 22-year-old child killer is sentenced to death, and is hanged by the neck until dead at Liverpool on the nineteenth of November. (43-year-old hangman Albert Pierrepoint carries out the execution) ... "Hello playmates!" - 48-

year-old Arthur Askey appears at the Palladium in front of King George VI. 33-year-old Norman Wisdom appears in a television variety 'special' called *Wit and Wisdom* - and viewers get a glimpse of his funny new 'gump' character - Norman in a tight suit and peaked cap ... "Since first I met you on the village green. Come to me, or my dream of love is over. I love you as I loved you when you were sweet..." *When You Were Sweet Sixteen* by 31-year-old Josef Locke is a popular gramophone record ... 26-year-old footballer Tom Finney (aka the 'Preston Plumber') scores for England in a 1-0 victory over Wales at Villa Park - it's Finney's twelfth goal in just fourteen games for wing commander Winterbottom's national team ... Cliff Britton's Everton play against George Kay's Liverpool in front of 78,299 at Goodison Park - Jock Dodds scores for Everton and Willie Fagan scores for Liverpool in a 1-1 draw ... 17-year-old John Charles has a trial with Leeds Utd ... 25-year-old Con Martin joins Alex Massie's Aston Villa for £10,000 ... 26-year-old MI6 officer George Blake is posted to Korea and assigned with the task of gathering intelligence on communist activity in the North ... Back in England - 22-year-old Princess Elizabeth gives birth to a baby boy. (A name for the newborn child is yet to be decided) ... *Bonnie Prince Charlie* - a film made in Technicolor is now showing at cinemas, with 38-year-old David Niven in the lead role ... 33-year-old Alec Guinness stars as Fagin in David Lean's *Oliver Twist* ... Radio Luxembourg (with popular disc jockeys Geoffrey Everitt and Teddy Johnson) broadcasts up-to-date music to the nation - on the long-wave frequency ... "H-h-h-har-har! H-h-h-har-har! Oh that's the Woody Woodpecker song" - *Woody Woodpecker* by 44-year-old Geraldo and his Orchestra (with vocals by Doreen Lundy and George Evans) is a popular tune of the day ... *The Cuckoo Waltz* - an instrumental by organist

Ken Griffin is also popular ... Wireless listeners hear all about a fire at Craddock's garage and Gwen's refusal to marry Dick Mutty in *Mrs. Dale's Diary* ... Life continues as normal in austere Britain ... 37-year-old Nellie Lovell from Birmingham takes a spin in the sidecar of her husband Bill's motorcycle ... 12-year-old Joey Scragg from Brereton in Staffordshire goes scrumping for apples ... *Dinky Toys* introduce a die-cast model (1:48 scale) of the Standard *Vanguard* motorcar in time for Christmas ... *Scrabble* is an exciting new board game ... The number of hats sold each year is declining ... Advertisements say, '*Brylcreem* - A little dab'll do ya' ... A pint of mild in the Red Lion costs one shilling.

Christmas 1948... Mrs. Dale's diary

"Salt' peanuts! Salt' peanuts!" - the 'killer diller' gramophone recording of Dizzy Gillespie's new tune, *Salted Peanuts*, is much sought after by 'hipsters' ... The slightly more traditional songs, *White Christmas* and *Silent Night Holy Night*, by 45-year-old Bing Crosby are the best selling records over the festive period ... The weather is unseasonably warm for December ... Temperatures of around 60 to 65 degrees Fahrenheit are recorded in the North of England and in Scotland ... Five footballers make their international debuts as wing commander Winterbottom's England team thrash Switzerland 6-0 at Highbury - Goalkeeper, Ted Ditchburn; full-back, Alf Ramsey; inside-right, Jack 'cannonball' Rowley; inside-left, Jack Haines and outside-left, Johnny Hancocks - all gain their first caps. Rowley, Haines (2) and Hancocks (2) get their names on the score-sheet, along with centre-forward Jackie Milburn ... 10-year-old schoolboy Gordon Banks from Sheffield dreams of being a goalkeeper in the First Division ... The new baby prince is christened Charles Philip Arthur George ... A road safety campaign gets underway with the slogan, 'Keep death off the road - carelessness kills' ... The new Ford *Anglia* motorcar is launched with a three-speed manual gearbox and a top speed of 57 mph ... Seventy new trolley-buses are now in service on the streets of London ... 29-year-old Jon Pertwee stars in *A Piece of Cake* at cinemas ... Bud Abbott and Lou Costello star in *Abbott and Costello Meet Frankenstein* ... "It's behind you!" - Middle-class families enjoy an evening at the Pantomime ... 33-year-old Norman Wisdom stars in *Robinson Crusoe* at the Alexandra Theatre in Birmingham ... 19-year-old Ronnie Barker makes his stage debut at the County Theatre in Aylesbury ... Bob Jackson's Portsmouth football team lead the way in Division One after two successive victories over Chelsea: The first, a 1-2 win on Christmas Day at Stamford Bridge. The second, a 5-2 victory at Fratton Park two days later ... George Martin's Newcastle Utd are just one point behind Pompey after beating Birmingham City 1-0 ... 35-year-old centre-forward Micky Fenton scores a hat-trick as David Jack's Middlesbrough thrash Alex Massie's Aston Villa 6-0 at Ayresome Park ... Two weeks later, Villa's 25-year-old centre-forward 'Terrible' Trevor Ford scores four goals as 'The Villains' beat Wolves 5-1 at Villa Park ... 51,517 spectators turn out at The Valley to watch Jimmy Seed's Charlton Athletic beat Tom Whittaker's Arsenal 4-3 ... Millions of people are now enjoying medical services, 'free at the point of use' from the NHS ... Political posters say, 'Labour's Health Service Covers Everyone - Tories Voted Against It' ... 210 million tonnes of coal have been mined in Britain this year - an increase of 10 million tonnes compared to last year ... 37-year-old Spike Jones and his City Slickers perform *All I Want for Christmas Is My Two Front Teeth* ("... my two front teeth, see my two front teeth!") ... 33-year-old Frank Sinatra sings *Have Yourself A Merry Little Christmas* ("... let your heart be light. From now on, your troubles will be out of sight") ... Lucky children get a *Slinky* on Christmas morning ... Wireless listeners are enthralled as Dr. Jim Dale saves a girl from drowning in *Mrs. Dale's Diary* ... Schoolboy David Nobbs enjoys playing Canasta (an exciting new card game) with his mother and father at their home in Orpington ... The word 'television' is now often abbreviated to 'TV' ... BBC broadcasts from 3.15 p.m. to 4.00 p.m. and then from 8.30 p.m. until 10.45 p.m. on Christmas Day ... *Alice's Adventures in Wonderland and Through the Looking Glass* is the main feature of the evening's schedule ... "Should you have the grace to go dancing, and if you want somewhere to go. Leicester Square's the place for romancing, so come along now to the show" - 48-year-old Harry Roy (aka the King of 'Hot-Cha') and his Band perform the *Leicester Square Rag* at dance halls ... Music-hall star Nellie Wallace dies aged 78 - just three weeks after performing in front of King George VI at the Palladium in the Royal Variety Performance ... *Polo* mints - 'the mint with the hole' - are now on sale.

New Year 1949... Stand by your beds

Clement Attlee's Labour government launches yet another productivity campaign - this one comes with the slogan, 'Productivity Pays' ... Firms, trade unions and households are encouraged to write off for a free booklet which explains how it all works ... The wheels of industry keep turning ... There are more than 1,000 coal mines in the country employing approximately 720,000 men ... Miners work long hours in dangerous conditions ... The average weekly wage in the collieries has risen from £6/3s/2d to £8/5s/2s since the industry was nationalised ... 11-year-old Arthur Scargill from Worsbrough Dale in Yorkshire plays out with his friends ... "I'd love to get you …" *On A Slow Boat To China* ("… all to myself, alone") by 35-year-old Tessie O'Shea is a popular new song ... 40-year-old Alvar Liddell announces the news on the wireless ... 42-year-old convicted murderer Margaret Allen is hanged by the neck until dead at Strangeways ... 'Stand by your beds, you 'orrible lot!' - Conscription begins and men aged 17 to 21 are now required to serve eighteen months national service in one of the armed forces ... 67-year-old Foreign Secretary Ernest Bevin takes part in negotiations with representatives from eleven other countries (including France, Denmark, Italy and the United States) all seeking to form a new international alliance for peace ... Relations between East and West remain strained ... An air-lift of essential supplies to people in West Berlin continues - as the Soviets maintain their blockade of the German city ... Back in England - comedian Tommy Handley dies of a brain haemorrhage at the age of 56 - his hugely popular radio show *It's That Man Again* (aka *Itma*) ends after running for almost ten years ... 53-year-old Jack Warner stars alongside 57-year-old

Kathleen Harrison, 19-year-old Susan Shaw and 16-year-old Petula Clark in the hugely popular film, *Vote for Huggett* ... 23-year-old Margaret Hilda Roberts is selected as the Conservative parliamentary candidate for Dartford ... 39-year-old John Haigh robs and murders an elderly lady at Crawley before disposing of her body in a 45-gallon drum containing sulphuric acid ... "Sir, I've been on the march for six days. I had no bible and no prayer book, but I have these cards. You see sir, when I look at the ace, it reminds me that there is one God" - a gramophone recording of 44-year-old Phil Harris telling the parable of the *Deck Of Cards* is a best seller ... "Hey! Sing temptation will ya" - *Cigareets, Whusky And Wild Wild Women* by 42-year-old Red Ingle is also popular ... Men and boys pack the terraces at football grounds ... 69,191 people turn out at Villa Park to watch a league match between Aston Villa and Arsenal - Billy 'Cowboy' Goffin scores for Villa in a 1-0 victory ... 55,019 people turn out at Boothferry Park to watch an FA Cup tie between Hull City and Manchester Utd - Stan Pearson scores for Utd in a 0-1 victory ... 22-year-old George Robledo makes his debut for Newcastle Utd ... 25-year-old Johnny Morris leaves Matt Busby's Manchester Utd and joins Stuart McMillan's Derby County for a new record transfer fee of £24,500 ... 26-year-old Ivor Broadis moves from Carlisle Utd to join Bill Murray's Sunderland for £18,000 ... 33-year-old actress Ingrid Bergman stars in glorious Technicolor as *Joan of Arc* at cinemas ... 41-year-old John Wayne and 28-year-old Montgomery Clift star in black and white as cowboys in *Red River* ... "There was a boy, a very strange, enchanted boy. They say he wandered very far. Very far, over land and sea" - 29-year-old Nat 'King' Cole sings *Nature Boy* ... Trombonist Pee Wee Hunt performs *Twelfth Street Rag* ... Instances of espionage are going undetected in the offices of some government departments

... 37-year-old German born scientist Klaus 'Karl' Fuchs of the highly secret Atomic Energy Research Establishment at Harwell in Oxfordshire passes confidential and classified information onto his Soviet handler ... "I'm rather worried about Jim" - Mrs. Mary Dale is a concerned about her husband Jim in *Mrs Dale's Diaries* on BBC radio's Light Programme ... Vauxhall launch the new *Velox* family saloon motorcar. It has a top speed of 74 mph and can reach 60 mph in 22.8 seconds ... A local call from a red telephone box costs tuppence ... People enjoy SPAM fritters for tea.

Spring 1949... Play up Pompey. Pompey play up

Rationing of clothes comes to an end ... Housewives scrub away on washing day and dry garments by squeezing them through the mangle in the back yard ... 38-year-old Olive Shapley is the new presenter of *Woman's Hour* on BBC's Home Service ... *The Green Cockatoo* - a lively Rumba - by Ethel Smith and the Bando Carioca is a popular gramophone record ... Britain signs the North Atlantic Treaty - along with the United States, Canada, Belgium, Denmark, France, Iceland, Italy, Luxembourg, Holland, Norway and Portugal ... US president Harry S. Truman says, "It is a simple document, but if it had existed in 1914 and in 1939, I believe it would have prevented the acts of aggression which led to two world wars." ... Britain's 68-year-old Foreign Secretary Ernest Bevin says the establishment of NATO is a huge step towards securing long lasting peace for the world ... 25-year-old Anne Shelton from Dulwich sings, *Put Your Shoes On, Lucy* ... 36-year-old Nellie Lutcher from Louisiana sings, *He's A Real Gone Guy* ... 39-year-old John Haigh is arrested and charged with murder after police find human remains in a 45-gallon drum at his workshop in Crawley ... Actor Will Hay dies aged 60 at his home in Chelsea ... "The sun comes up and the sun goes down, the hands of the clock go round and round, I just wake up and it's time to lay down..." *Life Gits Tee-jus Don't It?* by Peter Lind-Hayes is a popular new 78 rpm gramophone record ... *Candy Kisses* by 38-year-old Danny Kaye is also popular ... *Cottage Rake* wins the Cheltenham Gold Cup for the second year running ... The football season ends and Bob Jackson's Portsmouth are the new champions of Division One - after beating Bolton Wanderers 1-2 at Burndon Park on the twenty-third of April. 34-year-old Pompey centre-forward Ike Clarke has scored fourteen league goals in the season; 26-year-old outside-left 'Jolly' Jack Froggatt has scored fifteen; 31-year-old inside-right Duggie 'Thunderboots' Reid has scored seventeen; 23-year-old outside-right Peter Harris has scored eighteen ... Teddy Davison's Sheffield Utd and committee controlled Preston North End are relegated to Division Two ... Frank Osborne's Fulham and Jack Smith's West Bromwich Albion are promoted to Division One ... One-hundred thousand football fans converge on Wembley for the FA Cup final. 29-year-old Jesse Pye scores twice in a 3-1 victory for First Division Wolverhampton Wanderers over Second Division Leicester City. 23-year-old Princess Elizabeth presents the famous silver trophy to 25-year-old Wolves captain Billy Wright. A ticket for the standing enclosure at the Empire Stadium costs three shillings ... 34-year-old goalkeeper Frank Swift of Manchester City plays his final game for England ... 29-year-old Bert 'the cat' Williams of Wolverhampton Wanderers takes over 'in nets.' ... Two football pools companies (*Shermans* and *Zetters*) publish the Australian football results for the first time - enabling punters to continue filling out their weekly pools coupons during the close-season ... Radio listeners tune-in to BBC's Home Service for programmes such as *Music While You Work*, *Worker's Playtime*, *Children's Hour* and *Those Were The Days!* ... The latest gramophone tunes are broadcast on Radio Luxembourg ... "You sigh, a song begins. You speak, I hear violins…" *It's Magic* by 25-year-old Doris Day is frequently played ... *Is It True What They Say About Dixie* ("… does the sun really shine all the time?") by Al Jolson is also popular ... 34-year-old boxer Joe Louis retires as heavy-weight champion of the world after holding the title for eleven years ... 35-year-old Fred Davis retains his title of World's Professional Snooker Champion - beating Walter Donaldson by 80 frames to 65 in the final at

Leicester Square Hall ... 30-year-old racing driver Major Anthony Rolt finishes third in the British Grand Prix at Silverstone driving an Alfa Romeo. (Band leader Billy Cotton drives an ERA and finishes in eighth position) ... The new Vauxhall *Velox* family saloon car costs £430 (plus £120/3s/11d purchase tax) ... Boy Scouts carry out the first 'Bob-a-Job' campaign. Tasks such as hedge trimming and grass cutting are performed with great gusto by willing young chaps in neckerchiefs and woggles ... Wealthy, retired gentleman in the Home Counties shun 'Bob-a-Job' and manicure their own lawns ... The latest *Qualcast* motor lawn-mower costs £38 (plus £9/18s/7d purchase tax), and comes with a three year guarantee ... 45-year-old John Snagge announces the news on the wireless ... The Royal Navy ship HMS *Amethyst* is trapped by the People's Liberation Army on the Yangtse river in China ... The Berlin air-lift comes to an end as the Soviets abandon their year long blockade of the city ... Tension remains high between the East and the West ... The Labour government's expensive groundnut scheme at Tanganyika in Africa has been running for two years - and failed to reap any reward. 66-year-old prime-minister Clement Attlee is criticised in parliament and ridiculed by the newspapers ... "Down in the meadow in a little bitty pool, swam three little fishies and a mama fishie too. 'Swim' said the mama fishie, 'swim if you can', and they swam and they swam right over the dam" - 32-year-old Frankie Howerd performs his song *Three Little Fishes* ... The Radio Revellers perform *Far Away Places* ("… with strange soundin' names, far away over the sea") ... Ray Ellington and his Band perform *The Maharajah Of Magador* ... 29-year-old actor Richard Todd makes his film debut in *For Them That Trespass* ... 19-year-old Susan Shaw plays Primrose Brown in *It's Not Cricket* ... Newspaper advertisements advise people to, 'Enjoy Milk everyday while it's plentiful'.

Summer 1949... Wakey! Wakey!

An extremely hot and sunny summer ... Temperatures remain high throughout June, July and August ... Water levels fall and the country suffers the worst drought since 1911 ... Families clamber aboard steam trains and head off to the seaside ... Posters on railway station walls say, 'The beauty of Butlin's is that it's ALL sheer holiday' ... 40-year-old singer Donald Peers is the headline act at the Grand Theatre in Blackpool - 34-year-old comedian Norman Wisdom is also on the bill ... Sweets come off the ration, but demand for confectionery is so strong that the restrictions are soon put back in place ... 53-year-old Jack Warner stars alongside 57-year-old Kathleen Harrison, 28-year-old Dinah Sheridan, 19-year-old Susan Shaw and 16-year-old Petula Clark, in the hugely popular film *The Huggetts Abroad* ... Cricketers Len Hutton and Cyril Washbrook stride out together to open the batting for England against New Zealand at Headingley. 25-year-old Trevor Bailey makes his Test Match debut and takes six wickets. 18-year-old Brian Close makes his debut in the third Test at Old Trafford. The four match series ends in a draw ... A polio epidemic sweeps across the United Kingdom, and 7-year-old schoolboy Ian Dury contracts the disease in a swimming pool at Southend-on-Sea ... "Tek-eeee-laa! De-de, de-de-de-de, de-de. De-de, de-de-de-de, der" - *Tequila* by 47-year-old Ted Heath and his Music is a hugely popular tune at dance halls ... "Everybody's doing it, soon you'll be doing it" - *Leicester Square Rag* by 49-year-old Harry Roy (aka the King of 'Hot-Cha') and his Band is now a best selling 78 rpm gramophone disc ... 36-year-old Richard Dimbleby announces the news on the wireless ... 40-year-old John Haigh (the acid bath murderer) is hanged by the neck until dead at Wandsworth. (45-year-old hangman Albert

Pierrepoint carries out the execution) ... There's nationwide celebration as HMS *Amethyst* escapes from the People's Liberation Army in China and steams to safety ... 29-year-old Hughie Green presents *Opportunity Knocks* on BBC Home Service radio ... Matt Busby's Manchester Utd return to Old Trafford eight years after their stadium was destroyed by German bombs. 42,515 spectators turn out to see Utd beat Bolton Wanderers 3-0 with centre-forward Jack 'cannonball' Rowley and outside-left Charlie Mitten on the score-sheet ... The maximum wage for footballers is set at £12 a week ... "The toe bone's connected to the heal bone. The heal bone's connected to the foot bone. The foot bone's connected to the ankle bone. It's easy to connect those..." *Dry Bones* by Ted Heath and his Music (with Jack Parnell and the Kordites) is a hit record ... "Wakey! Wakey!" - *The Billy Cotton Band Show* is on the radio every Sunday ... The summer heat-wave continues ... Seaside resorts are crammed with sunburnt children, women wearing wide-brimmed straw bonnets and men wearing knotted handkerchiefs on their heads ... 45-year-old George Formby replaces Donald Peers as headline act at the Grand Theatre in Blackpool ... 'A hilarious study in the gentle art of murder' - 35-year-old Alec Guinness stars in *Kind Hearts and Coronets* at cinemas ... 'A highland fling on a tight little island' - 52-year-old Basil Radford stars in *Whisky Galore!* ... Petrol remains 'on the ration' and is at an all time high price of 4s/3d a gallon ... 'Big Brother is Watching You!' - *Nineteen Eighty Four*, a new novel by 45-year-old author George Orwell, is published ... The number of road accidents is on the increase ... A yellow and blue striped road crossing for pedestrians is trialled ... Triumph introduce the *Thunderbird* motorbike with a 650cc engine and a top speed of 100 mph ... The ultra-modern Austin *A90 Atlantic* motorcar has sweeping lines, enclosed rear wheels and three circular headlights. This remarkable new vehicle costs £784 (including purchase tax) ... A pint of mild in the Red Lion is 1s/1d ... A packet of twenty *Woodbines* is 2s/9d.

Autumn 1949... Passport to Pimlico

The warm weather continues into September and October ... People suffer with prickly heat ... Clement Attlee's Labour government continues its drive for greater productivity, but times are hard and shortages of food and fuel affect most families ... Rationing remains in place and small luxury goods such as household appliances are almost impossible to obtain ... Immigrants arrive from Commonwealth countries in search of work ... Many people are homeless and living in temporary accommodation - often sharing with other families ... Local councils are offered financial incentives to build new houses ... Economic growth is slow ... Chancellor of the Exchequer Sir Stafford Cripps is forced to devalue the pound - it's now worth just $2.80 ... "You can't push English people around like sacks of potatoes" - *Passport to Pimlico*, with 59-year-old Stanley Holloway, 57-year-old Margaret Rutherford and 34-year-old Charles Hawtrey, draws crowds to the cinema ... John McCallum, Patrick Holt and 23-year-old Honor Blackman star in *A Boy, a Girl and a Bike* ... The new school term is underway ... 14-year-old David Nobbs goes up to Marlborough as a border - and is sexually assaulted by an 18-year-old senior in the woods ... 11-year-old Diddy David Hamilton from Manchester plays gramophone records at home ... "Are the stars out tonight? I don't know if it's cloudy or bright, 'cause..." *I Only Have Eyes For You* by Nat 'King' Cole is the best seller ... *The Last Mile Home* by Bing Crosby is also popular ... 50-year-old John Christie murders Beryl Evans and her baby Geraldine at 10 Rillington Place. The subsequent police investigation is flawed and 24-year-old Timothy Evans (husband of Beryl) is apprehended for the crime instead of Christie ... 46-year-old writer George Orwell is admitted to hospital suffering with tuberculosis ... 37-year-old Kim Philby takes up a senior post for the British security services in Washington DC ... Former German paratrooper and prisoner of war, 26-year-old Bert Trautmann, signs for Jock Thomson's Manchester City football team as goalkeeper ... Footballers Len Shackleton and Dickie Davis are on the score-sheet as Bill Murray's Sunderland beat Manchester Utd 1-3 at Old Trafford ... Kevin Baron and 27-year-old Billy Liddell score for Liverpool, and Bobby Mitchell and 20-year-old Tommy 'Topper' Thompson score for Newcastle Utd, in a 2-2 draw at Anfield ... 25-year-old Jackie Milburn scores a hat-trick as England beat Wales 1-4 in Cardiff ... Singers Jo Stafford and Gordon MacRae perform the popular song *'A' - You're Adorable* ("... 'B' - You're so beautiful, 'C' - You're a cutie full of charms") ... *Come Dancing* is shown for the first time on BBC television ... 19-year-old Princess Margaret and 23-year-old Princess Elizabeth accompany the King and Queen to see Maurice Chevalier at the Royal Variety Show ... 21-year-old Ken Colyer plays trumpet in the Crane River Jazz Band at the White Hart pub in Cranford ... 37-year-old actor John Le Mesurier marries 27-year-old actress Hattie Jacques ... "There's a girl named Tessie Town, and she weighs about four hundred pounds. She's fat and fair, she don't care 'cause the boys all hang around" - 36-year-old Tessie O'Shea sings *Two Ton Tessie From Tennessee* ... The Ink Spots sing *You're Breaking My Heart* ("... 'cause you're leaving. You've fallen for somebody new. It isn't too easy believing, you'd leave after all we've been through") ... Advertisements advise, 'Keep your strength up the natural way. *Hovis* - the better balanced bread' ... A daring and dangerous trick by magician Alan Alan (aka the 'British Houdini') goes horribly wrong when the 23-year-old fails to dig himself out of a shallow grave. Alan is rescued by his assistants, just in the nick of time!

Christmas 1949...
Young Tommy Docherty to Preston North End

Schoolboys write out their Christmas wish lists ... *Dinky Toys* introduce a die-cast model (1:45 scale) of the Austin *A40 Devon* motorcar ... *Meccano* sets remain as popular as ever ... 'Automatic binding bricks' from *Lego* are now in stock at *Woolworths* ... 49-year-old Victor Silvester and his Ballroom Orchestra perform *December* - a popular new (slow) Foxtrot ... "It's behind you!" - Middle-class families enjoy an evening at the Pantomime ... 45-year-old entertainer George Formby appears in *Cinderella* at Leeds ... 34-year-old Norman Wisdom appears in a new production of *Robinson Crusoe* at the Grand Theatre in Wolverhampton ... 25-year-old Billy Wright scores a goal for wing commander Winterbottom's England football team in a 2-0 win against Italy at White Hart Lane ... 61-year-old Director General of MI5 Sir Percy Sillitoe receives a worrying report; instances of espionage have been detected in offices at some government departments ... 37-year-old German born scientist Klaus 'Karl' Fuchs of the highly secret Atomic Energy Research Establishment at Harwell in Oxfordshire is questioned on suspicion of being a Soviet spy ... "Jealous heart, oh jealous heart, stop beating. Can't you see the damage you have done" - *Jealous Heart* by 34-year-old Al Morgan from Chicago is a popular song of the day ... *Monday Tuesday Wednesday* ("... Thursday, Friday, Saturday, Sunday. I love you") by 29-year-old Betty Driver from Leicester is also popular ... 17-year-old actress Elizabeth Taylor from London stars alongside Robert Taylor in *Conspirator* at cinemas ... 30-year-old Richard Todd from Dublin stars in *The Interrupted Journey* - a new film featuring 22-year-old Roger Moore in a minor role ... 52-year-old Enid Blyton is the author of *Noddy Goes to Toyland* - a wonderful new book for children ... The BBC begins broadcasting to a wider audience as a new television transmitter opens in the Midlands ... A programme called *For The Children* is shown on weekday afternoons ... 218 million tonnes of coal have been mined this year under Lord Hyndley's National Coal Board ... Life remains hard under Clement Attlee's Labour government ... Working-class men and boys look forward to Saturday afternoons when they can escape the drudgery of everyday life by attending football matches ... League games kick-off at 2.15 p.m. ... George Kay's Liverpool are top of Division One. 32-year-old inside-left Willie Fagan scores twice as 'The Reds' defeat Everton 3-1 in front of 50,485 spectators at Anfield ... Matt Busby's Manchester Utd are two points behind Liverpool in second place ... 30-year-old inside-left Stan Pearson scores twice as Utd beat Arsenal 2-0 in front of 55,757 spectators at Old Trafford ... "Who can explain it? Who can tell you why? Fools give you reasons, wise men never try" - 37-year-old Perry Como has a hit record with *Some Enchanted Evening* ... 53,802 spectators turn out at Ayresome Park to see David Jack's Middlesbrough football team play against George Martin's Newcastle Utd in a mid-table clash in Division One - it's a 1-0 victory to Boro ... 47,817 turn out at Elland Road to see Major Frank Buckley's Leeds Utd play against Angus Seed's Barnsley in a mid-table clash in Division Two - it's a 1-0 victory to Leeds ... 21-year-old talented right-half Tommy Docherty transfers from Celtic (of the Scottish First Division) to Preston North End (of the English Second Division) ... A small number of middle-class families watch television sets in the parlour ... "Oh, splendid. Jolly good show" - *How Do You View*, a wonderful new comedy, starring 38-year-old actor Terry-Thomas is broadcast at 9 p.m. on Wednesday the twenty-first

December ... Courting couples enjoy an evening out, sitting side-by-side in cold, dreary cinema halls holding hands in the gloom ... *The Third Man* with Joseph Cotton and Orson Welles is now showing ... "I'm dreaming, of a..." *White Christmas* by 46-year-old Bing Crosby is the best selling gramophone record at Christmas - yet again! ... "Yippee-I-yay. Yippee-I-yo. Ghost riders in the sky" - *Riders In The Sky (A Cowboy Legend)* by 29-year-old Peggy Lee with the Jud Conlon Singers is also popular ... 26-year-old footballer 'Terrible' Trevor Ford scores for Aston Villa in a 1-0 victory over local rivals Birmingham City ... A BSA *Golden Flash* bicycle with three-speed hub gear and 'central-pull' caliper brakes costs £25/17s/1d ... A modern 'lightweight' Raleigh *Record Ace* bicycle with three-speed hub gear and a Brooks *B-37* leather saddle costs £39/9s/4d ... *Cluedo* is a new board game for all the family ... Middle-class people throw fancy dress parties on New Year's Eve ... Working-class people go to the pub or to the dance hall.

New Year 1950... Labour again

It's a mild winter ... A general election is held in February ... Posters depicting the Jarrow March (from 1936) say, 'Remember? Unemployment. Don't Give the Tories another chance. Vote Labour.' ... Clement Attlee is triumphant - winning a second term as prime-minister, but with a reduced majority. (Labour: 315 seats, Conservatives: 298 seats, Liberals: 9 seats). 62-year-old Hugh 'Comrade' Dalton is the new Minister for Town and Country Planning. Manny Shinwell is the new Minister for Defence. Sir Stafford Cripps continues as Chancellor. Aneurin Bevan remains at Health and Ernest Bevin remains at the Foreign Office. 33-year-old Harold Wilson from Huddersfield is the President of the Board of Trade ... 33-year-old Edward Heath is elected as Conservative MP for Bexley ... 32-year-old Reg Maudling is elected for the Conservatives in Barnet ... 24-year-old Margaret Hilda Roberts fails to get elected in Dartford ... 38-year-old German born scientist Klaus 'Karl' Fuchs of the highly secret Atomic Energy Research Establishment at Harwell in Oxfordshire confesses to being a Soviet spy - and is committed for trial ... "Are you sitting comfortably? Then I'll begin" - *Listen With Mother* is a new radio programme for children ... "Janet. John. Come, John, come. Look, John, look. Come, John, come and look. See the boats. Look, John. See the boats" - *Janet and John* books (published by James Nisbet & Co. Ltd.) are now on sale ... "Well it's you, oh my darling, yes it's you" - 26-year-old Anne Shelton from Dulwich sings *Oh! My Darling* ... 42-year-old John Wayne, from Iowa in the US, stars in the hit film *She Wore a Yellow Ribbon* ... 'Love held its breath as sudden terror held the stage!' - 33-year-old Jane Wyman and 48-year-old Marlene Dietrich star in Alfred

Hitchcock's new film *Stage Fright* ... 54-year-old Jack Warner stars as PC Dixon (and 28-year-old Dirk Bogarde plays Tom Riley) in *The Blue Lamp* ... 56-year-old Mao Tse Tung of China holds talks with 71-year-old Joseph Stalin of the USSR. The two leaders form a political alliance and the basis for a 'Cold War' between East and West is set ... Back in England - Timothy Evans (a lodger in the house belonging to John Christie at 10 Rillington Place) goes on trial accused of murder - the 25-year-old is found guilty and sentenced to death ... "Mule train! Gidduup! Yeaahh!" - 30-year-old Tennessee Ernie Ford sings *Mule Train* ... 44-year-old Mantovani performs *Legend Of The Glass Mountain* ... Writer George Orwell dies aged 46 in a London hospital ... Music-hall star Sir Harry Lauder dies aged 79 at Strathaven in Scotland ... "I've got a lovely bunch of coconuts. There they are all standing in a row. Big ones, small ones, some as big as your head" - 50-year-old Billy Cotton and his Band perform *I've Got A Lovely Bunch Of Coconuts* ... 29-year-old centre-forward Eddie Quigley leaves Sheffield Wednesday and joins Will Scott's Preston North End for a new record transfer fee of £26,500 ... George Kay's Liverpool continue to lead the way in Division One - 'The Reds' beat Birmingham City 2-0 at Anfield with 30-year-old Albert Stubbins on the score-sheet ... 14-year-old schoolboy David Nobbs plays rugger in the mud at Marlborough ... Young couples enjoy a Saturday night out ... 'Dancing Time For Dancers' - *The Kiss In Your Eyes* a Waltz performed by 40-year-old Joe Loss and his Orchestra is a popular tune ... The nation's landed gentry and a few wealthy businessmen order sleek new motorcars from London showrooms ... The latest Jaguar 3.5 litre *Mark V* saloon has a top speed of 90 mph and accelerates from 0-60 mph in 20.4 seconds ... Aston Martin launch the *DB2* sports car with a top speed of

116 mph and capable of 0-60 mph in 10.9 seconds ... Standard grade petrol costs 3s/2d a gallon ... *Your Wardrobe* is broadcast on BBC television - with Mary Malcolm and Elspeth Wilding giving hints and advice on getting 'the best service from your sewing machine' ... *Housewives' Choice* is broadcast on BBC radio's Light Programme - with 38-year-old Roy Rich playing record requests at ten past nine each morning ... *(Two Little Men In A) Flying Saucer* ("... flew down to Earth one day, listened to a radio, saw a television show, and said 'let's fly away'") by Billy Cotton and his Band is a new and popular tune ... The average weekly wage in Britain is £7/5s/6d ... A *Mars* bar costs 4d.

Spring 1950... Dan Dare in the Eagle

29-year-old outside-left Charlie Mitten scores four goals (including a hat-trick of penalties) as Matt Busby's Manchester Utd thrash Aston Villa 7-0 at Old Trafford ... 13-year-old schoolboy footballer Duncan Edwards plays a match for England's under-14 team at the Empire Stadium in Wembley ... 11-year-old schoolboy footballer Ron Atkinson from Liverpool has a kick-about with his friends in the park ... *Cottage Rake* wins the Cheltenham Gold Cup for the third year running ... Walter Donaldson wins the World's Professional Snooker Championship at the Tower Circus in Blackpool - he beats Fred Davis in the final ... There's heavy snow at the end of April ... 25-year-old convicted murderer Timothy Evans is hanged by the neck until dead at Pentonville ... "Bibbidi-bobbidi-boo" - Walt Disney's *Cinderella* is at cinemas ... Married couples enjoy a Saturday night at the local dance hall ... 50-year-old Victor Silvester and his Ballroom Orchestra perform *My Foolish Heart* - a popular new (slow) Foxtrot ... 'They had 30 days to teach their hearts to behave!' - 30-year-old Richard Todd, 24-year-old Patricia Neal and 38-year-old Ronald Reagan star in *The Hasty Heart* ... 18-year-old actress Elizabeth Taylor from London marries Nick Hilton (a super-rich heir to an international hotel business empire) at Beverley Hills in California ... Back in England - 56-year-old Stuart Hibberd reads the news for BBC radio's Home Service ... Eighty people are killed when an Avro *Tudor V* aeroplane crashes at Llandow in Glamorgan - it's the world's worst aviation disaster ... 38-year-old Soviet spy Klaus 'Karl' Fuchs is found guilty of breaking the Official Secrets Act - and is sentenced to fourteen years imprisonment ... 75-year-old Leader of the Opposition Winston Churchill ridicules Labour prime-minister Clement Attlee over his failed groundnut scheme at Tanganyika in Africa. The project has now been running for three years - without any reward ... 45-year-old George Formby sings *Come Hither With Your Zither* ("... make my dreams come true") ... 63-year-old Al Jolson sings *I'm Looking Over A Four Leaf Clover* ("... I overlooked before") ... 19-year-old Ronnie Corbett is called up for national service in the RAF ... Motorists take to the road as petrol rationing finally comes to an end ... Morris *Minors*, Standard *Vanguards* and Rover *P4s* clog the countryside trunk roads ... "How do you view? Are you frightfully well? You are? Oh, good show!" - 38-year-old actor Terry-Thomas returns in the wonderful TV comedy *How Do You View* ... "I'm rather worried about Jim" - millions of radio listeners tune-in daily to hear *Mrs. Dale's Diary* ... Portsmouth footballer Duggie 'Thunderboots' Reid scores a hat-trick on the last day of the football season - as Bob Jackson's Portsmouth thrash Alex Massie's Aston Villa 5-1 to become champions of Division One for the second year running. Ernie Butler, Jimmy Dickinson, Ike Clarke, 'Jolly' Jack Froggatt (with fifteen goals), Billy Hindmarsh, Peter Harris (with sixteen goals) and 32-year-old Duggie 'Thunderboots' Reid (with sixteen goals) have all been sensational for Pompey ... Stan Cullis' Wolverhampton Wanderers are runners-up - losing out only by goal average ... Notts County are champions of Division Three (South) - with 30-year-old centre-forward Tommy Lawton scoring thirty-three goals for the season ... 31-year-old sports all-rounder Denis Compton is on the winning side as Tom Whittaker's Arsenal beat George Kay's Liverpool 2-0 in the FA Cup final. A ticket for the standing enclosure at the Empire Stadium in Wembley costs three shillings ... "Have you ever passed the corner of Fourth and Grand, where a little ball of rhythm has a shoe-shine stand?

People gather 'round and they clap their hands, he's a great big bundle of joy. He pops the boogie woogie rag, the…" *Chattanoogie Shoe Shine Boy* by Bing Crosby is the best selling gramophone record ... "I name this ship 'Ark Royal'. May God protect her and all who sail in her" - 49-year-old Queen Elizabeth launches the 36,800 tonne HMS *Ark Royal* aircraft carrier on Merseyside ... Racing driver Giuseppe Farina wins the British Grand Prix at Silverstone in a red Alfa Romeo. (Farina's 39-year-old team mate Reg Parnell from Derby is third). The ultra-modern Austin *A90 Atlantic* motorcar zooms along English roads - it has a top speed of 90 mph ... 'EAGLE - the new national strip cartoon weekly' - *The Eagle* comic is launched, featuring 'Pilot of the Future' Dan Dare and a wonderful new character called Captain Pugwash - a lovable pirate ... 28-year-old footballer Tom Finney (aka the 'Preston Plumber') scores four goals - including two penalties - as England beat Portugal 3-5 in a friendly at Lisbon. (Stan Mortensen is also on the score-sheet for wing commander Winterbottom's national team) ... 27-year-old Jimmy Mullen of Wolverhampton Wanderers is the first ever substitute used by England, when he comes on to replace Jackie Milburn during a 4-1 win against Belgium ... "Well, well, well, look who's here, I haven't seen you in many a year…" *(If I Knew You Were Coming) I'd've Baked A Cake* ("… baked a cake, baked a cake") by 52-year-old Gracie Fields is a hugely popular new song ... "Put another nickel in. In the nickelodeon. All I want is having you and music, music, music" - 19-year-old Teresa Brewer performs *(Put Another Nickel In) Music! Music! Music!* - and the whole nation sings along ... Advertising posters proclaim, 'There are only two things a man can't resist - A pint of Guinness and another pint!'

Summer 1950...
Wright, Finney and Matthews at the world cup

It's a sunny summer, but with cool temperatures ... British Railway's fleet of steam locomotives haul millions of passengers off to the seaside ... A third-class return ticket between London's Victoria station and Ramsgate costs 21s/2d ... *Horizon* organise 'package' holidays to the exotic and faraway sunshine resort of Corsica ... As part of their honeymoon, 18-year-old actress Elizabeth Taylor and her new husband Nick Hilton have a gay old time at Ascot Races ... 23-year-old Alan Alan (aka the 'British Houdini') entertains crowds of holiday makers by performing daring escape routines, bound in a straitjacket and chains, whilst suspended high above the ground on a burning rope ... 37-year-old James Corbitt strangles his lover Eliza Wood at the Prince of Wales hotel at Ashton-under-Lyme ... *A Murder is Announced* - the latest 'whodunit' from 59-year-old Agatha Christie is on sale in book shops ... Hollywood blockbuster movie *Samson and Delilah* - starring 37-year-old Victor Mature and 35-year-old Hedy Lamarr (36-25-35), and directed by 69-year-old Cecille B DeMille, is now showing at picture houses - and it's in Technicolor! ... Prime-minister Clement Attlee sends British troops to Korea as part of a combined United Nations response to North Korea's invasion of South Korea ... 27-year-old MI6 officer George Blake is captured by the enemy and held by communists in North Korea ... Back in Blighty - cricketers 33-year-old Len Hutton and 30-year-old Reg Simpson stride out together at Old Trafford to open the batting for England in the first Test of the summer. Hutton retires hurt. 29-year-old wicket-keeper Godfrey Evans (batting at number eight) scores 104 runs, and England win the match. In the second Test, John Goddard's touring West Indians beat England at Lord's for the first time - and then go on to win the series 3-1 with further victories at Trent Bridge and the Oval ... The Calypso Rhythm Kings (with Lord Beginner) release a song called *Victory Test Match Calypso* ... 42-year-old Donald Peers from Ammanford in South Wales sings *Enjoy Yourself (It's Later Than You Think)* ... "My mom gave me a nickel to buy a pickle, but I didn't buy a pickle, I bought some choo'n gum" - 33-year-old Dean Martin from Ohio in the United States of America sings *Choo'n Gum* ... 31-year-old Florence May Chadwick swims across the English Channel in a new record time of 13 hours and 20 minutes ... 15-year-old schoolboy David Nobbs plays cricket at Marlborough, before joining his mother on a week long holiday in Frinton ... Families from the North head off for a day at Blackpool ... Children ride donkeys on the beach and enjoy *Wall's* ice-cream ... Nans wear rollers in their hair and smoke *Park Drive* cigarettes ... Grandads wear Fedora hats and inhale J&H Wilson Ltd's *S.P. No. 1* 'Celebrated Snuff' ... For the first time since the tournament began (in 1930), England's footballers take part in this year's FIFA World Cup in Brazil. 29-year-old Stan Mortensen (of Blackpool) and 32-year-old Wilf Mannion (of Middlesbrough) score for England in their opening game - a 2-0 victory over Chile. The next game ends in a humiliating defeat against the United States (1-0). A further defeat against Spain (1-0) sees England crash out of the tournament. Bert 'the cat' Williams, Alf Ramsey, John Aston, Billy Wright, Bill Eckersley, Eddie Bailey, Jimmy Dickinson, Laurie Hughes, Tom Finney (aka the 'Preston Plumber'), Stan Mortensen, Wilf Mannion, Jackie Milburn, Roy Bentley, Jimmy Mullen and 35-year-old Stanley 'wizard of dribble' Matthews - clutching a pair of new-fangled light-weight football boots that he's seen worn by the players of Brazil and

Uruguay - all return home disappointed ... 24-year-old inside-left Arthur Rowley leaves Fulham and joins Leicester City for £14,000 ... 29-year-old outside-left Charlie Mitten turns his back on Manchester Utd, and a wage of £8 a week, and joins Colombian club Santa Fe of Bogota - where he receives a staggering signing-on fee of £5,000, and a weekly wage of £40 ... "You're the end of the rainbow, my pot of gold. You're daddy's little girl, to have and hold" - Donald Peers sings *Daddy's Little Girl* ... "Mona Lisa, Mona Lisa, men have named you. You're so like the lady with the mystic smile. Is it only 'cause you're lonely they have blamed you, for that Mona Lisa strangeness in your smile?" - 31-year-old Nat 'King' Cole sings *Mona Lisa* ... 34-year-old Frank Sinatra appears for the first time in Britain - performing at the London Palladium, where he receives mixed reviews ... The Chiswick Palais features in the hit movie *Dance Hall* - the story of four factory girls looking for love: Eve (played by 19-year-old Natasha Parry), Mary (23-year-old Jane Hylton), Georgie (17-year-old Petula Clark) and Carole (18-year-old blonde sex-siren Diana Dors) ... "Andy Pandy's coming to play, la-la, la-la, lah-lah" - *Andy Pandy* makes his first appearance on television ... 24-year-old Princess Elizabeth and her husband Philip are proud parents of a second child - their newborn daughter is christened Anne Elizabeth Alice Louise ... BBC television transmits a 'live' broadcast from overseas - as 37-year-old Richard Dimbleby reports from Calais ... Three British soldiers are convicted of murdering an Egyptian watchman in the Suez Canal Zone - and sentenced to death. (45-year-old hangman Albert Pierrepoint carries out the executions) ... "There's a village, hidden deep in the valley, among the pine trees half forlorn. And there on a sunny morning, little Jimmy Brown was born. Bom-bom-bom, bom" - *Three Bells (The Jimmy Brown*

Song) by Les Compagnons de la Chanson is a popular choice on juke boxes ... The sun shines ... A bottle of lager beer in the Red Lion costs 1s/3d.

Autumn 1950... 'Serve yourself' at shops

Children return to school after the summer holidays ... Boys soak conkers in vinegar, or bake them in the oven, before taking part in conker 'battles' on the playground ... The BBC Home Service broadcasts the latest news on the wireless ... Eighty miners are killed in a colliery fire at Cresswell in Derbyshire ... Twenty-eight passengers and crew are killed when a *BEA* Vickers *Viking* aeroplane crashes in heavy fog at London Airport ... 39-year-old Frank Griffin murders Jane Edge (aged 74) at the Queen's Head pub at Ketley in Shropshire ... Edith Morrell (aged 81) dies in Eastbourne and Dr. John Bodkin Adams inherits her Rolls-Royce motorcar ... 11-year-old schoolboy John Cleese from Weston-super-Mare makes his friends laugh by performing a funny walk ... 50-year-old Harry Roy (aka the King of 'Hot-Cha') and his Band perform the popular song *He'd Have To Get Out And Get Under* ... 31-year-old Teddy Johnson from Surbiton sings *Beloved Be Faithful* ("... Beloved, be true. While I am away dear, I'll trust in you") ... 'At Sainsbury's Self-service shopping is EASY and QUICK' - *J. Sainsbury* opens a new-fangled 'self-service' supermarket at Croydon ... Housewives walk the aisles popping goods into a wire basket before joining the queue to pay at the check-out ... 29-year-old Peter Dimmock reports on sporting events for the BBC ... 30-year-old cyclist Reg Harris (of the *Raleigh* team) is voted the Sports Journalists' Association's 'Sportsman of the Year' ... 27-year-old footballer 'Terrible' Trevor Ford leaves Aston Villa and joins Sunderland for a new record transfer fee of £30,000 ... 24-year-old inside-left Arthur Rowley scores twice as Leicester City beat Hull City 1-3 in Division Two ... Amateur motorbike racer Frank Sheene and his wife Iris are proud parents of Barry - their new baby boy ... "De-

de-de-der, de-der. De-de-de-der, de-der." - *The Harry Lime Theme* (an instrumental tune from the film *The Third Man*) by Anton Karas is a popular gramophone record ... 42-year-old Gene Autry sings *Have I Told You Lately That I Love You* ("... could I tell you once again somehow") ... World famous singer and entertainer Al Jolson dies aged 64 in San Fransico ... Back in England - 54-year-old King George VI opens the newly restored House of Commons Chamber at Westminster ... MPs return to the green leather benches after sitting in the House of Lords since 1941 - when the Commons was destroyed by German bombs ... 44-year-old Hugh Gaitskell takes over as Chancellor of the Exchequer from Sir Stafford Cripps ... The rationing of soap comes to an end, but other goods such as meat, sugar and tea are still 'on the ration' ... Labour prime-minister Clement Attlee faces criticism for the prolonged period of austerity that's existed since the war ... The number of new houses being built each year has fallen - and many families are still without a home of their own ... 28-year-old Philip Larkin from Coventry takes up a new role as librarian at Queen's University in Belfast ... 25-year-old Anthony Wedgwood Benn is elected as a Labour MP at a by-election in Bristol ... 'A Story of Twelve Men as Their Women Never Knew Them...' - *Twelve O'Clock High*, starring 34-year-old Gregory Peck, is now showing at cinemas ... Comedians Max Miller, Frankie Howerd and 42-year-old Max Wall appear at the Royal Variety Show ... 48-year-old Jack Train returns to the wireless as Colonel Chinstrap in *The Great Gilhooly* ... "Oh, good show!" - 39-year-old actor Terry-Thomas returns to the TV in the hugely popular comedy *How Do You View* - 45-year-old Leslie Mitchell, 31-year-old Peter Butterworth and 32-year-old Avril Angers also feature in the show ... "Irene goodnight, Irene goodnight, goodnight Irene, goodnight Irene, I'll see you in my dreams" - 34-year-old Frank Sinatra sings *Goodnight Irene* ... Hundreds of thousands of men and boys pack the terraces of football grounds on Saturday afternoons ... 30-year-old winger Les Medley scores a hat-trick as Arthur Rowe's newly promoted Tottenham Hotspur (playing with a new, fast-moving, 'give-and-go' style) thrash Newcastle Utd 7-0 in front of 70,336 at White Hart Lane ... Tom Whittaker's Arsenal beat Matt Busby's Manchester Utd 3-0 in front of 66,157 at Highbury ... 20-year-old Roy Sproson makes his debut for Third Division (South) team Port Vale in a 1-1 draw away at Gillingham ... 25-year-old Nat Lofthouse scores twice on his debut for wing commander Winterbottom's international England team in a 2-2 draw with Yugoslavia at Highbury. (38-year-old full-back Leslie Compton of Arsenal scores an own goal in the same match) ... 'National Savings for Prosperity' - families are encouraged to buy National Savings stamps ... Motorcars are becoming slightly more affordable ... Approximately 500,000 cars have been produced this year - a record high figure ... A Morris *Minor Tourer* costs £382 (including taxes) and has a top speed of 64 mph ... *Dinky Toys* introduce a die-cast model (1:45 scale) of the Morris *Oxford* motorcar ... Prize money of £100,000 is paid out to one lucky 'treble chance' winner on the football pools ... 'The death of an angry old man' - George Bernard Shaw dies aged 94 in Hertfordshire ... Edward Cavendish, the Duke of Devonshire, dies of a heart attack aged 55 in Eastbourne ... Dr. John Bodkin Adams signs the Duke's death certificate ... A pint of pale ale in the Red Lion costs 1s/3d.

Christmas 1950... Pierrepoint hangs a friend

It's the coldest December for sixty years ... Road and rail services are affected by widespread snow and ice ... 10-year-old David Lovell and his friends 'lark about' on the frozen Birmingham and Fazeley Canal ... Albert Pierrepoint hangs a personal acquaintance at Strangeways - the 45-year-old executioner terminates the life of 37-year-old convicted murderer James Corbitt in just ten seconds ... Annabelle Kilgour dies in Eastbourne aged 89 and Dr. John Bodkin Adams inherits a large amount of money ... "If you want to, do the Mambo. Do the Mambo, Mambo Jambo" - *Mambo Jambo/ Mambo No. 5* by Perez Prado is a top selling 78 rpm gramophone disc ... Arthur Rowe's top-of-the-table ('give-and-go') Tottenham Hotspur football team beat Arsenal 1-0 at White Hart Lane. 25-year-old inside-forward Eddie Bailey scores the goal for Spurs and 31-year-old wing-half Bill Nicholson is man-of-the-match ... David Jack's Middlesbrough are close behind Spurs in Division One - separated only by goal average ... Newcastle Utd's manager George Martin leaves the club to take over at Aston Villa ... Schoolboys become excited as Christmas approaches ... A new table-top football game called *Subbuteo* is available by mail-order ... A zero-gauge clockwork train set costs seven shillings from *Woolworths* ... A hand-held 'Catch-It' ball game is 1s/9d ... 11-year-old schoolboy Ricky Tomlinson from Liverpool sits at home in an armchair, reading a book ... 21-year-old actress Jean Simmons from London marries Hollywood film star Stewart Granger ... "You used to be in silent pictures. You used to be big" - *Sunset Boulevard*, starring 51-year-old Gloria Swanson as Norma Desmond, is now showing at cinemas ... 58-year-old comedian Jimmy James stars in *Over The Garden Wall* ... 30-

year-old Freddie Brown leads England's cricketers on tour down-under. Trevor Bailey takes 3 for 28 and Alec Bedser takes 4 for 45 but England lose the first Test Match in Brisbane ... Back in England - viewers of BBC television are treated to a Laurel and Hardy film on Boxing Day ... "I taut I taw a puddy cat a-creeping up on me. I did! I taw a puddy cat, as plain as he could be" - 42-year-old Mel Blanc sings *I Taut I Taw A Puddy Cat* ... 42-year-old Donald Peers sings *Rudolph The Red Nosed Reindeer* ("… had a very shiny nose") ... 47-year-old Bing Crosby has the best selling record (yet again) at Christmas with the ever popular *White Christmas* ... 219 million tonnes of coal have been mined this year ... Lord Hyndley of the National Coal Board introduces a Plan for Coal - which aims to raise production to 250 million tonnes by the year 1970 ... The average weekly wage in Britain has risen slightly to £7/10s but times are hard and rationing remains in place ... 38-year-old architect Hugh Casson oversees the construction of a new national exhibition on the South Bank of the River Thames in London ... Clement Attlee's Labour government hopes the ambitious project will boost the morale of the nation.

New Year 1951... Dennis the Menace

Heavy snow falls across much of the country ... Advertisements say, 'Drink *Ovaltine* for Health - delicious hot or cold' ... 40-year-old convicted murderer Frank Griffin is hanged by the neck until dead at Shrewsbury ... "Come along with me to Paradise. I've a dreamboat that takes me there" - popular singer Donald Peers performs *Me And My Imagination* ... 18-year-old Petula Clark from Epsom sings *Tennessee Waltz* ... 18-year-old actress Elizabeth Taylor divorces Nick Hilton in the United States - the two had been married for just eight months ... 57-year-old Stuart Hibberd announces the news on BBC radio ... Trouble is brewing in Persia - a mass demonstration is held in Tehran with locals demanding the nationalisation of the Anglo-Iranian Oil Company ... Back in England - schools re-open after the Christmas break ... Classes of children listen to (and participate in) *Music and Movement* on BBC radio ... Boys wear grey flannel shorts with elasticated 'snake' belts and play British Bulldog on the playground ... Dennis the Menace makes his first appearance in *The Beano* comic ... 29-year-old Dirk Bogarde stars at cinemas in *The Woman In Question* ... 52-year-old Gracie Fields hosts her own show on Radio Luxembourg ... 34-year-old Len Hutton scores 79 and Reg Simpson is 156 not out as Freddie Brown's England cricket team win a Test Match against Australia for the first time in twelve years. It's a consolation victory only, as Lindsay Hassett's Aussies clinch the Ashes series 4-1. R T Simpson, C Washbrook, D S R Sheppard, T G Evans (wk), D C S Compton, J G Dewes, L Hutton, W G A Parkhouse, A J W McIntyre, F R Brown (cpt), T E Bailey, D B Close, A V Bedser, D V P Wright, R Tattersall and J J Warr are all downcast by another Ashes defeat - Australia have held the trophy since 1934

... "While I was walkin' down the beach one bright and sunny day, I saw a great big wooden box a-floatin' in the bay" - *The Thing* by 46-year-old Phil Harris is a top selling gramophone record ... *Woolworths* sell copies of sheet music for sixpence ... *The Petite Waltz (La Petite Valse)* is a popular tune of the day ... For the fifth successive year - the final of the World's Professional Snooker Championship is contested by Walter Donaldson from Edinburgh and Fred Davis from Chesterfield - Davis wins by 58 frames to 39 at the Tower Circus in Blackpool ... 35-year-old football star Stanley 'wizard of dribble' Matthews wears new-fangled light-weight boots as his team Blackpool beat Chelsea 0-2 at Stamford Bridge ... 31-year-old full-back Alf Ramsey scores a penalty as league-leaders Tottenham Hotspur beat Aston Villa 3-2 at White Hart Lane ... 23-year-old centre-half Malcolm Allison transfers from Charlton Athletic to West Ham Utd ... 59-year-old George Kay steps down as Liverpool's manager ... 29-year-old James Inglis murders 50-year-old prostitute Alice Morgan in Hull ... Labour prime-minister Clement Attlee finally abandons the costly groundnut scheme at Tanganyika in Africa - after wasting tax-payers money for four years ... 'Cars of Extremely Original Design, announced from the Dagenham factory' - Ford introduce two new medium sized cars: the 4-cylinder *Consul* and the 6-cylinder *Zephyr.* Both models have a front bench seat, wing mirrors and MacPherson strut independent front suspension ... 'Buy yourself some Spangles - the wonderful new fruity sweets!' - Packets of *Spangles* are now on sale for 3d - and just one point off the ration allocation! ... A pack of twenty *Woodbines* costs 2s/9d ... A nice cup of tea at the *J. Lyons & Co* teashop on Broadgate in Coventry is tuppence.

Spring 1951... Come on, you Spurs!

26-year-old footballer Len Duquemin scores a hat-trick as Tottenham Hotspur thrash West Bromwich Albion 5-0 in front of 45,353 spectators at White Hart Lane - Spurs stay top of Division One ... 11-year-old schoolboy footballer Jimmy 'Greavsie' Greaves from Manor Park in London scores goals in the park ... 24-year-old Arthur Rowley scores twice as Leicester City beat Luton Town 3-1 in front of 23,560 spectators at Filbert Street in Division Two ... The weather is cold, grey and wet *My Heart Cries For You* ("... sighs for you, dies for you") by 24-year-old American singer Guy Mitchell is the best selling gramophone record ... MPs urge the 68-year-old Labour prime-minister Clement Attlee to take action on the deepening oil crisis in Iran - Britain's access to fuel is under threat ... Standard grade petrol rises in price at the pumps - it's now 3s/5d a gallon ... 17-year-old Henry Cooper is called up for national service in the British Army ... 40-year-old civil servant Guy Burgess and 28-year-old civil servant Donald MacLean suddenly go missing. There's speculation that McLean was about to be interrogated by MI6 over allegations of spying for the Soviet Union - and may have fled the country. (In five years time, the government will acknowledge publically that both men were working for the KGB - and have defected to the USSR to evade arrest) ... *Crazy People* featuring 33-year-old Spike Milligan is a great new radio comedy ... The economy continues to flounder and Clement Attlee's Labour government is coming under more and more pressure ... 45-year-old Chancellor of the Exchequer Hugh Gaitskell delivers his first Budget ... The standard rate of income tax is increased from nine shillings in the pound to 9s/6d in the pound ... New prescription charges for false teeth and spectacles are announced

... 53-year-old Aneurin Bevan and 35-year-old Harold Wilson resign from the Cabinet in protest ... 63-year-old Herbert Morrison becomes Foreign Secretary after the recent death of Labour stalwart, Ernest Bevin ... 40-year-old Don Welsh is appointed manager of Liverpool Football Club after the retirement of George Kay ... "Just wear a red silken stocking and you'll get the fellas flocking" - 30-year-old Betty Driver from Leicester sings *Red Silken Stockings* with Sid Phillips and his Band ... "Be my love, for no one else can end this yearning, this need that you, and you alone, create" - 30-year-old Mario Lanza sings *Be My Love* ... Cambridge win the Boat Race for a fifth consecutive year ... *Nickel Coin* (ridden by John Bullock) wins the Grand National at Aintree at odds of forty to one ... *Royal Tan* is second. *Derrinstown* is third ... 24-year-old footballer Jackie Sewell leaves Notts County and joins Eric Taylor's Sheffield Wednesday for a new record transfer fee of £34,500 ... Swindon Town (of the Third Division - South) install new-fangled floodlights at their ground and play a 'friendly' match against Bristol City on a Monday night ... The new 'give-and-go' style of play used by Arthur Rowe's First Division Tottenham Hotspur has been successful; a 3-1 victory over Liverpool (with 29-year-old Pete Murphy scoring twice) secures the title for Spurs! Ted Ditchburn, Alf Ramsey, Eddie Baily, Ron Burgess, Harry Clarke, Len Duquemin, Sonny Walters, Les Medley and 32-year-old Bill Nicholson have all been outstanding ... 36-year-old Stanley 'wizard of dribble' Matthews is on the losing team in the FA Cup final as Newcastle Utd beat Blackpool 2-0. Both goals are scored by 26-year-old Jackie Milburn. A ticket for the standing enclosure at the Empire Stadium costs three shillings. A ticket for a North Terrace seat (uncovered) is 10s/6d ... 29-year-old Tom Finney (aka the 'Preston Plumber') scores for England in a 2-3 defeat against Scotland at Wembley ... 19-year-old blonde sex-siren Diana Dors (37-24-35) stars in *Worm's Eye View* at cinemas ... "She gets too hungry for dinner at eight. She likes the theatre and never comes late. She never bothers with people she'd hate. That's why, the lady is a tramp" - 49-year-old Ted Heath and his Music perform *The Lady Is A Tramp* ... Fathers and sons visit car-showrooms and dream of owning the latest, shiny model ... The new Ford *Consul* costs £710 (including taxes), has a top speed of 71 mph and accelerates from 0-60 mph in 28.3 seconds ... The stylish new *Zephyr Six* costs £812 (including taxes), has a top speed of 80 mph and accelerates from 0-60 mph in 20.2 seconds ... 'A tonic for the nation'- against a back drop of food rationing and rising taxes, 55-year-old King George VI opens the Festival of Britain on the South Bank of the River Thames in London. It's a celebration of industry, arts, science and design ... Up in Manchester, 29-year-old convicted murderer James Inglis is hanged by the neck until dead at Strangeways. (46-year-old hangman Albert Pierrepoint carries out the execution in just seven seconds).

Summer 1951 ... Festival of Britain

'The shape of things to come' - Eight-million people flock to see the 'Skylon' and the 'Dome of Discovery' at the Festival of Britain on the South Bank of the River Thames ... Schoolboys queue for a ride on the miniature railway around the Festival Pleasure Gardens ... 46-year-old Harry Perryman wins the annual *News of the World* darts tournament at Earls Court in London ... 11-year-old schoolboy Sid Waddell from Alnwick in Northumberland sits at home reading poetry ... *What's My Line?* makes its debut on BBC television ... 44-year-old Gilbert Harding is chairman for the first show - then 28-year-old Eamonn Andrews takes over ... '208 is Great!' - Radio Luxembourg moves from the long wave frequency to medium wave - and increases the number of listeners ... "When you are in love, it's the loveliest night of the year. Stars twinkle above, and you can almost touch them from here" - 30-year-old Mario Lanza sings *The Loveliest Night Of The Year* ... "If ever the devil was born without a pair of horns, it was you Jezebel, it was you" - 38-year-old Frankie Laine sings *Jezebel* ... 81-year-old entertainer George Robey (aka the Prime Minister of Mirth) appears in a Gala Performance at the London Palladium - and receives rapturous applause for his rendition of *If You Were The Only Girl In The World* ... Cricketers 34-year-old Len Hutton and 33-year-old Jack Ikin stride out together to open the batting for England against South Africa at Trent Bridge. Reg Simpson scores 137 runs and Denis Compton knocks 112, but England lose the match. Freddie Brown's England team recover from the defeat with victories at Lord's, Old Trafford and the Oval - and win the series 3-1 ... Promising schoolboy cricketer Geoffrey Boycott (aged 10) joins Ackworth Cricket Club in Yorkshire ... 34-year-old golfer Max

Faulkner from Bexhill-on-Sea wins the British Open at Royal Portrush ... 27-year-old Ian Appleyard wins the RAC Rally in a Jaguar *XK120* motorcar - crossing the finish line in Bournemouth, after travelling a route of approximately 1,800 miles ... 40-year-old Reg Parnell from Derby finishes sixth in the British Grand Prix at Silverstone driving a racing green BRM ... The latest Humber *Super Snipe* motorcar (with traditional running boards on each side) costs £1,471, has a top speed of 82 mph and can reach 60 mph in 19.1 seconds ... 39-year-old senior civil servant Kim Philby is forced to resign from MI6 amidst rumours that he was the 'third man' in the Burgess MacLean spy ring - and that he tipped the two men off before their mysterious disappearance ... 19-year-old Herbert Leonard Mills murders 48-year-old Mabel Tattershaw in Lincoln ... 'The men who broke the bank - and lost the cargo!' - *The Lavender Hill Mob*, starring 37-year-old Alec Guinness and 60-year-old Stanley Holloway, is now showing at cinemas ... "Spaceships Away!" - *The Adventures of Dan Dare* is on Radio Luxembourg ... Steam locomotives thunder through Leamington Spa railway station as a small 4-year-old boy called Peter Waterman looks on in awe ... A *Rovex* train set (with the 'Princess Elizabeth' locomotive) costs £2/16s/6d from *Marks & Spencer* ... 23-year-old bikini clad Kiki Hakansson from Sweden wins the first Miss World title at the Lyceum in London - 32-year-old Eric Morley hosts the contest ... 27-year-old Anne Shelton from Dulwich performs her own version of the hit song *The Loveliest Night Of The Year* ... 36-year-old Dorothy Squires from Pontyberem sings *My Resistance Is Low* ... 51-year-old Victor Silvester and his Ballroom Orchestra perform *The Minute Waltz* ... 23-year-old boxer Randolph Turpin from Warwickshire defeats Sugar Ray Robinson to become world middle-weight champion ... 32-year-old convicted murderer John Dand is hanged by the neck until dead at Strangeways. (Dand had robbed and killed an elderly man in York in January) ... The old electric powered trolley-buses in Birmingham are replaced by diesel vehicles ... 27-year-old centre-forward Jackie Milburn scores a hat-trick as Newcastle Utd beat Stoke City 6-0 on the opening day of the new football season ... 32-year-old centre-forward Jack 'cannonball' Rowley scores a hat-trick for Manchester Utd in a 3-3 draw against West Bromwich Albion (and follows up four days later with another hat-trick against Middlesbrough) ... 28-year-old Con Martin switches from left-back to goalkeeper for Aston Villa - and keeps the green goalie jersey for most of the season ... 25-year-old inside-left Arthur 'dead shot' Rowley bags a hat-trick for Leicester City in a 4-0 victory over Birmingham City in Division Two ... Labour prime-minister Clement Attlee and his Foreign Secretary Herbert Morrison meet to discuss the on-going oil crisis in Persia. The two men decide to impose economic sanctions on Iran ... British military resources are being stretched to the limit - troops have now been active in Korea for twelve-months as part of a United Nations coalition force ... Additional soldiers are sent to the Suez Canal Zone of Egypt to deal with the rising tide of protest against British imperialism ... Back in England - Winston Churchill's opposition Conservative party heaps even more pressure on Clement Attlee's government; claiming that the continuation of food rationing plus recent income tax rises and the failure to build sufficient quantities of new houses are all symptoms of a failing socialist system ... A general election is called and campaigning gets underway ... Posters in support of the Tories declare, 'They Don't Catch ME Again! I'm voting CONSERVATIVE!' ... There's a flurry of activity on football's transfer market ... 26-year-old footballer

'Tiny' Ernie Taylor moves from Newcastle Utd to Blackpool for £27,000 ... 31-year-old centre-forward Harry Catterick leaves Second Division Everton and joins Third Division (North) Crewe Alexandra ... 30-year-old Manchester Utd star Charlie Mitten (aka 'the Bogota Bandit') returns to England from Colombia and is banned from playing football for six months.

Autumn 1951... Churchill back at Number 10

The Festival of Britain ends ... Workmen move in to clear the site ... People go to the polls and vote in the general election ... 76-year-old Winston Churchill defeats Clement Attlee and the Conservatives are back in power. (Conservatives: 321 seats, Labour: 295 seats, Liberals: 6 seats) ... 41-year-old Labour candidate Barbara Castle retains her seat in Blackburn East ... 26-year-old Conservative candidate Margaret Hilda Roberts loses for a second time in Dartford ... 48-year-old Richard Austen 'Rab' Butler is the new Chancellor of the Exchequer ... 54-year-old Anthony Eden is Foreign Secretary ... 57-year-old Harold Macmillan is Minister for Housing ... Churchill's new government makes a commitment to increase national output, halt the rising cost of living, preserve social services and to build 300,000 new houses a year ... An ailing 55-year-old King George VI undergoes an operation to remove his left lung ... "They try to tell us we're too young, too young to really be in love" - 29-year-old Jimmy Young from Cinderford sings *Too Young* ... "Come on-a-my house, my house. I'm gonna give you candy" - 30-year-old Kay Starr sings *Come On-A-My House* ... 'M.G.M.'s Happy-Go-Lucky Technicolor Musical' - *Rich, Young and Pretty* is now showing at cinemas - starring 22-year-old Jane Powell ... A new production of the play *Zip Goes A Million* opens at the Palace Theatre in London - starring 47-year-old entertainer George Formby ... 28-year-old Eamonn Andrews introduces *Sports Parade* on BBC radio's Light Programme ... Ex-footballer 60-year-old Charles Buchan previews the upcoming football ties each Saturday afternoon ... Attendances at matches are at a record high ... 51,075 spectators turn out for a Second Division local derby between Sheffield Utd and Sheffield Wednesday at

Bramall Lane - Utd win the game 7-3 ... More than 14,000 spectators turn out for a Third Division (South) match between Port Vale and Torquay Utd - and see 20-year-old Roy Sproson score a goal for 'Vale' in a 2-2 draw ... Popular double-act Nervo and Knox appear in front of 51-year-old Queen Elizabeth and 21-year-old Princess Margaret at the Victoria Palace Theatre ... King George VI remains at home at Buckingham Palace, recovering from his recent operation ... 53-year-old Walter Pidgeon and 29-year-old Margaret Leighton star in *Calling Bulldog Drummond* at cinemas ... "But..." *Belle Belle My Liberty Belle* ("... I'm still in love with you") by 24-year-old Guy Mitchell from Detroit is a popular gramophone record ... *How D'ya Like Your Eggs In The Morning?* ("... I like mine with a kiss") by Dean Martin and Helen O'Connell is also popular ... 29-year-old George Blake is still being held prisoner by communists in North Korea - the MI6 officer has been in captivity for the past twelve months ... Back in England - black and white 'zebra' road crossings for pedestrians are introduced on busy roads ... A new television transmitter opens at Holme Moss and BBC is now available to people in the North ... "Oh, good show!" - 40-year-old actor Terry-Thomas returns in a new series of the popular comedy *How Do You View* ... 11-year-old schoolboy John Lennon from Liverpool learns to play guitar ... 10-year-old schoolboy David Lovell from Birmingham passes his 11-Plus examination and gains entry to Waverley Grammar School in Small Heath ... 29-year-old Birmingham City goalkeeper Gil Merrick makes his debut for wing commander Winterbottom's England football team in a 2-0 victory over Northern Ireland at Villa Park. (26-year-old Nat Lofthouse scores both goals) ... 45,389 spectators turn out to watch Bill Murray's Sunderland beat Bob Jackson's Portsmouth 3-1 at Roker Park in a mid-table clash. Sunderland's star player 28-year-old Ivor Broadis leaves the club to join Les McDowall's struggling Manchester City for £25,000 ... 25-year-old Billy Foulkes leaves Third Division (North) team Chester and joins Stan Seymour's First Division Newcastle Utd for £11,500 ... Tom Whittaker's Arsenal beat Hapoel Tel Aviv 6-1 under the new floodlights at Highbury ... Matt Busby's Manchester Utd move to the top of Division One with a 2-5 victory over Aston Villa. (32-year-old inside-forward Stan Pearson and 33-year-old centre-forward Jack 'cannonball' Rowley both score twice) ... The Five Smith Brothers perform their popular song *In The Cool Cool Cool Of The Evening* ("... tell 'em I'll be there") ... The Delta Rhythm Boys sing *Blow Out The Candle* ... The exciting new Austin *A30* motorcar (with a modern 'chassis-less' design) is shown at Earls Court - it's a small family car that'll be a competitor to the hugely popular Morris *Minor* ... *Dinky Toys* introduce a die cast model (1:45 scale) of the Hillman *Minx* ... 'New Chocolate Thrill!' - the exotic tasting *Bounty* bar is launched.

Christmas 1951... We want Muffin, Muffin the mule

Twenty-three people are killed at Chatham in Kent when a bus ploughs into a company of marine cadets ... Five British soldiers are killed in the Suez Canal Zone of Egypt - prompting the withdrawal of troops from the region ... Back in England - thousands of people enjoy a night out at the cinema ... 19-year-old Elizabeth Taylor from London stars alongside 31-year-old Montgomery Clift in *A Place in the Sun* ... 38-year-old Vivien Leigh stars alongside 27-year-old Marlon Brando in *A Streetcar Named Desire* ... 39-year-old Gene Kelly stars in *An American in Paris* ... 20-year-old blonde sex-siren Diana Dors (37-24-35) stars in *Lady Godiva Rides Again* ... Winston Churchill's new Conservative government makes a commitment to keep the coal industry in state ownership - 226 million tonnes have been mined this year - the highest level of output for eleven years ... The steel industry is to be re-privatised by means of repealing the previous Labour government's Iron and Steel Act ... 49-year-old Chancellor of the Exchequer Richard Austen 'Rab' Butler is working hard at Number 11 Downing Street, formulating his plan to take Britain out of austerity ... 62-year-old Education Secretary Florence Horsbrugh announces that GCE Ordinary and Advanced Level examinations are to be introduced in schools ... In other news, 19-year-old convicted murderer Herbert Leonard Mills is hanged by the neck until dead at Lincoln ... "Come on along and listen to, the lullaby of Broadway" - 27-year-old Doris Day sings *Lullaby Of Broadway* - and 16-year-old schoolboy David Nobbs develops his first teenage crush ... All across the country, men drink beer, smoke cigarettes and talk about football in pubs ... *Charles Buchan's Football Monthly* is on sale at newsagents for 1s/6d ... 25-year-old inside-left Arthur 'dead shot'

Rowley bags a hat-trick for Leicester City in a 4-0 victory over Queens Park Rangers in Division Two ... Manchester Utd manager Matt Busby sells 31-year-old Charlie Mitten (aka 'the Bogota Bandit') to Fulham for £22,000 ... "They call it vanity, because I'd rather be, all by myself instead of laughing with the crowd" - 30-year-old Jimmy Young from Cinderford sings *Vanity* ... 39-year-old Perry Como sings *It's Beginning To Look A Lot Like Christmas* ("... toys in ev'ry store") ... Excited children look forward to Christmas Day ... "We want Muffin, Muffin the Mule" - a push-along Muffin the Mule is the best selling toy this year ... A *Woolworths* cowboy set costing 1s/9d is also popular ... "I'm dreaming of a white Christmas. Just like the ones I used to know. Where the treetops glisten, and children listen, to hear sleigh bells in the snow" - for the fifth consecutive year, *White Christmas* by Bing Crosby is the best selling gramophone record ... Football fans pack onto the terraces and twirl wooden rattles urging on their favourite players ... 33-year-old centre-forward Jack 'cannonball' Rowley and 22-year-old outside-left Ernie Bond score goals in both matches as Matt Busby's Manchester Utd beat Fulham 3-2 at Old Trafford on Christmas Day and then draw 3-3 at Craven Cottage on Boxing Day ... Utd continue to lead the way in Division One ... Bob Jackson's Portsmouth are second ... Jackie Milburn and George Robledo are on the score-sheet as Newcastle Utd beat Sunderland 1-4 at Roker Park on Christmas Day ... 33-year-old Wilf Mannion lines up for Middlesbrough in a 3-1 defeat against Spurs ... "Silent night, holy night. All is calm, all is bright" - 30-year-old Mario Lanza sings *Silent Night* ... "Hey good lookin'. what you got cookin'? Hows about cookin' something up with me?" - 38-year-old Frankie Laine and 33-year-old Jo Stafford duet on *Hey Good Lookin'* ... 26-year-old Margaret Hilda Roberts marries 36-year-old businessman Denis Thatcher in London ... Motoring technology moves on apace ... The wonderful new Austin *A30* family motorcar has modern 'trafficators' fitted as standard ... The latest Vauxhall *Wyvern* has a gadget to open the boot lid from inside the car ... The weather turns cold ... Mothers look after their poorly children ... Catarrh and bronchitis can be treated with *Lantigen 'B'* - available at chemists for 1 guinea a bottle (plus 4s/8d purchase tax) ... *Lucozade* costs 2s/6d a bottle (plus a 3d returnable deposit).

New Year 1952...
The King is dead. Long live the Queen

'Broadcast on 208 metres medium wave' - 26-year-old disc jockey Peter Murray spins discs on Radio Luxembourg ... 10-year-old schoolboy Ed 'Stewpot' Stewart from Exmouth in Devon sits at home listening to the wireless ... "Unforgettable, that's what you are" - *Unforgettable* by 32-year-old Nat 'King' Cole is a hit song ... The upbeat instrumental *Down Yonder* performed by 31-year-old pianist Del Wood is also popular ... A new radio comedy called *The Goon Show* is broadcast on the BBC Home Service - featuring 26-year-old Peter Sellers, 30-year-old Harry Secombe, 30-year-old Michael Bentine and 33-year-old Spike Milligan ... 77-year-old prime-minister Winston Churchill travels to America on the *Queen Mary* liner - he meets president Harry S. Truman who tells Churchill, "Great Britain and the Commonwealth and the United States are the closest of friends and you and I want to keep it that way." ... 49-year-old Chancellor of the Exchequer Richard Austen 'Rab' Butler is at home in Number 11 Downing Street - working hard, formulating his plan to take Britain out of austerity ... Attendances at football matches remain at a record high ... 65,327 spectators turn out for a (Second Division) local derby between Sheffield Wednesday and Sheffield Utd at Hillsborough - Utd win 1-3 ... 56,122 spectators turn out for a (First Division) local derby between Manchester Utd and Manchester City at Old Trafford - it's a 1-1 draw ... John Snagge speaks on the radio ... "This is London. It is with the greatest sorrow that we make the following announcement. It was announced from Sandringham at ten forty-five today February the sixth 1952, that the King, who retired to rest last night in his usual health, passed peacefully away in his sleep early this morning" - The nation mourns as King George VI dies aged 56 ... The sad news is given to young Princess Elizabeth during a tour of Kenya with her husband Philip. Elizabeth becomes Queen at the age of 25 ... Back in England - children's entertainer Harry Corbett introduces his puppets Sooty and Sweep on television ... 37-year-old Captain Kurt Carlsen remains on board his sinking ship near Falmouth for twelve days in a forlorn attempt to save the vessel ... "Talk to her please, Mr. Sun. Speak to her, Mr. Rainbow" - 25-year-old angst-ridden Johnnie Ray sings *Please Mr. Sun* ... 43-year-old Donald Peers sings *There's Always Room At Our House* ... 20-year-old actress Elizabeth Taylor marries 39-year-old actor Michael Wilding in London - it's Taylor's second marriage ... "What are we gonna do, Charlie?" - 44-year-old Katharine Hepburn and 52-year-old Humphrey Bogart star in *The African Queen* at cinemas ... 42-year-old James Mason appears in *The Desert Fox* ... 43-year-old Ian Fleming begins writing stories about a fictional secret agent called James Bond ... 32-year-old footballer Tommy Lawton leaves Second Division Notts County and joins Brentford (also of the Second Division) as player-manager ... "Why don't you hurry, hurry, hurry home?" - 34-year-old Jo Stafford sings *Shrimp Boats (A-Comin' - There's Dancin' Tonight)* ... 25-year-old Lita Roza from Liverpool sings *Lullaby Of Broadway* with Ted Heath and his Music ... Ellen Sutton sings *I Wanna Say Hello!* and she's accompanied by Sir Hubert Pimm on piano ... Matt Busby's Manchester Utd remain top of Division One with a 0-3 victory over Derby County at the Baseball Ground ... Motoring technology moves on apace ... The wonderful new Austin *A30* family motorcar has a top speed of 67 mph and can reach 60 mph in 42.3 seconds ... Men enjoy a night at their 'local' ... Pub opening hours in England are strictly: Monday to

Saturday 11.00 a.m. to 2.40 p.m. and 5.00 p.m. to 10.30 p.m. Sundays and public holidays 12.00 noon to 2.00 p.m. and 7.00 p.m. to 10.00 p.m. ... A pint of best bitter in the Red Lion costs 1s/7d.

Spring 1952... The Goons on the wireless

Heavy snow descends on Britain - disrupting traffic on the roads and railways ... The Conservative government's health-minister, 58-year-old Harry Crookshank, announces that the National Registration identity card system is to be abolished ... 49-year-old Chancellor of the Exchequer Richard Austen 'Rab' Butler continues to work hard at Number 11 Downing Street - formulating his plan to take Britain out of austerity ... Wing commander Winterbotton's England football team (captained by 28-year-old Billy Wright) gain a 1-2 victory over Scotland in front of 134,504 spectators at Hampden Park ... 11-year-old schoolboy Bobby Moore from Barking in Essex dreams that one day he'll be captain of the England football team ... 33-year-old centre-forward Jack 'cannonball' Rowley scores his twenty-fourth league goal of the season as Manchester Utd move three points clear at the top of Division One with a 1-2 victory over Sunderland at Roker Park ... The first edition of the *New Musical Express* is published with an array of jazz musicians pictured on the front cover ... *There's A Pawnshop On A Corner In Pittsburgh Pennsylvania* by Bill Johnson with Ted Heath and his Music is a popular song of the day ... *Tell Me Why* ("... when we danced until three, tell me why, why my heart couldn't see") by The Four Aces is also popular ... 25-year-old footballer Arthur 'dead shot' Rowley scores twice as Leicester City beat West Ham Utd 3-1 in Division Two ... 38-year-old Fred Davis wins snooker's World Professional Match Play Championship (his fourth world title in five years) by beating Walter Donaldson in the final at the Tower Circus in Blackpool ... "You've been listening to the Goon Show, a recorded programme featuring Peter Sellers, Harry Secombe, Michael Bentine and Spike

Milligan; with the Ray Ellington Quartet, Max Geldray and the Stargazers" - *The Goon Show* has beome hugely popular and is enjoyed by millions of radio listeners on Tuesday evenings at 10 p.m. ... Chancellor of the Exchequer Richard Austen 'Rab' Butler delivers his first Budget for Churchill's Conservative government ... A gallon of petrol goes up from 3s/2d to 4s/2d ... Tax on car ownership goes up from £10 a year to £12 ... The car manufacturing industry is in growth - more than 600,000 vehicles have been produced in the last twelve months ... The Morris motor company (producer of the popular *Minor* model) and the Austin motor company (producer of the popular *A30*) come together to form the British Motor Corporation ... Jo Stafford from California sings *A-Round The Corner* ("... Ooh, ooh. Beneath the berry tree. A-long the footpath, behind the bush, looking for Henry Lee") ... Tony Martin from San Francisco sings *At Last! At Last!* ("... you're in my arms, you're in my arms where you should be") ... 47-year-old George Formby from Wigan survives a heart attack and spends nine weeks recovering in hospital before resting at his home in Lytham St Annes ... 38-year-old actress Vivien Leigh wins an Oscar for her role in *A Streetcar Named Desire* ... The racehorse *Teal* wins the Grand National at odds of one-hundred to seven ... Oxford beat Cambridge in the Boat Race for the first time in six years ... *Housewives' Choice* is on BBC radio's Light Programme each morning at ten past nine ... "I'm rather worried about Jim" - a repeat of the previous afternoon's edition of *Mrs. Dale's Diary* is on at eleven o'clock ... Convicted murderers Edward Devlin and Alfred Burns are hanged by the neck until dead at Liverpool. (47-year-old hangman Albert Pierrepoint carries out both executions) ... Julia Bradnum dies in Eastbourne aged 85 and Dr. John Bodkin Adams inherits a large amount of money ... 23-year-old footballer Jimmy Hill leaves Brentford and joins Fulham ... 42-year-old Matt Busby leads Manchester Utd to the First Division title ... Utd thrash Arsenal 6-1 in front of 55,516 at Old Trafford in their final league game of the season - with 33-year-old Jack 'cannonball' Rowley bagging a hat-trick and 33-year-old Stan Pearson scoring twice. Utd players Johnny Berry, Allenby Chilton, Henry Cockburn, Johnny Downie, Stan Pearson (with twenty-two goals), Jack 'cannonball' Rowley (with thirty goals) and 33-year-old captain Johnny Carey have all been outstanding ... Bill Dodgin's Fulham and Andy Beattie's Huddersfield Town are relegated to Division Two ... Stan Seymour's Newcastle Utd win the FA Cup for the second year running. 'Hot-shot' striker George Robledo scores the only goal of the final tie, as 'The Magpies' beat Arsenal 1-0 at the Empire Stadium in Wembley. A ticket for the standing enclosure costs three shillings ... 26-year-old Nat Lofthouse scores twice as England beat Switzerland 0-3 in Zurich ... 21-year-old Frank Burgess strangles and kills 22-year-old Johanna Hallahan at the Elgin Court hotel in East Croydon ... "I went walking down by the river, feeling very sad inside" - angst-ridden Johnnie Ray sings *The Little White Cloud That Cried* ... "I'm in your spell and there's no cure, I'm lost for sure, 'cause you're a weaver of dreams and I'm in love with you" - Billy Eckstine sings *A Weaver Of Dreams* ... 19-year-old Maurice Micklewhite is called up for national service in the British Army ... 18-year-old twins Reginald and Ronald Kray are also called up - but the pair go 'absent without leave' and end up serving nine months in detention at Shepton Mallet ... 37-year-old comedian Norman Wisdom signs a £5,000 film contract with the Rank Organisation ... 32-year-old footballer Jesse Pye transfers from First Division Wolverhampton Wanderers to Second Division Luton Town for £5,000 ... *BOAC* operate the first commercial 'jet powered' aeroplane (a de Havilland *Comet*) on flights between London and Johannesburg ... The wonderful new Austin *A30* family motorcar is in showrooms priced at just £507 (including taxes) ... A new *Vespa* motor scooter is £127/15s/7d (including taxes) ... Advertisements for petrol declare, 'You can be sure of Shell!'

Summer 1952... Pay a bob for your prescription

The weather is mostly dull and wet, with a few drier days in July ... *Horizon* organise 'package' holidays to faraway sunshine resorts ... Palma de Mallorca is popular this year ... Back in England - Winston Churchill's Conservative government introduces a one shilling charge for NHS prescriptions ... 39-year-old war hero Alan Turing is convicted of a homosexual act and then forced to choose between a form of chemical castration or imprisonment as his punishment ... 45-year-old jockey Charlie Smirke rides *Tulyar* to victory in the Epsom Derby ... *Time Gentlemen, Please!* is now showing at cinemas - starring 41-year-old Thora Hird, 29-year-old Dora Bryan, 39-year-old Sid James and 52-year-old Raymond Lovell ... 'A Stick of Rock, Cock?' - saucy postcards by Donald McGill are in high demand at seaside shops ... 20-year-old Des O'Connor from Stepney in London works as a Redcoat at *Butlin's* holiday camp in Filey ... 25-year-old Alan Alan (aka the 'British Houdini') entertains crowds of holiday makers by performing daring escape routines, bound in a straitjacket and chains, whilst suspended high above the ground on a burning rope ... *The Bristol Queen* paddle steamer takes paying passengers on day-long cruises in the Bristol Channel ... The last tram journey is made on the streets of London ... Dozens die in floods after heavy rain at Lynmouth in Devon - where a smell of sulphur in the air leads to a conspiracy theory that the government has been conducting 'cloud seeding' experiments in an attempt to manipulate the weather ... 21-year-old Lonnie Donegan performs a solo guitar act during a jazz night at the Royal Albert Hall ... 25-year-old Guy Mitchell from Detroit has a hit record with *Feet Up!* ("... pat him on the po-po. Let's hear him laugh. Ha ha") ... The Beverley Sisters sing

"Oh..." *Wheel Of Fortune* ("... please don't pass me by. Let me know the magic of a kiss and a sigh") ... 39-year-old Ted Drake is the new football manager of Chelsea - Drake takes over from 55-year-old Billy Birrell ... There's much consternation on the MCC cricket board when Len Hutton is appointed England's first 'professional' captain ... The controversial move pays off - as 36-year-old Hutton leads England to victory over India in a four match Test series. 21-year-old fast bowler Fred Trueman is in fine form - taking eight wickets at Old Trafford and five wickets at the Oval. Alec Bedser, David Sheppard and Peter May also play their part in England's splendid victory ... 17-year-old tennis player Maureen Connolly (aka Little Mo) from California wins the ladies' final at Wimbledon. Frank Sedgman from Australia beats 30-year-old Jaroslav Drobny from Czechoslovakia in the men's final ... 41-year-old racing driver Reg Parnell from Derby finishes seventh in the British Grand Prix at Silverstone in a green Cooper-Bristol ... Great Britain win a gold medal at the Helsinki Olympics in the Equestrian Team Jumping event - Harry Llewellyn, Duggie Stewart and Wilf White are the victors ... 23-year-old Sheila Lerwill wins silver in the Women's High Jump. "Auf wiedersehen, auf wiedersehen. We'll meet again sweetheart" - *Auf Wiederseh'n Sweetheart* by 35-year-old Vera Lynn (with the Soldiers and Airmen of HM Forces) is a top selling 78 rpm gramophone ... "I'll be loving you, eternally. With a love that's true, eternally. From the start, within my heart, it seems I've always known the sun would shine, when you are mine, and mine alone" - 30-year-old Jimmy Young from Cinderford signs to Decca and records a new 'pop' single called *Eternally* ... The new football season gets underway ... Johnny Berry and Johnny Downie score the goals as reigning champions Manchester Utd beat Ted Drake's Chelsea 2-0 in front of 43,629 at Old Trafford ... Len Duquemin is on the score-sheet as Tottenham Hotspur beat Manchester City 0-1 in front of 33,621 at Maine Road ... Doug Lishman and Don Oakes (making his debut) score the goals for Arsenal in a 1-2 victory over Aston Villa in front of 50,930 at Villa Park ... 26-year-old inside-left Arthur 'dead shot' Rowley scores four goals for Leicester City in a 6-1 victory over his old club Fulham in Division Two ... 50-year-old John Snagge announces the news on BBC radio ... 21-year-old convicted murderer Frank Burgess is hanged by the neck until dead at Wandsworth ... Traffic jams form and cars overheat as families take motoring trips to the seaside on the Summer Bank Holiday ... The latest Vauxhall *Velox* has a new improved engine giving a top speed of 80 mph ... Advertisements say, 'A bottle of *Idris* Lemon Squash has no rival as a pure and delicious thirst quencher, and is greatly appreciated by people of taste and discrimination'.

Autumn 1952... The end of tea rationing

Icy winds sweep across the country bringing heavy frosts ... It's the coldest September since 1807 ... The freezing temperatures continue into October ... Farmers in the North struggle to keep their livestock warm and safe ... Business commuters in London keep snug in *Burberry* raglan overcoats ... 49-year-old Chancellor of the Exchequer Richard Austen 'Rab' Butler delivers the first stage of his plan to take Britain out of austerity - tea rationing comes to an end after thirteen years and there's great joy all across the nation ... Bill poster advertisements say, 'Mummy always uses *Brooke Bond* dividend Tea' ... Newspaper advertisements say, '*Ty-Phoo Tea.* Goes further' ... "I'm once again back home in Innisfree" - 49-year-old Bing Crosby from Tacoma in Washington sings *The Isle Of Innisfree* ... 25-year-old Guy Mitchell from Detroit sings *My Truly, Truly Fair* ... 17-year-old schoolboy David Nobbs from Orpington is appointed House Prefect at Marlborough College ... 37-year-old John Profumo from Kensington is appointed Parliamentary Secretary in the Ministry of Transport ... New road safety measures come into effect as flashing orange beacons - atop black and white hooped poles - are used for the first time at pedestrian crossings ... Hundreds of thousands of people brace themselves against the cold weather and visit the Motor Show at Earls Court ... 54-year-old Donald Healey displays his new Healey *100* sports car ... The latest Morris *Minor* has a redesigned front grill and headlights - and a top speed of 64 mph ... The all new Humber *Super Snipe* motorcar is lower, sleeker and is the first of its marque to come without side running boards. The new model costs £1,481, has a top speed of 91 mph and can reach 60 mph in 14.7 seconds ... 30-year-old test pilot John Derry and his co-pilot Tony Richards are killed when their proto-type de Havilland jet plane breaks-up in mid air at the annual Farnborough Air Show. An engine from the aeroplane then falls to earth and lands on spectators below - twenty-nine people are killed ... *Forget Me Not* ("... today. Though I am far away") by 35-year-old Vera Lynn is a popular gramophone song ... One hundred and twelve people die and hundreds are injured in a train crash involving three locomotives at Harrow & Wealdstone station ... Prime-minister Winston Churchill sends troops to Nairobi to confront Mau Mau terrorists - a militia group revolting against British colonial rule ... 29-year-old American Rocky Marciano is the new heavy-weight boxing champion of the world - after knocking-out Jersey Joe Walcott in Philadelphia ... Back in Britain - 52-year-old 'daring' John Cobb is killed on Loch Ness as he attempts to break the world water speed record ... A 'hit parade' of popular music is published in the *New Musical Express* ... The 'Top 12' best selling songs are listed ... 25-year-old Al Martino is number one with *Here In My Heart* ... 33-year-old Nat 'King' Cole is number three with *Somewhere Along The Way* ... 25-year-old angst-ridden Johnnie Ray is number twelve with *Walkin' My Baby Back Home* ... 37-year-old football star Stanley 'wizard of dribble' Matthews is injured in a match playing for Blackpool against Tottenham Hotspur at White Hart Lane ... 16-year-old Duncan Edwards scores five goals in a match for Manchester Utd's youth team ... 29-year-old 'Terrible' Trevor Ford scores four as Sunderland beat Manchester City 5-2 at Roker Park ... 27-year-old Nat Lofthouse scores his tenth goal in just nine matches for wing commander Winterbottom's England football team ... Radio programme *Children's Hour* featuring 54-year-old Derek McCulloch as 'Uncle Mac' remains popular after thirty years on the wireless ... "Comes along a love suddenly, brother, are you excited?" - Kay Starr sings *Comes A-Long A-Love* - and it remains on the new hit parade for sixteen weeks ... "I'm walking behind you, on your wedding day, and I'll hear you promise to love and obey" - 24-year-old heart-throb Eddie Fisher sings *I'm Walking Behind You* - and it stays on the hit parade for eighteen weeks ... 63-year-old movie star Charlie Chaplin travels to London for the first time in twenty-one years - and attends the premiere of his new film *Limelight*. Chaplin's 27-year-old wife Oona O'Neill is at his side ... All around the country, crowds of people flock to cinemas for an evening of entertainment ... 20-year-old actress Elizabeth Taylor stars alongside 41-year-old Robert Taylor in an exciting new movie called *Ivanhoe* - and it's filmed in glorious Technicolor! ... Crowds of people continue to flock to football matches on Saturday afternoons ... 23-year-old centre-forward Cliff Holton scores a hat-trick as Tom Whittaker's Arsenal thrash Don Welsh's Liverpool 1-5 at Anfield in Division One ... 25-year-old centre-half Malcolm Allison is on the score-sheet for West Ham Utd in a 3-2 victory over Nottingham Forest in Division Two ... 22-year-old Roy Sproson is on the score-sheet as Port Vale beat Chesterfield 3-0 in Division Three (North) ... 19-year-old Gordon Nutt is on the score-sheet as Coventry City beat Reading 4-0 in Division Three (South) ... Crowds of people flock to theatres and enjoy more traditional forms of entertainment ... 26-year-old Queen Elizabeth II is at the Palladium to see Josef Locke, The Beverley Sisters and 37-year-old comedy star Norman Wisdom ... "Do not forsake me, oh my darlin', on this our wedding day" - *High Noon (Do Not Forsake Me)* by Frankie Laine moves up to number seven on the new hit parade ... "If you loved me half as much as I love you, you wouldn't worry me half as much as you do. You're nice to me when there's no one else around. You only build me up to let me down" - *Half As Much* by Rosemary Clooney is number three ... 16-year-old burglar Christopher Craig shoots and kills a policeman at a warehouse in Croydon. Craig's accomplice, 19-year-old Derek Bentley, now faces the hangman's noose as he was present at the murder scene and was reported to have uttered the words, "Let him have it." ... 11-year-old schoolboy Fred West from Much Marcle in Herefordshire kills a neighbour's cat and buries it in his garden ... 55-year-old actor Basil Radford dies of a heart attack in a radio studio in London ... *The Mousetrap* a wonderful new 'whodunit' play from 62-year-old Agatha Christie opens at the Ambassador's Theatre in the West End and features 29-year-old actor Richard 'Dicky' Attenborough ... Met Office warnings of thick smog over London go largely unheeded ... Men sit in saggy armchairs reading newspapers and smoking cigarettes ... The *Daily Mirror* costs 1½d ... A pack of ten *Bar One* costs 1s/4d.

Christmas 1952... Bill and Ben, the flower pot men

A thick blanket of smog - a real pea-souper - descends on London. For three days, visibility is barely more than a yard. Hospitals are at straining point as people seek treatment after inhaling noxious fumes. It's estimated that around four-thousand people lose their lives ... 53-year-old John Christie murders his wife Ethel at 10 Rillington Place and hides her body behind a false wall in the kitchen ... 19-year-old Derek Bentley is sentenced to death for the murder of a policeman. Bentley's accomplice, 16-year-old Christopher Craig (who fired the fatal shot), is detained at Her Majesty's Pleasure - as he's too young to face the death penalty ... Powerful centre-forward Nat Lofthouse scores two goals as wing commander Winterbottom's England football team gain a 5-0 victory over Belgium at Wembley ... 11-year-old schoolboy Geoff Hurst from Ashton-under-Lyne plays football with his friends in the park ... 78-year-old prime-minister Winston Churchill meets with his Foreign Secretary Anthony Eden ... British soldiers remain active in South Korea ... 30-year-old George Blake is still being held prisoner by communists in North Korea - the MI6 officer has been in captivity for the past two years ... "Your cheatin' heart will make you weep, you'll cry and cry and try to sleep. But sleep won't come the whole night through, your cheatin' heart will tell on you" - 29-year-old Hank Williams sings *Your Cheatin' Heart* ... "I went to your wedding, although I was dreading, the thought of losing you" - 19-year-old Alma Cogan sings *I Went To Your Wedding* ... Movie star Charlie Chaplin is told he cannot return to America because of his alleged sympathies with communism ... Chaplin's latest film, *Limelight* (with 21-year-old Claire Bloom), is hugely popular at cinemas ... 34-year-old Spike Milligan suffers a mental breakdown and is forced to take a break from popular radio comedy, *The Goon Show* ... "I'm rather worried about Jim" - *Mrs. Dale's Diary* (with 46-year-old Ellis Powell as Mrs. Mary Dale) continues to captivate listeners at 4 p.m. every weekday - with the programme repeated the following morning at 11 a.m. ... Will Scott's Preston North End football team are riding high in Division One with 30-year-old Charlie Wayman leading the attack ... Les McDowell's Manchester City are bottom of the table ... 32-year-old inside-left Harry Potts scores a hat-trick as Cliff Britton's Everton beat Bury 0-5 in league Division Two ... On the same day, 26-year-old inside-left Arthur 'dead shot' Rowley also scores a hat-trick as Norman Bullock's Leicester City beat Hull City 5-0 - also in Division Two! ... 'What a Glorious Feeling' - 40-year-old Gene Kelly and 20-year-old Debbie Reynolds star in *Singing In The Rain* at cinemas ... 'The story of a man who was too proud to run!' - 51-year-old Gary Cooper and 23-year-old Grace Kelly star in *High Noon* ... 21-year-old blonde sex-siren Diana Dors (37-24-35) plays Ruby Bruce in *The Last Page* ... "Flob-a-lob-lob" - Bill and Ben the flower-pot men make their first appearance on BBC television ... "It's Christmas!" - 6-year-old Neville Holder hangs a stocking on the wall at his family's council house in Walsall - hoping Santa Claus will pay a visit ... Lucky schoolboys unwrap a *Tri-ang Railways* trainset on Christmas morning ... *Dinky Toys* die-cast models of cars and lorries are also popular ... "Here in my heart, I'm alone, I'm so lonely. Here in my heart, I just yearn for you only" - *Here In My Heart* by Al Martino stays at number one on the hit parade for nine weeks! ... 63-year-old Hubert Houldsworth is chairman of the National Coal Board ... 228 million tonnes of coal have been produced this year - up slightly compared to 1951 ... Things seem to be improving ... 'Britain Strong and Free' -

prime-minister Winston Churchill is satisfied that his government is meeting the promises made in its manifesto ... 78-year-old Churchill looks to his much trusted Chancellor of the Exchequer, Richard Austen 'Rab' Butler, to keep the country's economy moving in the right direction ... The shortage of luxury goods is beginning to ease ... A new *Goblin* washing machine costs £34/7s/10d (plus £14/12s/2d purchase tax) ... 58-year-old Housing Minister Harold Macmillan is successfully delivering the required number of new houses - tackling the nationwide shortage of family homes. (More than 300,000 houses have been built in 1952) ... 'The cigarette for me' - *Craven 'A'* cigarettes are endorsed by non-smoking footballer Stanley 'wizard of dribble' Matthews.

New Year 1953... Severe floods along the East coast

37-year-old comedian Dick Emery stands in for mentally exhausted Spike Milligan on the popular radio comedy *The Goon Show* ... 26-year-old ex nude calendar girl Marilyn Monroe (36-22-36) stars in *Clash by Night* at cinemas ... 39-year-old Burt Lancaster stars in *The Crimson Pirate* ... Country singer Hank Williams dies aged 29 in Virginia ... 62-year-old Dwight D. Eisenhower is inaugurated as US president ... Back in Britain - there's great excitement when it's announced that this year's Coronation of young Queen Elizabeth II will be televised ... BBC TV broadcasts the weather forecast in sound only just before closedown each night ... Twenty-thousand homes are flooded and three hundred people are killed when a tidal surge from the North Sea devastates the east coast - the countryside from Lincolnshire to Kent is submerged in just one night and dozens of low lying areas including Canvey Island are evacuated. The total cost of the damage is estimated to be over £50 million ... Heavy snow descends on the country in February - blocking roads and railway lines ... The A6 at Shap in Cumbria is impassable and the movement of goods between England and Scotland comes to a standstill ... 53-year-old John Christie murders Rita Nelson and Kathleen Maloney at 10 Rillington Place in London ... Derek Bentley's appeal against his death penalty is unsuccessful - the 19-year-old from Southwark will go to the gallows on the twenty-eighth of January ... 30-year-old Eamonn Andrews introduces *Sports Parade* on Saturday afternoons on BBC radio's Light Programme ... 37-year-old Stanley 'wizard of dribble' Matthews returns from injury and scores a goal for Blackpool in a 1-2 victory against Sheffield Wednesday in the third round of the FA Cup ... Barnsley manager Angus Seed dies from chronic bronchitis aged 60 and Tim Ward takes over as boss at Oakwell ... 15-year-old schoolboy Bobby Charlton signs for Manchester Utd ... 29-year-old Doug Lishman scores twice for Arsenal in a 5-3 victory over Wolverhampton Wanderers ... Johnny Dixon, Billy 'Cowboy' Goffin and Tommy 'Topper' Thompson are on the score-sheet as Aston Villa thrash Portsmouth 6-0 at Villa Park ... 21-year-old John Charles scores a hat-trick for Major Frank Buckley's Leeds Utd in a 4-0 victory over Rotherham Utd ... 21-year-old centre-forward Tommy Taylor scores for Barnsley in a 2-2 draw against Hull City ... Sheffield Wednesday's Derek Dooley breaks his leg in a match against Preston North End. Complications arise during hospital treatment and gangrene sets in, leading to the 23-year-old striker having a leg amputated ... "See the pyramids along the Nile. Watch the sunrise on a tropic isle. Just remember darlin' all the while..." *You Belong To Me (See The Pyramids Along The Nile)* by 35-year-old Jo Stafford is the new number one song ... *Cowpuncher's Cantana* by 30-year-old Max Bygraves is number six ... Public outrage ensues and there are protests on the street as 19-year-old Derek Bentley is hanged by the neck until dead at Wandsworth. (47-year-old hangman Albert Pierrepoint carries out the highly controversial execution) ... The Rev. Richard Tatlock gives a late night homily on BBC television ... *Faith Can Move Mountains* by Johnnie Ray and The Four Lads plays on juke boxes in coffee bars ... The songs *Comes A-Long A-Love* by 30-year-old Kay Starr, and *Outside Of Heaven* by 24-year-old Eddie Fisher both spend a week at the top of the pop chart ... 11-year-old schoolboy Stephen Hawking from Oxford sits at home reading books ... 50-year-old Chancellor of the Exchequer Richard Austen 'Rab' Butler takes another step forward in his mission to move Britain out of austerity. Rationing of sweets and chocolate comes to an end - leading to scenes of great jubilation throughout the country. Children rush out to to buy liquorice strips, toffee apples and sticks of nougat ... The football season continues ... Tom Whittaker's Arsenal and Will Scott's Preston North End are neck and neck at the top of Division One ... 'The Gunners' beat Spurs 4-0 at Highbury with goals from Cliff Holton (2), Doug Lishman and Jimmy Logie ... 'The Lilywhites' beat Cardiff City 0-2 at Ninian Park - with goals from Charlie Wayman and Tom Finney (aka the 'Preston Plumber') ... Joe Smith's Blackpool knock Arsenal out the FA Cup - winning a quarter-final tie 1-2 in front of 69,158 at Highbury with goals from 'Tiny' Ernie Taylor and Allan 'bomber' Brown ... "Too many nights (too many nights). Too many stars (too many stars). Too many moons could change your mind (don't let the moon change your mind)" - *Don't Let The Stars Get In Your Eyes* by Perry Como climbs to number one in the Top 12 - and stays there for five weeks! ... Churchill's Conservative government is slowly moving the country out of austerity ... A record number of new houses have been built under the direction of 59-year-old Housing Minister Harold Macmillan - and the shortage of homes is beginning to ease ... The average price of a house in the UK is £1,800 ... Men go to the pub in the evening ... A pint of mild in the Red Lion is 1s/2d.

Spring 1953… Stanley Matthews' at the FA cup final

35-year-old star of radio Spike Milligan returns to *The Goon Show* after his recent illness. Milligan and his fellow Goons entertain millions of listeners with a new episode entitled, 'The Mystery of the Monkey's Paw' ... 50-year-old Chancellor of the Exchequer Richard Austen 'Rab' Butler presents his Budget to the country. In an effort to get people spending, Butler cuts the basic rate of income tax by 6d in the pound and slashes purchase tax by twenty-five percent ... Families enjoy taking a spin in their motor car on Sunday afternoons. Morris *Minors*, Austin *A30s*, Hillman *Minxs* and Ford *Consuls* clog the country's roads ... 21-year-old footballer Tommy Taylor transfers from Barnsley to Manchester Utd for £29,999 and scores twice on his debut in a 5-2 victory over Preston North End ... Men in grubby raincoats loiter on the streets of London ... 28-year-old Paul Raymond presents, 'The Sauciest Show of the Century', featuring the Monte Carlo Bikini Girls and Nudes in Ice, at Collins Music Hall ... "She wears red feathers and a hooly-hooly skirt" - *She Wears Red Feathers* by Guy Mitchell climbs to the top of the hit parade -and stays there for four weeks ... 24-year-old Ken Colyer forms a new jazz band, with banjo-playing Lonnie Donegan and trombone-blowing Chris Barber in the line-up ... 39-year-old Fred Davis wins snooker's World Professional Match Play Championship (his fifth world title in six years) by beating Walter Donaldson by 37 frames to 34 in the final at Leicester Square Hall ... An expedition to climb Mount Everest (with Edmund Hillary and Tenzing Norgay in the team) sets up base camp in the Himalayas ... Back in England - 45-year-old coal miner Joe 'Yorky' Henry is killed in a pit explosion at Horden Colliery near Sunderland ... 53-year-old John Christie murders

Hectorina MacLennan at 10 Rillington Place in Notting Hill ... 46-year-old Louisa May Merrifield murders Sarah Ricketts at 339 Devonshire Road in Blackpool ... Queen Mary dies peacefully in her sleep aged 85 at Marlborough House in London ... "Because you're mine the brightest star I see looks down, my love, and envies me..." *Because You're Mine* by 32-year-old Mario Lanza is number three in the popular music chart ... "Rise up, Sir Winston!" - the nation celebrates as 78-year-old prime-minister Winston Churchill is knighted by the young Queen Elizabeth at Buckingham Palace ... 61-year-old Charles Buchan previews the upcoming FA Cup semi-final football matches on BBC radio's *Sports Parade* programme ... 33-year-old Tottenham Hotspur full-back Alf Ramsey misplaces a back-pass in the semi-final at Villa Park, and Jackie Mudie scores a late winner for Blackpool. 'The Seasiders' (with 38-year-old Stanley 'wizard of dribble' Matthews in the team) are off to Wembley! ... In the other semi-final tie at Maine Road, Bolton Wanderers beat Everton 4-3 and 'The Trotters" (with 27-year-old Nat Lofthouse in the team) are also off to Wembley! ... W. J. Hicks previews Football League matches on BBC radio's *Sports Parade* programme ... 27-year-old inside-left Arthur 'dead shot' Rowley bags a hat-trick (including two penalties) as Leicester City beat Lincoln City 3-2 in Division Two ... 34-year-old Wilf Mannion scores twice as Middlesbrough thrash Manchester Utd 5-0 in Division One ... 18-year-old Brian Clough is called up for national service in the RAF ... Middle-class families gather in living-rooms and parlours to watch TV programmes on Ferguson *9916T* or Cossor *930* television consoles. Both 'sets' come with a large 17-inch screen ... 33-year-old actor Patrick Troughton stars as *Robin Hood* on Tuesday evenings at 5 p.m. ... 30-year-old Eamonn Andrews hosts *What's My Line* on Sunday evenings at 8 p.m. ... The football season draws to a close ... 54-year-old Tom Whittaker's Arsenal are champions of Division One for a record seventh time. Ray Daniel, Joe Wade, Don Roper, Jimmy Logie, Doug Lishman, Peter Goring, Cliff Holton and 38-year-old captain Joe Mercer have all been outstanding ... Preston North End (with Willie Cunningham, Joe Marston, Charlie Wayman, Tom Finney - aka the 'Preston Plumber' and talented 25-year-old right-half Tommy Docherty) are runners-up by the narrowest of margins - on goal average only! ... 17-year-old Jack Charlton from Ashington in Northumberland makes his debut at centre-half for Leeds Utd in Division Two ... 38-year-old outside-right Stanley 'wizard of dribble' Matthews is on the winning side (after three attempts) in the FA Cup final, as Joe Smith's Blackpool come back from 3-1 down, to beat Bill Ridding's Bolton Wanderers 4-3, in a thrilling match at the Empire Stadium in Wembley - Lofthouse, Moir and Bell score the goals for Bolton. Mortensen bags a hat-trick and Perry scores the winning goal for Blackpool. A ticket for the standing enclosure costs 3s/6d ... Courting couples spend their evenings at the cinema - seeking glamour and excitement ... 'Scorching the Screen with Violent Passions and Passionate Violence!' - 20-year-old actress Joan Collins (36-23-37) stars in *The Good Die Young* ... 51-year-old actor Gary Cooper wins an Oscar for his role in *High Noon* ... "With broken wings, no bird can fly. And broken promises mean love must fade and die" - *Broken Wings* by The Stargazers is new at number one in the pop chart ... "Oh, please come back I beg you, please baby please. What fools are we who cannot see the forest for the trees" - *Downhearted* by 24-year-old heart-throb Eddie Fisher is number three ... 11-year-old schoolboy Ian Dury from Harrow in Middlesex sits in his bedroom listening to records and reading books ... "The name's Bond. James Bond" -

Casino Royale by Ian Fleming is the first James Bond novel to be published ... 35-year-old William Holden stars in *Stalag 17* at picture houses ... "Yes, yes, she'll run. She's as good as she ever was" - 67-year-old George Relph plays Sam Weech in the quintessentially English film *The Titfield Thunderbolt* - and it's in Technicolor ... 39-year-old Raich 'Silver Fox' Carter takes over from 70-year-old Major Frank Buckley as football manager of Leeds Utd ... Working-class families gather in front-rooms and parlours to listen to music on Sobell *519P* 5-valve radio receivers ... *(How Much Is) That Doggie In The Window* ("… the one with wag-er-ly tail") by 27-year-old Lita Roza from Liverpool is top of the hit parade ... "I love the hills, I love the prairie, I love Jane and I love Mary. But pretty little black eyed Susie, but pretty little black eyed Susie, cross my heart, I love ya best of all" - *Pretty Little Black-Eyed Susie* by 26-year-old Guy Mitchell from Detroit is number two ... The Moka coffee bar opens on Frith Street in Soho - serving cups of cappuccino to stylish young customers ... 53-year-old John Christie of 10 Rillington Place is arrested in London and charged with multiple counts of murder ... Leo and Hazel Blair of Edinburgh are proud parents of Anthony - their newborn baby boy ... Unemployment has fallen to 380,000 under Sir Winston Churchill's Conservative government ... 'Well-to-do' young men race along England's narrow country roads in sports cars ... The new Triumph *TR2* has a top speed of 107 mph and can reach 60 mph in 12.4 seconds ... The new Aston Martin *DB2/4* has a top speed of 118 mph and can reach 60 mph in 10.5 seconds ... 'Come and get it! … and banish Pinking' - BP *Super* petrol is now available at roadside garages ... Schoolboys peer through toy shop windows ... *Dinky Toys* introduce a die-cast model (1:45 scale) of the Austin *A40 Somerset* in two-tone black and cream ... *All The Time And*

Everywhere by 23-year-old Dickie Valentine from London is number nine in the pop chart ... Television sets are in demand as people prepare for the Coronation ... A Regentone 14-inch set costs 62 guineas - tax paid ... A Regentone 17-inch set is 89 guineas - tax paid.

Summer 1953... God save the Queen

Britain endures cool temperatures and drizzling rain in early June ... *The Cardiff Queen* paddle steamer takes thousands of holiday makers on cruises on the Bristol Channel ... *Butlin's* holiday camp in Filey now has a miniature railway ... 'It's my little Rosie behind I want photographed' - saucy postcards by Donald McGill are in high demand ... 33-year-old Edmund Hillary and 39-year-old Tenzing Norgay complete the final ascent to the summit of Mount Everest. The two men stand for fifteen minutes at a height of 29,028 - on top of the world! ... Back in England - millions of viewers watch television as the Coronation of 27-year-old Queen Elizabeth II is broadcast live by the BBC. The nation looks on as the young Queen is crowned by the Archbishop of Canterbury. The congregation at Westminster Abbey proclaim, "God save the Queen!" ... Comedians Peter Sellers, Harry Secombe and Spike Milligan perform a 'Coronation Special' of *The Goon Show* on the wireless ... Young people gather together in milk bars and coffee shops - and listen to the latest hit songs ... 23-year-old Dickie Valentine from London sings *In A Golden Coach (There's A Heart Of Gold)* ... 39-year-old pianist Winifred Atwell from Trinidad performs the *Coronation Rag* ... Young Queen Elizabeth attends the Epsom Derby a few days after her Coronation and watches her own horse *Aureole* come in second - four lengths behind *Pinza* (ridden by 49-year-old Sir Gordon Richards) ... Jimmy Carr - representing the Red Lion public house at Dipton in County Durham - wins the annual *News of the World* darts tournament at Earls Court in London ... *I Believe* ("... for every drop of rain that falls, a flower grows. I believe that somewhere in the darkest night, a candle glows") by Frankie Laine is top of the hit parade for a total of eighteen weeks ... 7-

year-old Neville Holder (soon to aquire the nickname ‘Noddy’) performs his very own rendition of *I Believe* on stage at the Labour Club in Walsall - and there’s not a dry eye in the house ... 11-year-old Neil Kinnock from Tredegar in Wales plays out with his friends ... 54-year-old convicted murderer John Christie (of 10 Rillington Place) is hanged by the neck until dead at Pentonville. (48-year-old hangman Albert Pierrepoint carries out the execution) ... BBC’s science-fiction thriller *The Quatermass Experiment*, starring 56-year-old Reginald Tate, keeps television viewers gripped on Saturday evenings ... 33-year-old Edith Atkins from Bilston rides a bicycle from Land’s End to John O’Groats in a new record time of 2 days, 18 hours and 4 minutes ... Cricketers 36-year-old Len Hutton and 29-year-old Don Kenyon stride out together to open the batting for England against Australia at Trent Bridge in the opening Test Match of the summer. The first four matches all end in draws (Len Hutton scores 145 runs at Lord’s). In the fifth and final Test at the Oval - Hutton scores 82, Trevor Bailey hits 64, Graham Lock takes 5 wickets for 45 runs and 22-year-old fast bowler ‘fiery’ Fred Trueman takes 4 wickets for 86. England secure an historic victory - it’s their first Ashes series win for nineteen years. L Hutton (cpt), D Kenyon, W J Edrich, R T Simpson, D C S Compton, T W Graveney, W Watson, P B H May, T E Bailey, T G Evans (wk), J C Laker, J H Wardle, F R Brown, G A R Lock, A V Bedser, R Tattersall, J B Statham and F S Trueman have all played a part in this wonderful Ashes victory ... 22-year-old all-rounder Richie Benaud is dropped from the Australian team after poor performances at Trent Bridge and Lord’s ... *I’m Walking Behind You* (“… on your wedding day, and I hear you promise, to love and obey”) by Eddie Fisher and Sally Sweetland is top of the pop chart ... 26-year-old Lord Edward Montague of Beaulieu hosts an intimate (male only) beach party - with Peter Wildeblood and Michael Pitt-Rivers among the guests ... 18-year-old schoolboy David Nobbs and his friends get drunk on cheap wine - to mark the end of their 'A' level examinations ... 38-year-old singer Dorothy Squires marries 25-year-old clothes model and actor Roger Moore ... "Pretend you're happy when you're blue, it isn't very hard to do" - *Pretend* by Nat 'King' Cole is number two on the hit parade ... *Hold Me, Thrill Me, Kiss Me* by Muriel Smith is number three ... People form queues outside cinemas, eager see the latest movies - especially those in glorious Technicolor! ... 39-year-old Alan Ladd stars alongside Jean Arthur and Van Heflin in the 'Western' blockbuster *Shane* ... 38-year-old Kenneth More and 26-year-old Kay Kendall star in the quintessentially English film *Genevieve* ... 27-year-old Margaret Thatcher gives birth to twins Carol and Mark in Hammersmith ... 15-year-old school leaver Arthur Scargill from Worsbrough Dale goes to work 'down the pit' ... 28-year-old Nat Lofthouse and 31-year-old Tom Finney (aka the 'Preston Plumber') both score twice as wing commander Winterbottom's England football team beat the USA 3-6 in New York ... *Say You're Mine Again* by June Hutton and Axel Stordahl with the Boys Next Door enters the Top 12 hit parade at number ten ... The new football season gets underway ... Reigning champions Arsenal are bottom of Division One after losing three of their first four matches ... Vic Buckingham's West Bromwich Albion are top of the league after beating Jim 'Scot' Symon's Preston North End 0-2 at Deepdale ... Stan Cullis' Wolverhampton Wanderers beat Bill Murray's Sunderland 3-1 in front of 41,442 at the Molineux ... 27-year-old inside-left Arthur 'dead shot' Rowley scores twice and centre-forward Derek Hines bags a hat-trick as Leicester City thrash Leeds Utd 5-0 in Division Two ...

The Song From Moulin Rouge (with its sweeping, dreamy strings) by 47-year-old Mantovani is number one in the pop chart ... *Rachel* ("... Oh, Rachel. I should have known you were never my own but I love you") by 25-year-old Al Martino is number ten ... The Bristol Motor Company launches the stunning *403* luxury saloon. Top speed is 102 mph and acceleration from 0-60 mph takes 13.4 seconds ... Standard grade petrol is 4s/2d a gallon ... The average waist size for men in the UK is thirty-two inches ... Rationing of sausages comes to an end.

Autumn 1953... Tetley introduce teabags!

44-year-old Henry Longhurst commentates on golf's Ryder Cup from Wentworth for BBC television ... 35-year-old Peter O'Sullevan commentates on the horse racing from Ascot ... 11-year-old schoolboy Des Lynam from Brighton plays out with his friends ... Footballers 27-year-old Dennis Wilshaw and 28-year-old Nat Lofthouse both score twice as wing commander Winterbottom's England football team beat Wales 1-4 at Ninian Park ... 30-year-old MI6 officer George Blake receives a hero's welcome as he returns to England after being held as a prisoner for three years by communists in North Korea ... Crowds gather to see 49-year-old entertainer George Formby perform the 'switching on of the lights' ceremony at Blackpool Illuminations ... 53-year-old Queen Elizabeth the Queen Mother opens a new reservoir at Blithfield near Rugeley in Staffordshire - it's taken six years to construct ... Young schoolboys become excited when Lesney Products introduce *Matchbox* sized die-cast toy vehicles for 1s/6d - a road roller, a dumper truck and a cement mixer are first in the wonderful new range ... Older schoolboys play conkers in the corner of the playground ... 10-year-old John Major attends Rutlish Boys School wearing a second-hand blazer and worn-out shoes ... 18-year-old David Nobbs begins his national service in the Royal Corps of Signals ... 18-year-old footballer Jack Charlton begins his national service in the Household Cavalry ... Millionaire businessman W. J. Bassett-Lowke dies aged 76 in Northampton ... Welsh poet Dylan Thomas dies aged 39 in New York ... Back in England - people are aghast as *Tetley* introduce teabags ... *Green Shield Stamps* are also new ... Millions tune-in to the BBC radio's Home Service on Friday nights and enjoy the latest series of *The Goon Show* featuring 28-year-old Peter Sellers, 32-year-old Harry Secombe and 35-year-old Spike Milligan ... 6-year-old Prince Charles and his 3-year-old sister Princess Anne travel by train on a visit to Scotland ... *Let's Walk That-A-Way* by Doris Day and angst-ridden Johnnie Ray is number four on the Top 12 hit parade ... *Hot Toddy* by Ted Heath and his Music reaches number six ... 78-year-old Sir Winston Churchill is partially paralysed by a stroke at his home in 10 Downing Street. 56-year-old Foreign Secretary Anthony Eden wonders how long the great man can continue as prime-minister ... The Ministries of Transport and of Civil Aviation become one department, under the control of 48-year-old Alan Lennox-Boyd ... A British Hawker *Hunter* jet-powered fighter plane piloted by 31-year-old Neville Duke sets a new air speed record of 727.63 mph ... Hollywood comedy icons 63-year-old Stan Laurel and 61-year-old Oliver Hardy begin an eight month tour of the UK and Ireland - opening at the New Theatre in Northampton ... Thieves break into the *Maples* shop in London and make off with cash and valuables worth £38,000. Police track down the culprits and 36-year-old Alfred Hinds is one of five men arrested and charged with robbery. Hinds stands trial, is found guilty and sentenced to twelve years imprisonment ... 34-year-old footballer Tommy Lawton transfers from Brentford to Arsenal for £10,000 and makes his debut for 'The Gunners' in a 2-2 draw against Manchester City at Highbury ... 20-year-old Albert Quixall of Sheffield Wednesday wears new-fangled 'abbreviated' shorts - instead of knee-length, baggy ones ... 43-year-old Eric Houghton is the new manager at Aston Villa ... The television programme *Panorama* is new - it's broadcast fortnightly on Wednesday evenings ... "Look at the way she walks. Listen when she talks. With each word my heart just skips, h-oh, if I could kiss those lips. Mmm..." *Look At That Girl* by 26-year-old Guy Mitchell from Detroit is the number one popular song ... "Tell me that old love story, but not the same old lies. You know my heart is waiting for you dear, here on the ..." *Bridge Of Sighs* by 28-year-old David Whitfield from Hull is number nine ... "Just like that!" - 32-year-old comedian Tommy Cooper (in trademark fez hat) is on the bill at the Royal Variety Show ... England's footballers are humiliated in a 3-6 defeat to Hungary at Wembley - Bill Eckersley (Blackburn Rovers), Alf Ramsey and George Robb (Tottenham Hotspur) and Harry Johnston, Stan Mortensen and 'Tiny' Ernie Taylor (Blackpool) will never be chosen to play for the national team again ... *Hey Joe* ("... where'd you find that pretty girly? Where'd you get that jolly dolly? How'd you make me wish that dish was mine") by 43-year-old Frankie Laine is new at number one on the hit parade ... 24-year-old centre-forward Cliff Holton scores a hat-trick for Tom Whittaker's Arsenal in a 4-3 win over Bolton Wanderers ... Stan Cullis' Wolverhampton Wanderers thrash Ted Drake's Chelsea 8-1 at the Molineux and move up to third in Division One ... 46-year-old convicted murderer Louisa May Merrifield is hanged by the neck until dead at Strangeways. (48-year-old hangman Albert Pierrepoint carries out the execution) ... "Answer me, Lord above, just what sin have I been guilty of?" - *Answer Me* by 40-year-old Frankie Laine moves to the top of the pop chart - and stays there for eight weeks! ... "Chicka-boom, chicka-rack, chicka-boom, chicka-rack, chicka-boom, chicka-rack, she's singin'" - *Chicka Boom* by Guy Mitchell is number five ... The Morris *Minor Traveller* estate car - with distinctive varnished wooden frame at the rear - is unveiled at the Earls Court Motor Show ... Reliant introduce a three-wheeler called the *Regal* - with a 747cc engine and aluminium body panels fixed onto a wooden frame ... 25-year-old footballer Tommy 'Topper'

Thompson scores a hat-trick as Eric Houghton's Aston Villa beat Walter Rowley's Middlesbrough 5-3 at Villa Park ... Chelsea supporters are despondent after seeing their team thrashed 5-2 by top-of-the-table West Bromwich Albion ... A charitable group called The Samaritans begin a new telephone help line service.

Christmas 1953...
Zephyr Zodiac with two-tone paintwork

There's mild weather and dull skies over much of the country ... 39-year-old Winifred Atwell from Trinidad reaches number two on the hit parade with her piano medley *Let's Have A Party* (comprising of the songs: *If You Knew Suzie, The More We Are Together, That's My Weakness Now, Knees Up Mother Brown, Daisy Bell, Boomps A Daisy, She Was One Of The Early Birds and Three O'Clock In The Morning*) ... Manufacturing output slows as the Amalgamated Engineering Union calls for industrial action to be taken by its members - and thousands of engineers stage a 24-hour strike ... Coal production remains at the same level as last year ... 83-year-old mining Safety Officer James Edward Ogdon retires from his work at the Parkhouse Colliery in Chesterton, Staffordshire. Mr. Ogdon began his working life as an underground pony driver at the Black Bull Colliery in the year 1897 ... A record number of houses - more than 320,000 - have been built this year under the direction of 59-year-old Housing Minister Harold Macmillan ... The economy continues to improve under 51-year-old Chancellor of the Exchequer Richard Austen 'Rab' Butler, with people spending more money on luxury goods ... The new 'up-market' Ford *Zephyr Zodiac* motorcar has leather trim, two-tone paintwork, a top speed of 81 mph and costs £850 (including purchase tax) ... 79-year-old prime-minister Sir Winston Churchill attends a conference in Bermuda along with US president Dwight D. Eisenhower and French prime minister Joseph Laniel ... Back in England - Laurel and Hardy's tour of the UK moves onto the Hippodrome in Birmingham and then the Empire in Nottingham ... 21-year-old footballer John Charles scores a hat-trick for Raich 'Silver Fox'

Carter's Leeds Utd in a 2-4 victory over Rotherham Utd in Division Two ... New film *From Here to Eternity*, starring 40-year-old Burt Lancaster and 33-year-old Montgomery Clift, is hugely popular at cinemas ... 32-year-old Jane Russell (38-24-36) and 27-year-old Marilyn Monroe (36-22-36) star in *Gentlemen Prefer Blondes* ... 26-year-old Gina Lollobrigida (36-22-35) stars in *Beat the Devil* ... 22-year-old 'would be' actress Dana Wynter (35-22-35) leaves Britain and heads for America in search of fame and fortune ... "Thumbelina, Thumbelina tiny little thing. Thumbelina dance. Thumbelina sing" - 42-year-old Danny Kaye sings *Thumbelina* ... "They're not making the skies as blue this year. Wish you were here" - 25-year-old heart-throb Eddie Fisher sings *Wish You Were Here* ... *Answer Me* by Frankie Laine remains at number one on the hit parade ... 'Minnie the Minx' makes her fist appearance in *The Beano* comic ... 18-year-old Signalman David Nobbs learns how to send and receive Morse code as part of his national service ... There's a full program of football fixtures over the festive period ... On Christmas Day - 24-year-old centre-forward Ronnie Allen scores as Vic Buckingham's West Bromwich Albion stay at the top of Division One by thrashing Don Welsh's Liverpool 5-2 at the Hawthorns ... Wolverhampton Wanderers stay close on the heels of their Black Country rivals by beating Manchester City 3-1 at the Molineux ... 21-year-old Tommy Taylor scores a hat-trick for Matt Busby's Manchester Utd in a 5-1 victory over Sheffield Wednesday ... 27-year-old inside-left Arthur 'dead shot' Rowley scores a hat-trick for Leicester City in a 4-1 victory over Rotherham Utd in Division Two ... On Boxing Day - Joe Smith's Blackpool draw 2-2 with Tom Whittaker's Arsenal in front of 29,347 spectators at Bloomfield Road ... 'My Cup Winning Boots' - a pair of men's *CWS Stanley Matthews* football boots cost 33s/11d ... "That's the

Stuff. Wren's Dubbin keeps boots tip-top" - a tin of *Wren's* dubbin costs 7d ... *The Kinsey Report* - a new book about sexual behaviour - becomes a best seller. Shorter skirts for women are in fashion - some are an astonishing (and leg-revealing) eighteen inches off the floor! ... *I Saw Mommy Kissing Santa Claus* ("... underneath the mistletoe last night") by The Beverley Sisters is a popular gramophone record ... 28-year-old June Whitfield sings *Diamonds Are A Girl's Best Friend* ... Children enjoy *Rag, Tag and Bobtail*, *Andy Pandy* and *Rufty Tufty the Golliwog* on BBC television ... The *Boy's Own Paper* is on sale for one shilling and still remains popular with schoolboys - ninety-seven years after it was first launched ... All around the country, crowds flock to *Odeon* cinemas to see 38-year-old comedy superstar Norman Wisdom in the hilarious new film *Trouble in Store* ... 43-year-old convicted murderer Stanislaw Juras is hanged by the neck until dead at Strangeways ... 22-year-old convicted rapist and murderer Alfred Whiteway is hanged by the neck until dead at Wandsworth ... "I'm rather worried about Jim" - millions of radio listeners tune-in daily to hear *Mrs. Dale's Diary* ... 30-year-old Sunderland footballer 'Terrible' Trevor Ford transfers to Cardiff City for £30,000 ... Lucky young boys get a metal *Tri-ang Sixty* pedal car for Christmas ... Lucky young girls get a *Pelham Puppet* ... The 'missus' gets a bottle of Estee Lauder *Youth Dew*.

New Year 1954... Here, have a Capstan

10-year-old schoolboy, John Major, from Worcester Park in South London, listens to the wireless ... "To begin at the beginning" - BBC radio broadcasts *Under Milk Wood* by the late Dylan Thomas - and with Richard Burton as First Voice ... A new report is published - showing a link between smoking and lung cancer ... Advertisements say, 'Have a Capstan - Made to Make Friends' ... A *BOAC* de Havilland *Comet* passenger jet (flying between Rome and London) crashes into the Mediterranean Sea killing all thirty-five people on board ... Back in England - a campaign featuring Tuffty Fluffytail warns children to be safe when crossing the road ... Flashing indicator lights become a legal requirement on motor vehicles ... Laurel and Hardy's tour moves onto the Theatre Royal in Portsmouth ... John Webster presents *Family Favourites* on BBC radio ... "Oh my papa, to me he was so wonderful" - *Oh Mein Papa* by Eddie Calvert is number one on the weekly hit parade ... "A man, oh a man, any woman will say, whatever he is, we like him that way" - *Man (Uh-Huh)* by 25-year-old Rosemary Clooney is number seven ... Clara Miller dies in Eastbourne aged 87 and Dr. John Bodkin Adams inherits £1,000 ... Ex borstal boy 23-year-old Milton Taylor strangles and kills his 25-year-old lover Marie Bradshaw at Nantwich in Cheshire ... Crowds flock to picture houses to see *The Robe* - it's the first movie to be shown in CinemaScope and stars 28-year-old Richard Burton, 41-year-old Victor Mature and 25-year-old Jean Simmons ... *Roman Holiday* with 24-year-old Audrey Hepburn (34-20-34) is also now showing ... "When the moon hits your eye like a big pizza pie, that's amore" - 36-year-old Dean Martin sings *That's Amore* ... 27-year-old footballer Arthur 'dead shot' Rowley bags a hat-trick for Second Division Leicester City in a 3-2 victory over First Division Middlesbrough in the third round of the FA Cup ... 18-year-old Signalman David Nobbs spends a day square-bashing as part of his national service ... "I love to go a-wandering along the mountain track, and as I go, I love to sing, my knapsack on my back. Val-deree, val-derah, val-deree, val-derah" - The Obernkirchen Children's Choir perform *The Happy Wanderer* ... "I'm not good looking, I'm not too smart. I may be foolish, but I've got a heart" - 38-year-old Norman Wisdom sings *Don't Laugh At Me ('Cause I'm A Fool)* ... Approximately one in four households now has a television set ... 39-year-old Edward Evans stars in a soap-opera called *The Grove Family* on the BBC ... 33-year-old George Cowling presents the weather forecast - and informs housewives which day of the week is likely to be the most suitable to get the washing dry ... A new comic strip called 'When the Bell Rings' appears in *The Beano* - it's the first story featuring kids from Bash Street School ... *Charles Buchan's Football Monthly* is on sale for 1s/6d with Jimmy Hagan of Sheffield Utd on the front cover ... 30-year-old Jimmy Glazzard scores twice for Andy Beattie's Huddersfield Town in a 2-2 draw with Chelsea in Division One ... 22-year-old centre-forward John Charles scores a hat-trick for Raich 'Silver Fox' Carter's Leeds Utd in a 5-2 win over Lincoln City in Division Two ... 25-year-old goalkeeper Peter Taylor plays for Jack Fairbrother's Coventry City in Division Three (South) - and keeps a clean sheet as City beat Torquay Utd 4-0 at Highfield Road ... Conservative Home Secretary Sir David Maxwell Fyfe is on a mission to keep English society wholesome and pure ... 27-year-old Lord Edward Montague of Beaulieu is arrested and charged with homosexual offences. 30-year-old Peter Wildeblood and 36-year-old Michael Pitt-Rivers are arrested on similar charges ...

35-year-old Billy Graham (an evangelical Christian from America) arrives in Britain - ready to start his crusade preaching the 'transforming message of Jesus' to people gathered at Haringey Arena. Despite freezing temperatures and driving sleet and snow, thousands turn out to hear the inspirational speaker, and to let Jesus into their hearts ... "Go on, laugh - and the best of luck!" - *The Runaway Bus*, a new film starring 36-year-old Frankie Howerd, 21-year-old Petula Clark and 61-year-old Margaret Rutherford, is a hit at picture houses ... "Hey Johnny, what are you rebellin' against?" / "What've y' got?" 29-year-old Marlon Brando stars in *The Wild One*, riding a Triumph *Thunderbird 6T* motorbike - the film is banned in the UK ... Hamburgers are on the menu at a new 'fast-food' counter in the *J. Lyons & Co* Corner House restaurant on Coventry Street in London - it's the UK's first *Wimpy* bar!

Spring 1954... Bannister's four minute mile

Harold Abrahams commentates for BBC radio and the whole country marvels as 25-year-old athlete Roger Bannister runs a mile in under four minutes at a race meeting in Oxford - the official time is given as 3 minutes and 59.4 seconds ... 40-year-old snooker player Fred Davis wins the World Professional Match Play Championship at Houldsworth Hall in Manchester - it's Davis' sixth world title and it's the eighth year in succession that he's faced Walter Donaldson in the final ... The headline in the *Daily Mirror* proclaims, 'Guilty. Montague - 12 months' after 27-year-old Lord Edward Montague is convicted at Winchester Assizes for homosexual offences and is sentenced to a year in prison. Co-defendants Michael Pitt-Rivers and Peter Wildeblood are each sentenced to eighteen months ... 11-year-old schoolboy Tony Blackburn from Guildford in Surrey listens to popular songs on the radio ... *Changing Partners* by Kay Starr enters the hit parade at number six ... *Tennessee Wig Walk* by Bonnie Lou is number four ... The *Elizabethan Express* steam train departs from Kings Cross Station in London at 9.30 a.m. and arrives at Edinburgh Waverley at 4 p.m. - as a daily service on the East Coast mainline. The buffet is somewhat limited ... 'The Collapse of the British Railways Sandwich System' is the latest episode of popular radio comedy *The Goon Show* ... All de Havilland *Comet* airline jets are grounded after a spate of crashes ... Reliant introduce a 'new and improved' three-wheel motorcar - the *Regal MkII* ... "You start to die the moment you are born." - *Live and Let Die* by Ian Fleming is the second James Bond novel to be published ... "Take me in your arms and never let me go. Whisper to me softly, while the moon is low" - 28-year-old Lita Roza from Liverpool sings *Make Love To Me* ... "If you're a guy who's had a gal in each and every port, and you've forgot the rules of love that life has always taught" - 30-year-old Anne Shelton from Dulwich sings *Cross Over The Bridge* ... The failing health of 79-year-old prime-minister Sir Winston Churchill continues to give concern to senior civil servants and cabinet ministers ... 56-year-old Foreign Secretary Sir Anthony Eden attends the Geneva Conference in Switzerland along with representatives from the US, the Soviet Union, France and China. Eden is praised for his contribution at the conference - and is widely tipped to become prime-minister as soon as 'Winny' steps aside ... Back in England - 51-year-old Chancellor of the Exchequer Richard Austen 'Rab' Butler oversees a healthy, growing economy ... The gross domestic production figure is 4.5% higher than last year ... 28-year-old disc jockey Pete Murray spins discs on Radio Luxembourg ... "Over the mountain, over the sea, back where my heart is longing to be. Please let the light that shines on me, shine on the one I love" - *I See The Moon* ("... the moon sees me") by The Stargazers is number one in the pop chart ... "I got the bell bottom blues 'cause my sweetie is a sailor, and he's sailing somewhere on the sea" - *Bell Bottom Blues* by Alma Cogan is number four ... 45-year-old Olive Bennett is strangled to death at Stratford-upon-Avon and her body is left on the bank of the river ... 40-year-old Arthur White is battered to death in Bradford. Edward Reid is arrested and charged with murder ... Actor Arthur Lucan dies in his dressing room at the Tivoli Theatre in Hull aged 68 - just minutes before he's due on stage as *Old Mother Riley* ... Audrey Hepburn (34-20-34) wins an Oscar for her role in *Roman Holiday* ... "Once I had a secret love that lived within the heart of me" - *Secret Love* by Doris Day climbs to number one on the hit parade - and stays for a total of nine weeks! ... 33-year-old Peter Dimmock presents

Sportsview on Thursday nights - BBC's new weekly sports television programme ... Oxford win the hundredth Boat Race on the River Thames - beating Cambridge by four lengths ... 39-year-old Arsenal captain Joe Mercer suffers a double fracture to a leg after a bad tackle in a match against Liverpool - and his playing career comes to an end ... Stan Cullis' Wolverhampton Wanderers are champions of Division One - after beating Tottenham Hotspur 2-0 in front of 44,055 at the Molineux on the final day of the football season. Bert 'the cat' Williams, Bill Slater, Bill Shorthouse, Johnny Hancocks, Dennis Wilshaw, Roy Swinbourne, Jim Mullen, Peter Broadbent and 30-year-old captain Billy Wright have all been outstanding for Wolves ... Don Welsh's Liverpool are relegated to the Second Division ... 28-year-old inside-left Arthur 'dead shot' Rowley scores twice as Leicester City beat Blackburn Rovers 4-0 in front of 40,040 spectators at Filbert Street - and 'The Foxes' go on to become champions of Division Two, gaining promotion to Division One along with Cliff Britton's Everton ... "Heart of my heart. I love that melody" - *(The Gang That Sang) Heart Of My Heart* by 31-year-old Max Bygraves enters the pop chart at number eleven ... 100,000 people travel to Wembley on a warm, sunny Saturday in May for the FA Cup final between Vic Buckingham's West Bromwich Albion and Jim 'Scot' Symon's Preston North End. 26-year-old Tommy Docherty and 32-year-old Tom Finney (aka the 'Preston Plumber') are part of the losing Preston team, as West Brom emerge as 3-2 victors. Centre-forward Ronnie Allen scores twice for 'The Baggies' and outside-right Frank Griffin scores the decisive goal with just two minutes of the match remaining. 35-year-old Arthur Luty from Leeds is referee. A ticket for the standing enclosure at the Empire Stadium costs 3s/6d ... England's international team are totally out-played in a shock 7-1 defeat against Hungary. (31-year-old Ivor Broadis scores England's solitary goal) ... 32-year-old Tom Finney (aka the 'Preston Plumber') is voted Footballer of the Year ... Hollywood comedy icons Laurel and Hardy are forced to end their UK tour when 62-year-old Oliver Hardy suffers a mild heart attack in Plymouth ... "Thousands are turning to God, and to finding peace, security, happiness and joy in this age of uncertainty and confusion" - Billy Graham's evangelical crusade in London has been a resounding success. 120,000 people travel to Wembley on a grey, overcast Saturday in May to see the 35-year-old American preach the closing message after his tour of Britain ... "Oooh that night. Oooh what a night it was, it really was..." *Such A Night* by 27-year-old angst-ridden Johnnie Ray is number one on the hit parade ... *Make It Soon* by Tony Brent is number nine ... The term 'Teddy-boys' is now being used to describe young men in long Edwardian-style jackets and 'brothel creeper' shoes ... Advertisements say, 'For Clean Grooming - *Brylcreem* Your Hair'.

Summer 1954... Hurrah! Ration books ripped up

It's a dull, wet summer with little in the way of sunshine ... *Horizon* organise 'package' holidays to faraway sunshine resorts ... Benidorm is popular this year ... Back in Britain - holiday makers enjoy cruising along English and Welsh coastlines on *White Funnel* paddle ships ... 'I Wish I Could See My Little Willy' - saucy postcards by Donald McGill are in high demand at seaside shops ... 'It's turned out nice again!' - 50-year-old entertainer George Formby appears in summer season at Blackpool ... 41-year-old Eric Winstone and his Orchestra appear in summer season at *Butlin's* in Clacton ... *(Oh Baby Mine) I Get So Lonely* by American group the Four Knights is number five on the hit parade ... *The Kid's Last Fight* by Frankie Laine is number three ... 'Be the girl with the Bush' - advertisements for a new transistor portable radio are aimed at women ... Myxomatosis is killing millions of rabbits in the British countryside. The Conservative government designates rabbits as pests - and allows the epidemic to run its natural course - 11-year-old schoolboy John Humphrys from Cardiff questions this controversial political decision ... 19-year-old Signalman David Nobbs is admitted to the Royal Naval Hospital in Plymouth to be treated for psoriasis ... 18-year-old jockey Lester Piggott from Wantage wins the Epsom Derby riding *Never Say Die* - a thirty-three to one outsider ... Motor car design takes a huge step forward ... The all new Morris *Oxford* has smooth, curved lines and integral front wings to give a unitary 'modern look' ... 40-year-old Ernie Watkins from Towcester takes his family for a Sunday drive in his Morris *Minor* and parks-up on a layby in the country-side to enjoy the view ... 30-year-old Eileen Sheridan from Coventry rides a Hercules sports bicycle from Land's End to John

O'Groats in a new record time of 2 days, 11 hours and 7 minutes ... After three days of no play because of rain, cricketers 37-year-old Len Hutton and 34-year-old Reg Simpson stride out together to open the batting for England against Pakistan at Lord's. The match ends in a draw. England win the second Test at Trent Bridge - with 36-year-old Denis Compton scoring 278 runs and 30-year-old spin bowler Bob Appleyard taking five wickets. There's another draw in a rain-affected match at Old Trafford, before Pakistan gain a victory in the final Test at the Oval to tie the series 1-1 ... 29-year-old Richard Baker reads the news on BBC television ... There's nationwide jubilation as *all* rationing finally comes to an end - and people take great delight in ripping up their ration books ... Posters declare, 'The Conservatives Get Things Done!' Sir Winston Churchill's Tory government (with 51-year-old Richard Austen 'Rab' Butler as Chancellor of the Exchequer) have succeeded where Clement Attlee's Labour government couldn't - rationing has ended! ... The country's finances are improving. People are being encouraged to spend money - it's the early stages of a new consumer driven boom in the economy ... 79-year-old prime-minister Sir Winston Churchill travels to the United States for a meeting with 63-year-old president Dwight D. Einsenhower in Washington ... Back in Britain - 56-year-old senior Labour MP Aneurin Bevan calls for Attlee to step down as Leader of the Opposition ... 41-year-old war hero Alan Turing commits suicide by eating a poisoned apple ... 23-year-old ex borstal boy and convicted murderer Milton Taylor is hanged by the neck until dead at Liverpool ... "Cara Mia why, must we say goodbye? Each time we part, my heart wants to die" - *Cara Mia* by David Whitfield with Mantovani and his Orchestra tops the hit parade for ten weeks ... "Blow me a kiss from across the room, say I look nice when I'm not. Touch my hair as you pass my chair…" *Little Things Mean A Lot* is a hit song for 32-year-old Jimmy Young from Cinderford ... Petty criminal Norman Stanley Fletcher is king of the teddy-boys in Muswell Hill ... Wing commander Winterbottom's England football team take part in the FIFA world cup competition in Switzerland. A 4-4 draw against Belgium and a 2-0 victory over the host nation sees England into the knock-out stages. 28-year-old Nat Lofthouse and 32-year-old Tom Finney (aka the 'Preston Plumber') both score goals in England's next match against Uruguay but 32-year-old goalkeeper Gil Merrick is slow to react to a couple of free kicks and England lose 4-2 and are out of the tournament. Gil Merrick, Ron Staniforth, Roger Byrne, Billy Wright (captain), Jimmy Dickinson, Ivor Broadis, Nat Lofthouse, Tommy Taylor, Jimmy Mullen, Tom Finney, Dennis Wilshaw, Bill McGarry and 39-year-old Stanley 'wizard of dribble' Matthews all return home disappointed ... 19-year-old Australian tennis player Ken Rosewall loses in the final at Wimbledon to Jaroslav Drobny from Czechoslovakia - 32-year-old Drobny is a popular champion with the centre-court crowd. 19-year-old Maureen Connolly (aka Little Mo) from California wins the women's final ... 'Somebody's Going To Pay … Because He Forgot To Kill Me' - *The Big Heat* with Glenn Ford and Gloria Grahame is now showing at cinemas ... "Wanted, someone who kissed me" - *Wanted* by 42-year-old Perry Como is number four in the pop chart ... "You send me someone else's roses. The note you sent, I wasn't meant to see. Why did they bring me…" *Someone Else's Roses* by 26-year-old Joan Regan from Romford is number five ... An unknown 19-year-old American singer called Elvis Presley records *That's Alright* at Sun Studios in Memphis ... Back in England - 79-year-old seaside postcard designer Donald McGill is prosecuted under the Obscene Publications Act ... *The Fellowship of the Ring* - the first volume in the new epic novel *Lord of the Rings* by 62-year-old J. R. R. Tolkien is now on sale in book shops ... 25-year-old racing driver Mike Hawthorn from Mexborough finishes second in the British Grand Prix at Silverstone in a red Ferrari. 38-year-old Ken Wharton from Smethwick finishes eighth in a red Maserati ... The new football season gets underway ... 26-year-old footballer Tommy Docherty (a talented right-half) transfers from Preston North End to Arsenal for £28,000 ... 30-year-old Eric 'Rabbit' Parsons is on the score-sheet as First Division Chelsea beat Burnley 1-0 in front of 30,239 at Stamford Bridge ... 23-year-old Roy Sproson scores for Second Division Port Vale in a 1-1 draw with Notts County in front of 26,805 at Vale Park ... People continue to spend their hard earned wages on motorcars and house-hold goods - and seem perfectly happy to do so ... A traditionally styled Ford *Popular* motorcar (based on a pre-war design) is available in showrooms for just £275 (plus £115/14s/2d purchase tax). It has a top speed of 62 mph and accelerates from 0-60 mph in 58.2 seconds ... The contemporary 'modern-looking' Ford *Anglia 100E* costs £360 (plus £151/2s/6d purchase tax). It has a top speed of 70 mph and accelerates from 0-60 mph in 29.4 seconds ... A new G.E.C. fourteen-inch television-set costs 60 guineas, or can be obtained on hire-purchase ... A nice cup of tea at the *J. Lyons & Co* teashop on North Street in Brighton costs tuppence.

Autumn 1954... Roy of the Rovers

Freezing fog descends on the country ... Ted Fenton's West Ham Utd football team beat Bristol Rovers 5-2 in League Division Two - with 26-year-old Frank O'Farrell and 24-year-old Dave Sexton on the score-sheet for 'The Hammers' ... Jimmy Anderson's Tottenham Hotspur beat West Bromwich Albion 3-1 in League Division One - with 34-year-old Alf Ramsey scoring a penalty for Spurs ... 10-year-old schoolboy Martin Peters from Plaistow in Essex plays football with his friends in the park ... 79-year-old prime-minister Sir Winston Churchill makes changes to his Cabinet. 50-year-old Sir David Eccles is the new Minister for Education and 60-year-old Harold Macmillan moves from Housing to become Minister for Defence ... Britain's first supersonic fighter plane - the *P1 Lightning* - embarks on test flights ... "Smile, though your heart is aching. Smile, even though it's breaking" - *Smile* by 35-year-old Nat 'King' Cole is number two on the hit parade ... *My Friend* by 41-year-old Frankie Laine is number three ... *Woolworths* introduce *Embassy* 78 rpm cover-version records for just four shillings ... 28-year-old Queen Elizabeth II welcomes 62-year-old Emperor Haile Salassie of Ethiopia on an official state visit to Britain ... A 'Super New Paper for Boys!' with 'Space Gun Novelty - Free Inside!' - *Tiger* is launched (3d a copy) featuring the characters 'Bulldog Bryant', 'The Speedster from Bleakmoor' and 'Roy of the Rovers' ... "I coulda been a contender. I coulda been somebody" - 30-year-old actor Marlon Brando stars in *On the Waterfront* at cinemas ... "Three coins in the fountain, each one seeking happiness. Thrown by three hopeful lovers, which one will the fountain bless?" - *Three Coins In The Fountain* by 38-year-old Frank Sinatra is number one in the pop chart ... *West Of Zanzibar* by

Anthony Steel and The Radio Revellers is number eleven ... The Swallow Doretti open-top sports car is exhibited at Earls Court ... 17-year-old blonde-bombshell Barbara Windsor (36-23-34) gets male pulses racing in new movie *The Belles of St. Trinian's* ... 28-year-old Marilyn Monroe (36-22-36) stands over an air vent and her skirt balloons up, as she films a scene for *Seven Year Itch* ... 24-year-old convicted murderer Edward Reid is hanged by the neck until dead at Leeds. (66-year-old hangman Stephen Wade carries out the execution) ... 25-year-old racing driver Mike Hawthorn from Mexborough wins the Spanish Grand Prix ... 43-year-old Juan Manuel Fangio from Argentina is world champion - for a second time ... The hit parade of pop songs is extended from a Top 12 to a Top 20 ... *Hold My Hand* by 35-year-old Don Cornell is number one for a total of five weeks. *My Son, My Son* by 37-year-old Vera Lynn is number one for two weeks ... 19-year-old footballer Johnny Haynes of Fulham scores on his debut for England in a 0-2 win over Northern Ireland. (27-year-old Don Revie of Manchester City is also on the score-sheet) ... Stan Cullis' Wolverhampton Wanderers lead the way in Division One after winning five of their opening seven matches ... 40-year-old Alan Brown is the new manager of Burnley - taking over from Frank Hill who's left recently to join Preston North End ... 30-year-old centre-forward Roy Bentley of Chelsea scores a hat-trick for England at Wembley ... Antique book dealers Peter and Helen Kroger from Canada set up home at 45 Cranley Drive in Ruislip ... *The Two Towers* - the second volume in the epic novel *Lord of the Rings* by 62-year-old J. R. R. Tolkien is now on sale in book shops ... An ailing and forgetful Sir Winston Churchill celebrates his 80th birthday - still prime-minister of the country. The great man is presented with a portrait (painted by Graham Sutherland) at a ceremony at Westminster Hall. 'Winny' describes the painting as, "a remarkable example of modern art." ... "Hello children, everywhere!" - 56-year-old Derek McCulloch is 'Uncle Mac' on Saturday morning radio show *Children's Favourites* ... 30-year-old Tony Hancock stars in *Hancock's Half Hour* on Tuesday evenings at 9.30 p.m. - 41-year-old Sid James also features in the show ... "This ole house once knew his children, this ole house once knew a wife. This ole house was home and comfort, as we fought the storms of life" - Rosemary Clooney tops the pop chart with *This Ole House* ... "There's a tiny house, by a tiny stream, where a lovely lass, had a lovely dream" - *Gilly Gilly Ossenfeffer Katzenellen Bogen By The Sea* by 32-year-old Max Bygraves is number seven ... The dreaded 'Lurgi Strikes Britain' - is the latest episode of *The Goon Show* ... Veteran entertainer Sir George Robey (aka the Prime Minister of Mirth) dies at the age of 85 in Saltdean ... Advertising posters for beer claim, '*A Double Diamond* works wonders!'

Christmas 1954...
Wolves dazzle under Molineux floodlights

The weather is cold and foggy ... Schoolboy friends Mick Jagger (aged 11) and Keith Richards (aged 10) from Dartford in Kent chase after girls on the playground ... "Oh, life could be a dream (sh-boom, sh-boom), if I could take you up in paradise up above, (sh-boom, sh-boom)" - *Sh-Boom* by The Crew Cuts is a popular song on juke boxes all around the country ... A rockin' new song called *Shake Rattle And Roll* by Bill Haley and his Comets plays on Radio Luxembourg - but is ignored by the BBC ... *Lucky Jim* - a brilliant new novel from 32-year-old Kingsley Amis is on sale now in bookshops ... Twenty-eight people are killed when a New York bound *BOAC* Boeing *377* passenger plane crash-lands at Prestwick in Scotland ... Political maneuvering is underway in the Conservitive party. 52-year-old Chancellor of the Exchequer Richard Austen 'Rab' Butler and 57-year-old Foreign Secretary Sir Anthony Eden demand that 80-year-old prime-minister Sir Winston Churchill sets a date for his retirement ... Political maneuvering is also underway in the opposition Labour ranks. 57-year-old Aneurin Bevan and 48-year-old Hugh Gaitskell both hold ambitions to take over from 71-year-old leader Clement Attlee ... 21-year-old tear-away twins Reginald and Ronald Kray 'take over' the management of an old billiard hall in the East End of London ... 28-year-old footballer Danny Blanchflower transfers from Aston Villa to Tottenham Hotspur for £30,000 - and makes his debut for Spurs in a 0-0 draw against Manchester City at Maine Road ... 36-year-old Jack 'cannonball' Rowley scores his final league goal for Manchester Utd (in a 3-1 victory over Leicester City) before transferring to Plymouth Argyle ... Police drama *Fabian of the Yard* (starring 45-year-old Bruce

Seton) is on television ... Crowds flock to the cinema to see the latest movie *Beau Brummell* starring Stewart Granger, Peter Ustinov and 22-year-old Elizabeth Taylor ... *I Need You Now* by 26-year-old heart-throb Eddie Fisher is number thirteen on the hit parade ... *No One But You* by 40-year-old Billy Eckstine is number three ... "Maybe there's a beast. Maybe it's only us." - gripping new novel *Lord of the Flies* by William Golding is published by Faber & Faber ... "John, see the aeroplanes. One, two, three aeroplanes. I can see three aeroplanes" - *Janet and John* books are published by James Nisbet & Co. Ltd ... 23-year-old athlete Christopher Chataway is BBC's 'Sports Personality of the Year'. (Chataway was the selfless pace setter for Roger Bannister's record breaking mile run in May) ... 32-year-old Len Shackleton scores an audacious chip shot as wing commander Winterbottom's England football team defeat West Germany 3-1 at Wembley in the first football match between the two countries since the war. 30-year-old Billy Wright is England's captain, 34-year-old Bert 'the cat' Williams is goalkeeper and 39-year-old Stanley 'wizard of dribble' Matthews is outside-right - and the undisputed man-of-the-match! ... In an amazing night under the new floodlights at Molineux stadium - 38-year-old Stan Cullis' Wolverhampton Wanderers come back from 0-2 down to beat the crack Hungarian side Honved 3-2 in front of 55,000 spectators ... 53-year-old convicted female murderer Styllou Christofi is hanged by the neck until dead at Holloway. (49-year-old hangman Albert Pierrepoint carries out the execution) ... England's cricketers (under the captaincy of 38-year-old Len Hutton) travel to Australia for an Ashes series ... Back in England - lucky schoolboys get a *Bayko* building set on Christmas morning. A *Matchbox* die-cast model of a red London bus is also popular ... Dads take their sons to football matches on Boxing

Day ... 47,450 turn out at Leeds Road to see Andy Beattie's Huddersfield Town draw 1-1 with Bill Murray's top-of-the-table Sunderland ... 42,734 turn out at Hillsborough to see Eric Taylor's bottom-of-the-table Sheffield Wednesday draw 2-2 with Jimmy Seed's Charlton Athletic ... 40-year-old Winifred Atwell from Trinidad is number one at Christmas with her piano medley, *Let's Have Another Party* (comprising of the songs: *Another Little Drink*, *Broken Doll*, *Bye Bye Blackbird*, *Honeysuckle And The Bee*, *I Wonder Where My Baby Is Tonight*, *Lily Of Laguna*, *Nellie Dean*, *Sheik Of Araby*, *Somebody Stole My Gal* and *When The Red Red Robin*) ... 55-year-old Alfred Hitchcock's new thriller *Rear Window* (starring 46-year-old James Stewart and 25-year-old Grace Kelly) is now showing at cinemas ... BBC TV programmes on a Saturday night include: *Association Football Results*; *Weather Chart*; *In Town Tonight* - with John Ellison; *The Crosby Christmas Hour* - showing selected extracts from Bing Crosby films; *Panto Parade*; and *Birds in Close-Up* - presented by 45-year-old ornithologist Peter Scott ... 227 million tonnes of coal have been mined in Britain this year ... Sir Winston Churchill's Conservative government presides over an unemployment figure of just 250,000 ... A record number of new houses - approximately 340,000 - have been built this year under the guidance of two Housing Ministers - Harold Macmillan (up until October) and Duncan Sandys (since October) ... The wider economy also continues to improve under the guidance of 52-year-old Chancellor of the Exchequer Richard Austen 'Rab' Butler ... 22-year-old Alma Cogan from Whitechapel sings *I Can't Tell A Waltz From A Tango* ("… I never know what my feet are gonna do. Oh I can't tell a waltz from a tango, darling when I dance with you") ... 19-year-old Ruby Murray from Belfast sings "Hear it. Hear it. Hear my…" *Heartbeat* ("…

pounding, pounding like a drum") ... 27-year-old footballer Andy Graver (a prolific goal scoring centre-forward) leaves Lincoln City and joins Norman Bullock's Leicester City for £29,500 ... A special Christmas pack of fifty *Senior Service* cigarettes costs 9s/9d.

New Year 1955... Shake, rattle and roll

A severe winter freeze affects most of the country, and some communities are cut off for several days ... 31-year-old Benny Hill stars in a new comedy show on BBC television ... 60-year-old Annette Mills, the popular host of children's programme *Muffin the Mule,* dies of a heart attack ... 29-year-old Anthony Wedgwood Benn MP fails in an attempt to renounce his official title of Viscount Stansgate ... "Someone broke into my heart and stole a beat or two..." *The Finger Of Suspcion* ("... points at you") by 25-year-old Dickie Valentine is new at number one in the weekly singles chart ... Long playing gramophone discs, containing up to ten songs, are becoming more and more popular ... Decca release *New Orleans Joys* - the debut album from Chris Barber's Jazz Band and Skiffle Group (featuring 23-year-old Lonnie Donegan on banjo) ... Cricketers Len Hutton, Denis Compton, Peter May, Trevor Bailey, Frank 'typhoon' Tyson, Brian Statham and 22-year-old Colin Cowdrey all play magnificently and help England retain the Ashes down-under - winning the series 3-1 against Ian Johnson's Aussies. England's full squad, comprising of L Hutton (cpt), R T Simpson, W J Edrich, P B H May, T W Graveney, M C Cowdrey, T E Bailey, F H Tyson, A V Bedser, K V Andrew (wk), T G Evans (wk), J H Wardle, J B Statham, D C S Compton and R Appleyard, all return to Blighty in buoyant mood after a wonderful series victory ... 32-year-old Max Bygraves sings *You're A Pink Toothbrush* ("... I'm a blue toothbrush, have we met somewhere before?") ... 37-year-old Dean Martin sings *The Naughty Lady Of Shady Lane* ("... has hit the town like a bomb. The back fence gossip ain't been this good since Mabel ran off with Tom") ... 18-year-old footballer Duncan Edwards scores his first goal for Matt

Busby's Manchester Utd in a 4-1 victory over Blackpool ... 28-year-old inside-left Arthur 'dead shot' Rowley bags a hat-trick for struggling Leicester City in a 6-3 victory over West Bromwich Albion at Filbert Street ... 23-year-old Billy Bingham and 29-year-old Ken Chisholm are in tremendous form for Bill Murray's league leaders Sunderland - but Ted Drake's Chelsea are closing the gap at the top of the Division One table ... Roy Bentley, Eric 'Rabbit' Parsons, Frank Blunstone and Les Stubbs are on the score-sheet as 'The Blues' beat Huddersfield Town 4-1 in front of 35,786 at Stamford Bridge ... "Hey mambo, mambo Italiano" - *Mambo Italiano* by 26-year-old Rosemary Clooney is number one in the pop chart ... "Get out from that kitchen and rattle those pots and pans" - the rockin' new sound of *Shake Rattle And Roll* by Bill Haley and his Comets climbs to number four ... Teddy-boys wear narrow boot-lace ties and style their hair into a 'quiff' ... Footballers 33-year-old Billy Liddell and 20-year-old Alan A'Court are among the goal scorers when Second Division Liverpool beat First Division Everton 0-4 in an FA Cup tie in front of 72,000 at Goodison Park ... 'Stars Love Mars!' - Vera Lynn, Petula Clark and 26-year-old Bob Monkhouse promote *Mars* bars ... 31-year-old Jack Hill takes over the running of his father's toy shop at Rugeley in Staffordshire ... New *Airfix* kits are popular with schoolboys - 1:72 scale models of the Gloster *Gladiator* and *Spitfire* fighter planes are in high demand ... Britain's naval defence is boosted by a new 'state-of-the-art' aircraft carrier - when HMS *Ark Royal* is commissioned into the Royal Navy fleet under the control of 47-year-old Captain Dennis Royle Farquharson Cambell ... 80-year-old Sir Winston Churchill's Tory government announces plans to build three-lane motorways throughout the country ... Plans to electrify the railway network are also unveiled ... "Earth angel, earth angel, will you be mine?" - Milk bar juke boxes play *Earth Angel* by The Crew Cuts ... Crowds flock to the cinema to see 39-year-old comedy superstar Norman Wisdom in *One Good Turn* ... 46-year-old John Mills stars in *The Colditz Story* ... "I'm rather worried about Jim" - Mrs. Mary Dale is concerned about her husband Jim in *Mrs Dale's Diary* on BBC radio's Light Programme ... The average price of a house has risen slightly to £1,900 ... Ford launch the new *Squire* motorcar - a small estate with a heater as an optional extra ... The last MG *TF* sports car rolls off the production line at Abingdon and the all new, super-sleek MG *A* takes its place.

Spring 1955... Sir Winston Churchill steps down

Maintenance workers at the printing presses in Fleet Street go on strike, and newspaper offices are forced to close down ... After much speculation, 80-year-old Sir Winston Churchill resigns as prime-minister and is succeeded by 57-year-old Sir Anthony Eden ... 52-year-old Richard Austen 'Rab' Butler remains as Chancellor of the Exchequer ... A general election is called ... 'Stick to Success - Vote Conservative' / 'Put the Family First with Labour' - campaigning gets underway and people go to the polls on the twenty-sixth of May ... Sir Anthony Eden defeats 72-year-old Labour leader Clement Attlee and increases the Tory majority. (Conservatives: 345 seats, Labour: 277 seats, Liberals: 6 seats) ... Newspapers remain off-sale due to the on-going strike by maintenance workers ... The number of aeroplanes flying in and out of London Airport is on the increase ... A new 'state-of-the-art' air-traffic control tower (measuring 130-feet) opens ... 32-year-old Philip Larkin from Coventry becomes head librarian at the University of Hull ... 48-year-old entertainment impresario Lew Grade commissions *Robin Hood* - an exciting new TV drama for the new commercial channel (which is due to start in the Autumn) ... "Softly, softly come to me, touch my lips so tenderly. Softly, softly turn the key, and open up my heart" - *Softly Softly* by 20-year-old Ruby Murray from Belfast is top of the hit parade ... 41-year-old Fred Davis beats 31-year-old John Pulman in the final of snooker's World Professional Match Play Championship at the Tower Circus in Blackpool - it's Davis' seventh world title in eight years ... The University Boat Race, the Grand National and the FA Cup semi-finals all take place on Saturday the twenty-sixth of March ... Cambridge win the Boat Race by sixteen lengths ... Pat Taaffe rides *Quare Times* to victory in 'The National' at Aintree ... Manchester City beat Sunderland 1-0 at Villa Park to make it through to the cup final ... Newcastle Utd draw 1-1 with York City at Hillsborough, and then win a replay at Roker Park 2-0 - with goals from 25-year-old Len White and 24-year-old Vic Keeble ... "Take my hand, I'm a..." *Stranger In Paradise* by 28-year-old Tony Bennett is a new entry in the pop chart at number ten ... 28-year-old Eric Morecambe and 29-year-old Ernie Wise (a popular new comedy double act) are currently appearing on stage in Blackpool ... 42-year-old Wallace Greenslade reads the news on BBC radio ... A strike by rail and dock workers gets underway ... The nation's transport system grinds to a halt and thousands of commuters are unable to get to work ... 28-year-old night club hostess Ruth Ellis shoots dead her racing driver boyfriend David Blakely in Hampstead ... 21-year-old tear-away twins Reginald and Ronald Kray confront established London gangsters Billy Hill and Jack 'Spot' Comer at a race meeting in Epsom. (Over the next few months, the Kray gang will become the most feared criminal Firm in the capital) ... The Warsaw Pact treaty is signed between the USSR, Poland, Hungary, East Germany, Czechoslovakia, Romania, Bulgaria and Albania ... The clash of ideologies between East and West hardens the state of Cold War ... 31-year-old MI6 officer George Blake is dispatched to Berlin to recruit Soviet officers as double agents ... Back in England - Helen and Peter Kroger of 45 Cranley Drive, Ruislip are purporting to be law-abiding antique book dealers, when in fact they are Soviet spies - passing on classified information to the USSR ... Daily newspapers are back on-sale after maintenance workers in Fleet Street agree to end their industrial action ... Distinguished scientist Albert Einstein dies aged 76 in New Jersey ... "A blossom fell from off a tree, it settled softly on the lips you turned to me" - *A Blossom Fell* by 25-year-old Dickie Valentine from London reaches number ten on the hit parade ... *Give Me Your Word* ("... your love will never die. Give me your word, you feel the same as I") by Tennessee Ernie Ford is new at number one ... The wonderful new MG *A* sports car zips along England's narrow and twisty roads - its top speed is 98 mph and acceleration from 0-60 mph comes in 16 seconds ... A new series of the comedy show *Hancock's Half Hour* begins on the wireless with 30-year-old Tony Hancock and 41-year-old Sid James ... 30-year-old actor Marlon Brando wins an Oscar for his role in *On the Waterfront* ... 30-year-old Eva Marie Saint is the Best Supporting Actress ... 18-year-old footballer Duncan Edwards makes his debut for England in a 7-2 victory over Scotland ... 21-year-old footballer Charlie Dutton of Coventry City marries his sweetheart Patricia Hammersley ... Ted Drake's Chelsea beat Bill Murray's Sunderland 2-1 in a top-of-the-table clash at Stamford Bridge - and then go on to complete victories over Tottenham Hotspur, Wolverhampton Wanderers and Sheffield Wednesday to become the new champions of Division One ... Bill Robertson, John Harris, Chick Thompson, Stan Willemse, Stan Wicks, Ron Greenwood, Peter Sillett, Ken Armstrong, Derek Saunders, Frank Blunstone, Eric 'Rabbit' Parsons, Johnny McNichol and 30-year-old centre-forward Roy Bentley (with twenty-one goals) have all been outstanding for Chelsea ... *Under The Bridges Of Paris* by Eartha Kitt from America is number seven in the pop chart ... *Let Me Go Lover* by Ruby Murray from Belfast is number five ... 34-year-old footballer Jackie Milburn scores after just forty-five seconds as Doug Livingstone's Newcastle Utd beat Les McDowell's Manchester City 3-1 in the FA Cup final ... A ticket for the standing enclosure at the Empire Stadium in Wembley costs 3s/6d ... "It's..." *Cherry Pink And Apple Blossom White*

("… when your true lover comes your way") by Perez Prado tops the hit parade for a couple of weeks ... Another version of the same song, by 33-year-old Eddie Calvert from Preston, also reaches number one - and stays there for four weeks ... High winds rage across the east of the country ... Buildings are damaged and trees uprooted in Norfolk ... The national rail strike continues - causing major disruption for thousands of commuters ... Food shortages are expected as the movement of supplies slows to a near standstill ... Prime-minister Sir Anthony Eden consults with 29-year-old Queen Elizabeth II and declares a State of Emergency ... Troops are put on stand-by ... "Take my hand, I'm a…" *Stranger In Paradise* by 28-year-old Tony Bennett is new at number one in the Top 20 pop chart ... "Things will turn out fine…" *Tomorrow* by 29-year-old Johnny Brandon and the Phantoms is number eight ... Sixteen teddy-boys are arrested at a dance hall in Bath.

Summer 1955... Blue jeans

It's a long, hot summer ... Public parks are packed with families enjoying the sun. 'Aqua-lung thrills! Jane Russell as you've never seen her before!' - crowds flock to the cinema to see 34-year-old Jane Russell (38-24-36) in *Underwater* ... 'The sweet with the hole' - a roll of *Navy Fruits* sweets cost tuppence ... 'Levi's - America's finest overall since 1850' - Hip teenagers wear blue denim jeans and loiter inside record shops - taking turns to stand in sound-proofed booths, while listening to the latest tunes ... "Lonely rivers flow to the sea, to the sea. To the open arms of the sea" - *Unchained Melody* by 33-year-old Jimmy Young from Cinderford reaches number one - and stays there for three weeks ... 11-year-old schoolboy Paul Gadd from Banbury dreams that one day he'll become a famous singer ... A high-speed car crash at the Le Mans 24 hour race in France takes the life of racing driver Pierre Levegh and eighty-three spectators ... Track safety is called into question and a number of racing circuits around the world are forced to close ... Back in England - the rail strike comes to an end and trains begin running again after three weeks of transport chaos ... The sun continues to shine ... A family 'brick' of *Wall's* ice-cream costs 1s/6d ... Wireless technology moves on apace ... The BBC transmit radio broadcasts in super high-quality VHF ... The economy remains buoyant ... Jobs are easy to come by ... Unemployment is at an all-time low of just 215,000 ... The Conservative government claims to have put Britain 'back to work.' ... 58-year-old prime-minister Sir Anthony Eden and 52-year-old Chancellor of the Exchequer Richard Austen 'Rab' Butler both take a well earned holiday ... "I wonder who paints the skies so blue, who paints the snowflakes white" - *I Wonder* by 25-year-old Dickie Valentine from London climbs to number four in the pop chart ... 28-year-old convicted murderer Ruth Ellis is hanged by the neck until dead at Holloway. The execution of this vulnerable young woman gives rise to a sense of unease across the country - with many people believing capital punishment is wrong in a modern day society ... 'And Now His Happiest Motion Picture!' - 53-year-old American movie magnate Walt Disney releases a new animated film called *Lady and the Tramp* ... 25-year-old racing driver Stirling Moss wins the British Grand Prix at Aintree in a Mercedes. The brilliant 44-year-old Juan Manuel Fangio from Argentina finishes in second place and leads the way in the Formula One Drivers' Championship ... 34-year-old Donald Campbell sets a new water speed record of 202 mph in *Bluebird K7* on Ullswater ... Standard grade petrol is 4s/6d a gallon ... Families take Sunday drives in their motor cars. Children sit in the back and remind their fathers to use the 'winkers' when turning ... "You dreamboats, you lovable dreamboats" - *Dreamboat* by 23-year-old Alma Cogan moves to the top of the hit parade ... 40-year-old Joe Mercer takes over from Reg Freeman as football manager at First Division Sheffield Utd ... 39-year-old Maurice Lindley takes over from Ralph Ward at Third Division (North) Crewe Alexandra ... 21-year-old striker Eddie Firmani leaves Charlton Athletic and joins Sampdoria for a new record transfer fee of £35,000 ... 27-year-old goalkeeper Peter Taylor leaves Coventry City and joins Middlesbrough for £3,500 - where he teams up with a young centre-forward called Brian Clough ... "Oh Rose, my r-hose Maria!" - *Rose Marie* by Slim Whitman reaches number one in the Top 20 - and stays there for eleven weeks! ... England's cricket team secure a Test series win against South Africa - with 26-year-old Peter May, 26-year-old Tony Lock and 33-year-old Jim Laker all playing their part ... 'Music, Laughter, Suspense: 208 Has Got Everything!' - advertisements for Radio Luxembourg appear in British newspapers ... *The Dam Busters*, with 47-year-old Michael Redgrave and 35-year-old Richard Todd, is now showing at cinemas ... "Evening All" - *Dixon of Dock Green* debuts on television, with 59-year-old Jack Warner in the title role ... Actor Reginald Tate (famous for playing Professor Bernard Quatermass in *The Quatermass Experiment*) dies of a heart attack aged 58 in London ... 41-year-old Ernie Watkins from Towcester takes his wife for a spin in his Morris *Minor* and the two sit together in a layby near Stow-on-the-Wold sipping hot tea from a Thermos flask ... In light of the terrible motor racing tragedy at Le Mans earlier in the summer, three Grands Prix (at Germany, Switzerland and Spain) are cancelled - and the brilliant Juan Manuel Fangio from Argentina is confirmed as world motor racing champion for the third time in his career ... Back in England - the new football season gets underway ... Eddie Lewis, Albert Scanlon and Dennis Viollet score the goals as Manchester Utd beat West Bromwich Albion 3-1 in front of 32,267 spectators at Old Trafford ... 35-year-old Tommy Lawton scores a hat-trick as Arsenal beat Cardiff City 3-1 in front of 31,361 at Highbury ... 24-year-old Billy Bingham scores twice as Sunderland thrash Aston Villa 5-1 in front of 33,761 at Roker Park ... On Sunday afternoons, families enjoy Coronation Chicken for dinner, followed by a piece of swiss roll for pudding.

Autumn 1955... Commercial television

Commercial television arrives! ... Associated-Rediffusion begin transmitting in the London region ... Gibbs *SR* - 'the tingling fresh toothpaste' is the first advert broadcast on the small screen ... "Robin Hood, Robin Hood, ridin' through the glen. Robin Hood, Robin Hood, with his band of men. Feared by the bad, loved by the good. Robin Hood. Robin Hood. Robin Hood." - *The Adventures of Robin Hood* (with Richard Greene in the title role and with Alexander Gauge as Friar Tuck) captivates viewers ... "The man from Laramie, he was a man with a warm and gentle heart" - *The Man From Laramie* by 34-year-old Jimmy Young from Cinderford is number one on the hit parade ... 20-year-old David Nobbs completes his national service and goes up to Cambridge to read Classics ... 18-year-old footballer Duncan Edwards scores both goals as Matt Busby's Manchester Utd beat Tottenham Hotspur 1-2 at White Hart Lane - with the Blanchflower brothers (29-year-old Danny of Spurs and 22-year-old Jackie of Utd) lining up on opposite sides ... 11-year-old schoolboy Graham Taylor from Worksop in Nottinghamshire plays football with his friends in the park ... "I know - a dark - secluded place. A place - where no - one knows your face" - *Hernando's Hideaway* by 28-year-old angst-ridden Johnnie Ray climbs to number eleven in the pop chart. Another version of the same song, by The Johnston Brothers, makes it to number one! ... "This pound note. What colour was it? / Green / It's mine! Mine was green!" - 30-year-old Peter Sellers is Major Bloodnok and 34-year-old Harry Secombe is Neddie Seagoon in a new series of *The Goon Show* on BBC Home Service radio ... 35-year-old Barbara Mandell announces the news on the new commercial television channel in London ... Speculation that former MI6 senior officer Kim Philby was the 'third man' in the Burgess MacLean spy ring is rife. 61-year-old Foreign Secretary Harold Macmillan makes a public statement saying there is no evidence to support the notion that Philby is a spy. 43-year-old Philby himself then holds a press conference to re-affirm his own innocence ... 72-year-old Clement Attlee steps down as Labour leader - and leaves the way open for either Hugh Gaitskell or Aneurin Bevan to take over ... 36-year-old singer turned disc jockey Teddy Johnson from Surbiton plays popular tunes on Radio Luxembourg ... 29-year-old Sammy Davis Jr. from New York sings *Love Me Or Leave Me* - and it climbs to number eight on the hit parade ... 31-year-old Gary Miller from Blackpool sings *The Yellow Rose Of Texas* - and it peaks at number thirteen ... Boys 'play out' after school ... Conkers, British Bulldog and football (played in the street) are popular games ... Joe Smith's Blackpool (with 40-year-old Stanley 'wizard of dribble' Matthews and 34-year-old Stan Mortensen) defeat Wolverhampton Wanderers 2-1 in front of 38,098 at Bloomfield Road and move two points clear at the top of Division One ... 22-year-old Dennis Viollet scores twice as Matt Busby's Manchester Utd beat Charlton Athletic 5-1 in front of 44,838 spectators at Old Trafford ... 35-year-old Tommy Lawton plays in his final league game as Arsenal lose 3-1 to Bill Murray's Sunderland at Roker Park ... 24-year-old Roy Sproson is on the score-sheet for Second Division Port Vale in a 2-0 victory over Leeds Utd at Vale Park ... 25-year-old racing driver Stirling Moss from London achieves the fastest lap in his Mercedes at the Monza Grand Prix but is forced to retire from the race with engine problems. The brilliant Fangio from Argentina wins the race ... Back in England - Standard-Triumph introduce the new *TR3* sports car - with disc brakes on the front wheels. The car costs

£950 and has a top speed of 105 mph ... Jaguar launch a new 2.4 litre saloon (priced from £1,344) with a top speed of 101 mph and capable of accelerating from 0-60 mph in 14.4 seconds ... Schoolboys crave a *Matchbox* die-cast model of a green Land Rover ... 24-year-old film star James Dean is killed in America driving his Porsche *550 Spyder* ... 60-year-old Labour MP Sydney Silverman introduces a Bill to abolish capital punishment - it's rejected by the House of Lords ... 28-year-old angst-ridden pop star Johnnie Ray appears at the Royal Variety Show in front of 29-year-old Queen Elizabeth II and the 34-year-old Duke of Edinburgh ... 19-year-old 'pin-up girl 'Sabrina (41-19-36) stars alongside Arthur Askey in a new television show called *Before Your Very Eyes* ... Children tune-in to watch *Crackerjack!* - hosted by 32-year-old Eamonn Andrews ... 47-year-old Franklin Engelman is the new presenter on BBC radio's *Down Your Way* ... "I put my finger in a woodpecker's hole, the woodpecker said, 'Cor bless my soul. Take it out. Take it out. Take it out. Remove it!'" - Billy Cotton and his Band perform *The Woodpecker (Would Peck Wood)* with 46-year-old Alan Breeze on vocals ... 30-year-old footballer Nat Lofthouse of Bolton Wanderers and 28-year-old Don Revie of Manchester City both score twice in England's 5-1 victory over Denmark. (28-year-old Geoff Bradford of Bristol Rovers is also on the score-sheet) ... 'Gang leaders will take the place of parents - if you don't stop them!' - Cinema goers are shocked as violent new American movie *Blackboard Jungle* hits the big screen ... Teenagers 'go wild' for rock'n'roll music ... "We're gonna..." *Rock Around The Clock* ("... tonight. We're gonna rock, rock, rock 'til broad daylight") by Bill Haley and his Comets climbs to number one on the hit parade - and stays there for three weeks ... *Go On By* by 23-year-old Alma Cogan is number sixteen ... There're widespread rumours and much speculation that the four year marriage between 43-year-old Michael Wilding and 23-year-old actress Elizabeth Taylor is on the rocks ... Adverts say, 'When a man notices a girl's hair, she's using *Silvikrin* shampoo - Liquid 6d & 1s/5d, Powder 4½d' ... Bird's Eye Foods introduce *Fish Finger*s.

Christmas 1955... Floodlights at the Empire Stadium

A heavy smog lingers over Birmingham, Wolverhampton, Stoke-on-Trent, Manchester and Liverpool ... 226 million tonnes of coal have been mined in Britain this year - it's been roughly the same amount for each of the past four years ... 11-year-old schoolboy Ron 'chopper' Harris watches the greyhound racing at Hackney Wick Stadium ... Ted Drake's Chelsea football team beat Newcastle Utd 2-1 in front of 37,327 spectators at Stamford Bridge ... "You made me cry, when you said goodbye..." *Ain't That A Shame* by 21-year-old Pat Boone climbs to number seven on the hit parade. (The original version of the song, by Fats Domino, is not available in the UK) ... *Meet Me On The Corner* by 33-year-old Max Bygraves is number two ... More and more passengers are travelling through London Airport ... "Whatever form air travel may take in the future, and we may be certain that striking changes lie ahead, London Airport will, I am sure, continue to grow in importance as one of the world centres of air traffic" - 29-year-old Queen Elizabeth II opens the new Europa terminal building ... 38-year-old convict Alfred Hinds (currently serving a twelve year sentence for robbery) escapes from Nottingham Gaol and goes on the run ... 33-year-old MI6 officer George Blake meets his KGB contact in Berlin and hands over confidential Defence information. (Blake is now a double agent working to undermine Britain's security interests) ... Back in England - men rush to cinemas to see 29-year-old Marilyn Monroe (36-22-36) in *The Seven Year Itch* ... 40-year-old comedy superstar Norman Wisdom appears in *Man of the Moment* ... 51-year-old 'hasbeen' movie star George Formby appears in Pantomime at Liverpool ... 41-year-old Winifred Atwell from Trinidad reaches number three in the pop chart with her piano medley *Let's Have A Ding Dong* (comprising of the songs: *Ain't She Sweet, Oh Johnny Oh Johnny Oh, Oh You Beautiful Doll, Yes We Have No Bananas, Happy Days Are Here Again, I'm Forever Blowing Bubbles, I'll Be Your Sweetheart, If These Lips Could Only Speak and Who's Taking You Home Tonight*) ... "When you've climbed the highest mountain, when a cloud holds the sunshine in, suddenly there's a valley where the earth knows peace with man" - *Suddenly There's A Valley* by 23-year-old Petula Clark is number seven ... Floodlights are used for the first time at an international football match at Wembley - John Atyeo, Bill Perry and 33-year-old Tom Finney (aka the 'Preston Plumber') score in a 4-1 victory for England over Spain ... 24-year-old Christopher Chataway announces the news on the new commercial television channel ... Thirteen people are killed when an electric passenger train crashes into a steam freight train at Barnes in South London ... 49-year-old Hugh Gaitskell is the new Leader of the Opposition after defeating 58-year-old Aneurin Bevan in Labour's leadership contest ... 61-year-old Harold Macmillan takes over from 53-year-old Richard Austen 'Rab' Butler as Chancellor of the Exchequer in Sir Anthony Eden's Tory government. (Butler becomes Lord Privy Seal and Leader of the House) ... Commercial TV is extremely popular - transmitting to the London area ... Michael Miles hosts *Take Your Pick*, Hughie Green hosts *Double Your Money* and Richard Greene stars in *The Adventures of Robin Hood* ... "You lucky people!" - 46-year-old comedian Tommy Trinder hosts *Sunday Night At The London Palladium* ... Frank Osborne's Fulham football team beat Dave Russell's Bury 3-1 at Craven Cottage in Division Two ... The gramophone recording of *The Singing Dogs Medley* by The Singing Dogs is heard frequently on Radio Luxembourg ... Families go to church and take part in carol singing during the festive period ... *The Christmas Alphabet* by 26-year-old Dickie Valentine from London is number one in the weekly Top 20 pop chart ... *Black & Green's* tea is a popular hot drink ... Dr. Spock's *The Common Sense Book of Baby and Child Care* is a popular new journal ... *The Return of the King* - the third volume in the epic novel *Lord of the Rings* by 63-year-old J. R. R. Tolkien is now on sale in all good book shops ... 55-year-old band leader Harry Roy (aka the King of 'Hot-Cha') features on the front cover of the *New Musical Express* ... 20-year-old Ruby Murray from Belfast performs *The Very First Christmas Of All* ... 31-year-old Anne Shelton from Dulwich performs *Arrivederci Darling* ... Matt Busby's Manchester Utd football team are top of Division One after a 5-1 victory over Charlton Athletic at Old Trafford ... Joe Smith's Blackpool are second - after beating Huddersfield Town 4-2 ... Dally Duncan's Luton Town are third - after beating Sheffield Utd 4-0 ... 30-year-old Noel Kinsey scores a hat-trick as Arthur Turner's Birmingham City beat Cliff Britton's Everton 6-2 at St. Andrew's ... 33-year-old Billy Liddell scores a hat-trick (and 18-year-old Jimmy Melia makes his debut) as Don Welsh's Liverpool beat Nottingham Forest 5-2 in Division Two ... The average weekly wage in Britain has increased under Sir Anthony Eden's Conservative government - it now stands at £11 ... Lucky schoolboys get a *Meccano* construction set on Christmas morning ... Very lucky schoolboys get a 5-speed Claud Butler *Buccaneer* racing bicycle with polished duralumin alloy 'dropped' handlebars and Brampton racing pedals ... Men go to the pub ... Bottles of Tennent's Lager at the Red Lion cost 1s/3d ... "1-2-3 O'Clock, 4 O'Clock, Rock!" - Teenagers really dig the crazy new sound of rock'n'roll - *Rock Around The Clock* by Bill Haley and his Comets moves back to the top of the hit parade.

Printed in Great Britain
by Amazon

49344745R00194